Managing Understanding
in Organizations

Managing Understanding in Organizations

Jörgen Sandberg
Axel Targama

SAGE Publications
London ● Thousand Oaks ● New Delhi

First published 2007

SAGE Publications Ltd
1 Oliver's Yard
55 City Road
London EC1Y 1SP

SAGE Publications Inc.
2455 Teller Road
Thousand Oaks, California 91320

SAGE Publications India Pvt Ltd
B-42, Panchsheel Enclave
Post Box 4109
New Delhi 110 017

British Library Cataloguing in Publication data

A catalogue record for this book is available
from the British Library

ISBN-10 1-4129-1065-X   ISBN-13 978-1-4129-1065-1
ISBN-10 1-4129-1066-8   ISBN-13 978-1-4129-1066-8 (pbk)

Library of Congress control number 2006921668

Typeset by C&M Digitals (P) Ltd, Chennai, India
Printed on paper from sustainable resources
Printed and bound in India by Gopsons Papers Ltd

Contents

ONE Understanding becomes a key issue

A paradigm shift is taking place in management

During the last two decades, we have witnessed a substantial shift within both management practice and academic discussions concerning how human action can be managed effectively in an acceptable way. Some writers, like Beckérus et al. (1988), have described it as a doctrinal shift while other scholars, such as Clark and Clegg (2000) and Pearce and Conger (2003), have portrayed it as a paradigm shift in management. The central message is that a shift is taking place in management from using direct techniques, such as specific rules and instructions, to the development and use of more indirect techniques, such as vision, mission, culture and values, together with a leadership based more on dialogue rather than authority for managing human action. There are two main reasons for this shift.

The first is that since 1980 society has undergone a range of social and economic changes, such as rapid technological development, increasingly knowledge-intensive industry and intensified global competition. These changes have given rise to new organizational forms, where the degree of freedom has increased at every level and individuals have received more independence at work. A key consequence of employees' greater autonomy is that management has lost its direct control over their behaviour. Managers must, to a much larger extent than previously, trust that their staff act and make judgements in accordance with the company's strategic direction. To maintain some control over employees' work performance, managers have become more dependent on being able to influence people's *understanding* of their own and their companies' task. The increased need to manage understanding has led to the development and use of more indirect management techniques (vision, values, culture, etc.) and a more dialogue-based leadership.

A second reason for the paradigm shift is that management by ideas and visions have received strong support from more recent research. During the last thirty years, a growing body of interpretative research shows that understanding of work forms the basis for human action in organizations. The findings demonstrate that people's work performance is not primarily influenced by external conditions such as specific rules and instructions *per se*. Instead, work performance is first and foremost defined by people's understanding of their work and how they understand the rules and instructions imposed upon them. This insight suggests that in order to create effective work performance managers need to develop and maintain a shared understanding among the employees about the company's task. Formulating the company's task in a set of central ideas and values that the employees can themselves commit to has thus become a chief managerial task.

The difficult art of 'understanding understanding'

Even if managers realize that the way people understand their work is fundamental to their performance, most companies still have difficulty influencing the way employees accomplish their work. Why? A central argument in this book is that the paradigm shift has only taken place at a rhetorical, but not at a practical, level. Managers have not been able to implement the change in practice because they have tried to do so by following the traditional leadership principles within the rationalistic management tradition. By following the rationalistic principles, they are unable to understand how employees' understanding of their own and their company's task forms the basis for their work performance and, thus, how understanding can be managed more effectively.

A capacity to influence understanding presupposes knowledge of how understanding operates. In this book, we propose an interpretative management perspective as an alternative to the prevalent rationalistic perspective on management. This shift in perspective makes it possible to 'understand understanding' and, thus, to develop practical ways of managing understanding that can enhance work performance in organizations.

Socio-economic forces behind the paradigm shift

To manage employees so as to achieve a competitive advantage, managers need to know what to influence and how to influence. Throughout the twentieth century, a rationalistic perspective has characterized management research and management practice. In such a perspective, the *top-down principle* has been the dominant principle. To influence employees' work performance, managers plan the work to be performed and how it is to be performed. With support from administrative specialists, managers formulate specific rules and instructions about work, which they impose on their staff through a hierarchy of authority and responsibilities. Two main managerial strategies can be distinguished: one emphasizing the process and the other emphasizing the outcome of employees' work performance. When focusing on the process, managers try to influence employees' work performance by imposing detailed instructions and rules about how staff should accomplish their work (the bureaucratic and the technocratic principles, respectively). When emphasizing outcome, managers specify details about the outcome of the work assigned to employees (management by objectives). The latter is, however, usually combined with a considerable amount of instructions and rules concerning work processes.

During the last two decades the dominant rationalistic management perspective has been heavily criticized as being inadequate for the effective management of people's work performance. One main reason derives from the socio-economic changes taking place in society today, such as rapid technological change, more knowledge- and service-based industry, intensified global competition, a more diverse workforce, an increased compression of time and space, and shifts in values.

Technological changes

Over the past three decades, we have witnessed an increasing rate of technological innovation in areas like biotechnology, microelectronics and telecommunications. The most profound technological advance is the development of information technologies such as the computer and the internet. The computer and, subsequently, the internet are themselves crucial vehicles in this technological development (Castells, 1996). Moreover, many of the new technologies are applicable to almost all aspects of the world economy. For example, computers and the internet have had an immense impact on national and international financial systems, creating radically new conditions for creating and producing goods and services in many industries. Flexibility in terms of products and the production process has increased dramatically, while the life cycles of both products and production process have been substantially reduced. Taken together, such technological changes have created new requirements for managing people's work performance. In particular, to a much larger extent than previously, managers are now required to facilitate an ongoing development and renewal of staff competence as demand for new and varying competence at work arises. As Ellström (1992) argued, a difficulty employees often encounter when confronted with new technology is not learning to use it, but

3

rather learning to use its potential to increase productivity. Orlikowski (1993) made a similar observation in her study of the implementation of new information technologies in European, Japanese and US firms. She found that most of the implementations failed because the companies had overlooked the most critical aspect of technology implementation, namely to prepare the employees to use the full potential of the new technology.

More knowledge- and service-based industries

Another important development is the structural changes occurring in the industrialized world as a result of a shift towards more knowledge- and service-based industries. Many current studies of economic development in the industrialized world, such as Ekstedt (1988), Eliasson et al. (1990) and Neef (1998), conclude that the production of services is increasing in relation to the production of goods, while both entities become increasingly knowledge-intensive. An expression of this change is the emergence of the so-called knowledge-intensive firms – conspicuously IT companies during the last two decades (Alvesson, 1993a, 1995, 2004; Starbuck, 1992). R&D based companies, various consultant companies, law firms, accountancy firms, universities and schools, and similar organizations also represent various forms of knowledge-intensive industries.

The growth of knowledge-intensive work creates an even greater need for a continuous development of employees' competence for improving work performance. Moreover, Bäcklund (1994) also demonstrated that the increasing rationalization of capital, decentralization, customer orientation and technical renewal that take place in companies today have led to a need for the continuous development of new and more advanced competence in work that is usually regarded as uncomplicated and simple. In addition, the complex, dynamic and interactional nature of knowledge-intensive work (Alvesson, 2004; Newell et al., 2002) makes it particularly problematic to represent in a simple set of static rules and instructions imposed by hierarchical authority. Instead, because of the high degree of independence and discretion to use their own judgement, knowledge workers and other professionals often require a leadership based on informal peer interaction rather than hierarchical authority.

Intensified global competition

The rapid technological advances and a more knowledge- and service-intensive industry have led to increased globalization of the economy, in conjunction with intensified competition. The new information technology has made it possible to integrate companies and whole industries into large global economic systems. For example, we have witnessed an enormous increase in the globalization of financial capital, the rate of the global diffusion of new technological innovations and the importance of multinational corporations (Gilpin, 2000). These and other trends towards increased global economic integration have intensified competition. Such competition necessitates new ways of managing people that permit greater flexibility and speed in product development and production processes. For example, most problems are identified at the operative level by staff who deal with customers or work in production. But sending these problems several levels up the hierarchy to be solved, and then sending them back down to the people who are affected by them, would take too long. In the interest of speed, problems should be solved directly by the people who encounter them. But operations should then be organized in such a way that operative personnel are permitted more independence and extended autonomy in performing their tasks.

Increased competition has also brought about a stronger focus on customers' interests and preferences. A greater consideration of customers' interests means that companies have to be more flexible and spontaneous to satisfy customers' varying preferences. To enable staff to develop such ability, managers must provide them with greater independence at work. As a further effect of increased customer orientation, quality has become a more important competitive factor. Quality is partly related to the design of products and production systems, but is also to a large extent an effect of the day-to-day actions of operative personnel. It is they who create quality, primarily through the sum total of their dealings with customers.

In the public sector, the deregulation that took place in the 1980s and 1990s has meant that most public organizations have been exposed to similar competition as global industrial companies. In addition, reduced financial support to the public sector has required public organizations such as hospitals, universities and schools to be more efficient and creative in developing new ways of delivering service to society. In particular, it has been argued that public organizations need to move from a bureaucratic to a more entrepreneurial governance, which embraces a decentralized authority and participatory management (Osborne and Gaebler, 1992).

A more diverse workforce

During the last twenty years, we have witnessed the emergence of an increasingly diverse workforce. The employees in most organizations are becoming

5

more diverse in terms of ethnicity, religious beliefs, gender, education, social background and age (Ashkanasy et al., 2002). An overarching force behind the increased diversity is the intensified globalization and the technological advances taking place in society. While the intensified globalization has encouraged a more mobile workforce, the technological advances have made it possible to connect work groups around the world. Following Ely and Thomas (2001), it is possible to identify three more specific forces behind the increase in diversity. First, a diverse workforce is seen as central because it provides organizations with different insights, knowledge and experience, which can form alternative views of work and how best to accomplish it. Secondly, it is argued that employees in organizations should reflect the diversity in markets to obtain access and legitimacy with those markets. Finally, there is a moral and political push for a more diverse workforce to ensure justice and fair treatment for all members in society.

A more diverse workforce creates pressure for finding new ways of managing people. A particular challenge is to coordinate all the experiences, knowledge and interests employees bring to work into a shared understanding about what the company is supposed to do. Creating a shared understanding within a diverse workforce by using specific rules and instructions from above will not suffice. Instead, it requires a more dialogue-based leadership that enables managers to access how employees understand their own and the company's task.

An increased compression of time and space

Rapid technological advancement and an increased globalization have led to a greater compression of time and space that deeply affect the way we live, work and manage organizations (Harvey, 1989; Sennett, 1998). As Harvey noted: 'As space appears to shrink to a "global village" of telecommunication' and 'time horizons shortens to the point where the present is all there is ... so we have to learn how to cope with an overwhelming sense of compression of our spatial and temporal worlds' (1989: 240). How the compression of space and time have affected work can be illustrated by the changes that have taken place in corporate law during the last twenty years (Sandberg and Pinnington, forthcoming). As one corporate lawyer expressed it: up to about mid-1980s corporate law was to a large extent seen as:

the old gentlemen's profession of practising law. You could work civilized hours and do all that sort of thing because of course what happens, the secretary or yourself, would craft a letter and do whatever. ... Then you send it, and then you think, great, that's off my desk. Now it's going to take a day to get there, and then it's going to take them a day to have a look at it, and it's going to take another day to come back again so how wonderfully civilized. With fax, that began to end. And then of course with email and all of the electronic communications flow, it's gone. Because now it's a matter of drafting [a document], very regularly on your own computer, rather than dictating, and having an assistant help you type it. Zing it down the line and then go out for lunch and then come back and it's sitting there in your in box and you go 'bloody hell that's too fast, I didn't even get to digest my lunch properly', and that's how it's changed.

Such a compression of time and space at work has led to increased pressure for new ways of managing people. In particular, the compression has made work much more fluid and ephemeral. To be able to adopt and adjust quickly to market shifts employees need to a greater extent to be involved in continuous sense making of what their work is about and how to accomplish it. The need to be involved in an ongoing sense making demands a leadership based on dialogue rather than hierarchical authority.

Change in values

Pressure from the new market conditions and technological development demands new ways of managing and organizing businesses. This tendency is reinforced by the trend to consider freedom and independence as important features of a desirable job. Younger people especially tend to look for freedom and independence at work (Zemke et al., 2000). As noted by Sennett (1998), there is also an indication that younger generations today tend to regard high uncertainty and risk taking as central features for a challenging work. Consequently, to recruit attractive employees, companies have to offer jobs that include risk taking, independence and freedom to use your own judgement at work.

The magnitude and complexity of the socio-economic forces

While the above socio-economic changes occur in most of the industrialized world, caution needs to be exercised with respect to both the magnitude and complexity of the changes, in particular with regard to their impact on the management of organizations. As Thomson and Warhurst (1998) pointed out, while we can witness a rapid increase in the professionalization of the workforce, we can also witness a growth in less qualified service work such as telesales and call centres. This kind of service work is still primarily managed by strict standardization of the work process, which provides little individual freedom. Research also suggests that even those who are doing knowledge-intensive work may not always experience high work autonomy (Harley

7

et al., 2005). For example, Felstead et al. (2002) showed that there has been a noticeable decline in work autonomy among technical and professional employees in the UK between 1986 and 2001. There has also been a considerable job loss together with an increased stress of the possibility of losing a job through the many mergers and acquisitions, restructuring and downsizing that have taken place during the last two decades (Cooper, 2002; Wheeler, 2002). Studies such as Littler and Innes (2003), using longitudinal firm-level data on organizational restructuring, suggest that the ongoing downsizing in the economy has also led to a 'de-knowledging of the firm'. Moreover, research suggests that the changes may not only have a profound impact on our work but also on our character. According to Sennet (1998: 25), today's, 'short-term capitalism' may corrode our character in fundamental ways. This is because 'no long term' means keep moving, don't commit yourself, and don't sacrifice'. As Cooper (2002) argued, this raises the question, among other things, to what extent individuals can commit to organizations that do not commit to them.

An attempt to sum up

The socio-economic changes described above require ways of managing companies that promote a high degree of flexibility, customer orientation, quality, efficiency, worker autonomy and ongoing competence development. With these new requirements, the rationalistic management perspective has been shown to be too rigid and inflexible for managing people's work performance in a way that makes competitive renewal and growth possible (Alvesson, 1993a; Beckérus et al., 1988; Clark and Clegg, 2000; Kanter, 1990; Morgan, 1993; Pearce and Conger, 2003; Schein, 1985). This has caused companies to search for organizational structures and management methods strongly focusing on the management of knowledge and competence development, and the permission of more individual freedom and local independence at work. For example, there has been a gradual shift in management philosophy in many companies. Instead of organizing work in a bureaucratic and hierarchical manner with strong specialization and job demarcation, many companies are trying to develop more decentralized and horizontal organizations which emphasize 'the capability of the workers' group to cope with local emergencies autonomously, which is developed through learning by doing and sharing knowledge on the shop floor' (Aoki, 1988, cited in Castells, 1996: 159). The reduction in levels of management has meant that self-managed teams are now one of the fastest-growing organizational units. The lack of a strong hierarchical authority in team-based organizations typically requires a different leadership from that stipulated by the rationalistic management tradition. Instead of relying on hierarchical authority, leaders in such organizations are more dependent on their peers for managerial success (Pearce and Conger, 2003). This is particularly true for professional organizations and more knowledge-intensive companies. Another response to the new conditions is the development of inter-organizational networks. One such business network is when companies operate on the basis of licensed commercial franchises under an umbrella corporation. Two such very successful networks are Benetton and McDonalds, which both consist of several thousand companies in many different countries coordinated by one core firm. Such a network enables its members to adapt more quickly to new demands on the market. A third response is a strong increase in various forms of strategic alliances between organizations. Such alliances have been particularly prominent among high-technology firms as a way of sharing R&D costs but, even more importantly, as a way of sharing knowledge that will enable the development of innovative new products.

Above all, the management principles in these new organizational models are not characterized by hierarchy and bureaucracy, but by networks (Castells, 1996). Managing network organizations consisting of relatively autonomous individuals and groups are not primarily about communicating each individual's duties in a top-down manner. Instead, management is essentially an ongoing dialogue between managers and staff with the aim of developing a shared understanding of how to best run the business. This means that the initiative to develop and improve the business is not only considered to be a question for managers and experts, but also for operative personnel. As a consequence of the need for ongoing competence development and greater staff independence, we identify three management problems that are becoming increasingly significant:

1   The company becomes *more dependent on employees' understanding* of their tasks and of the reality in which they act. As soon as people are given more freedom, they will act in accordance with their understanding of their work situation in general, with the effect that different ways of understanding work will emerge and, hence, different ways of performing work. Previously, people acted according to their understanding of the rules and routines governing their work. The scope for interpretation was generally not particularly wide.

2   People in management positions need to develop a more important pedagogical role. One of their key opportunities to influence operations is *to influence employees' understanding* of the company's strategic direction and the main ways that should be used to achieve its strategic goals. Formulating the company's task in a clear and stimulating way becomes an important managerial challenge.

3   *Increased dependency on human competence for competitive success.* The strong emphasis on knowledge for competitive success has been accompanied by a greater dependency on human competence and its development. It is no longer sufficient to provide occasional opportunities

for competence development. It is instead necessary to provide ongoing opportunities for competence development throughout the organization and sometimes also among the members of the business network. Moreover, as staff autonomy increases, it is not enough for them to master only a few techniques or routines. They must also be able to detect and evaluate problems, develop alternative ways of solving problems and foresee the future effects of different ways of solving problems.

Research emphasizes understanding as the basis of human action

Another main reason for the paradigm shift in management derives from the criticism of the rationalistic management perspective raised by interpretative studies. As pointed out previously, management researchers using interpretative approaches have shown that people's work performance is not primarily based on external stimuli such as rules and instructions, as assumed within the rationalistic management tradition. Instead, work performance is based on people's *understanding* of their particular work and the situation in which it is embedded. This insight can be illustrated with the following simple example.

Tom is given five cards from an ordinary pack of cards. Tom has knowledge that can be of use here. He knows what a pack is, how many cards it contains and that the cards are classified according to a particular system. But this knowledge does not become interesting until he has found out what it means to play a card game such as poker.

Let us imagine that Tom has recently learnt to play poker as an innocent party game. He learns that the idea is to get the best possible combination of cards according to certain rules. Tom is clever at head counting and also good at statistics, and his ability to do probability calculations means that he asserts himself well in the party game. Over a period of time he wins more often than his fellow players do.

Tom's friends recognize his ability and one of them says: 'You are really good at this. You ought to go to a game club and test your ability because you could probably get rich playing cards.' It is a challenge hard to resist and as soon as Tom has learned the basic rules of playing for money, he goes and finds a club. He starts off cautiously, calculating as carefully as he can, but despite this he loses more often than his fellow players do. How is this possible?

Based on our framework, we would argue that the problem is related to his understanding of the situation. In the first case, the party game, he did have an accurate understanding of the situation. The trick was *to choose the cards to maximize the probability of obtaining the best outcome in terms of a specific combination of cards*. Since he was clever at probability calculations, he did well. However, at the game club, he applied the same understanding of the task. The main problem was that he was still angling for the best possible hand. What he did not realize was that another understanding of the situation would have been more appropriate. This was because at the game club holding the best cards is not the main object. There, the point is *to make your opponent think that you hold the best cards*. Once one realizes that, one also understands that calculating probability is only a small part of a game of poker. The main part is being skilful in the psychological play, mastering body language, being able to read the degree of certainty and sincerity in fellow players' bids or counter-bids, to discern whether they are holding first-class cards or just bluffing. The example shows that:

- our understanding of a task and its context shapes our attention and determines what is interesting and relevant and what is not,
- we may have knowledge and skills but they only become useful through our understanding of a specific situation,
- understanding is not a given that automatically follows from a situation. We learn to interpret reality in a particular way, so our understanding is coloured by our previous experiences.

Consequently, the same task can be understood in different ways and the more complex the task, the greater the number of possible ways of understanding it. With a task as complex as managing a company, obviously there are several ways of understanding what it is about, what is more or less important, what resources are useful and how to achieve a favourable result.

Even the results favoured by management by objectives rely on our general understanding of the particular business situation. To discuss the success of any business, it must be possible to evaluate results. For a defined task such as a poker game, it is rather obvious how the result can be evaluated. But for the more complex tasks performed in companies, the results become full of nuances. For example, say we want to achieve something in the short term and at the same time create opportunities to achieve strong results in the longer term. We want to meet quality requirements, create a stimulating working environment and keep the costs down – all at the same time. Moreover, in industry, someone often evaluates results other than the person producing the results. The results that are to be achieved may be formulated by managers, customers or other stakeholders.

The paradigm shift: from instruction to vision

The growing dependency on knowledge and the ability to apply it, that is, human competence (Alvesson, 2004), greater independence and the insight that people's work performance is based on their understanding of work, have given rise to support from an increasing number of practitioners and management researchers for a shift from management by specific rules to management by ideas and visions, together with a leadership based on dialogue rather than hierarchical authority. As pointed out previously, this is a shift from using direct management techniques, such as rules and instructions, to the development and use of more indirect techniques, such as vision, mission, culture and values. Beckérus et al. argued in their book, *The Doctrinal Shift,* that such a shift implies:

> [a] new leadership ideal derived from a developmentally oriented view of human beings, which has a particularly strong link to corporate thinking. The new keywords are *competence mobilization* and *competence development*, where the staff members' knowledge, experience and problem-solving capacity are assumed to be integrated in a shared network of *commitment* and *involvement* concerning the company's business idea and its relation to the market (customers, suppliers and other interest groups).
>
> No longer is the task of the leadership to limit responsibility and influence, and to increase control and ability to direct by regulating details. Its new function is to break up rigid structures, to create commitment and local freedom to act, and to reduce control of details and governing by rules. In this way, opportunities to use experience and knowledge 'from floor to ceiling' within the company are created – something that is central to the new corporate thinking. (1988: 27, translated from Swedish, italics in original)

More than a decade later Clark and Clegg, in their extensive overview of the paradigm shift in management, argued in a similar vein:

> All business is becoming knowledge-based – that is, the utilization of state-of-the-art knowledge is now the critical ingredient for commercial viability. Developing better information systems is only part of this challenge. It is necessary to create collaborative cultures, group technologies, supportive infrastructures and sensitive measurement systems to facilitate the effective acquisition and deployment of new knowledge.
>
> In knowledge-based business, learning and innovation are the critical drivers of business development. Redefining the workplace as a central mechanism for knowledge exchange encourages the discovery and utilization of knowledge at every level, making the organization more alert, informed and responsive. (2000: 431)

The above arguments have been intensified even further more recently with an increased emphasis on the importance of knowledge for growth and survival. As Newell et al. argued:

> In these dynamic and global environments, it is not possible to expect managers to do all the thinking – in other words, the separation between thinking and doing (or decision and action knowledge) is no longer appropriate. Success depends, rather, on harnessing the intellectual capital of all employees. Moreover, in such situations people will often work together in teams to create new solutions, integrating their knowledge and experience to develop new products and services. (2002: 173)

As mentioned previously, these principles have received broad attention from the business community throughout the industrialized world. Most corporate leaders believe in these principles and try to apply them in some form or other. But despite claims that a shift from management by rules to management by ideas has taken place, a range of problems usually associated with traditional management styles seems to remain. Let us describe some typical situations of that kind.

1   The board of a company has observed that the company is strongly production-oriented while market indications seem to call for a more customer-oriented approach. When earnings decline, the current CEO resigns and the new CEO is given a clear mandate by the board to make the company more customer-oriented. The new leader and key senior managers elaborate a number of central ideas that combine to form a more customer-oriented vision of the company. Then, the new CEO launches a comprehensive information campaign to propagate the company's new vision. All employees in management positions and several others participate in courses and seminars. The organization is restructured, and managers with a more customer-oriented approach are brought in. Two years later, it can be observed that numerous discussions have been held and a range of changes has occurred, but the company's way of thinking is more or less the same as before. Very few of its grand ambitions have been realized.

2   One company takes over another company in the same industry. The management of the over-taking company carries out a comprehensive and expensive campaign about the advantages and positive synergies it will achieve through the merger. There is little protest. Most employees seem to support the managers' ideas. But after a while, it becomes clear that it will be difficult to achieve the expected synergies. The two companies still operate in very different ways, and their employees have difficulties coming up with shared solutions, and are complaining that they 'talk past each other'.

3   In a certain industrial company, it is observed that 72 per cent of middle managers are men and 28 per cent are women. The company has declared that it should strive towards a more equal distribution. The equality committee has suggested various activities to support this aim. For instance, an internal survey showed that of the resources available for training and developing middle managers, 80 per cent had been used by men and only 20 per cent by women. The equality committee recommended that women should be encouraged more to take advantage of training and development opportunities. The general managers of the company supported the recommendations and decided that in two years' time 65/35 per cent distribution should be the norm. This policy was also discussed extensively at various management seminars. However, after the two years had elapsed, a new investigation showed that of the employees who have received training and development support, 78 per cent were men and 22 per cent were women.

What these examples have in common is that the management techniques used did not play out as expected. Despite management's clear formulation of ideas, visions and principles towards a desired change in work performance and their communication to employees, they seem not to have influenced the employees' performance in any particular way. How is this possible? As mentioned above, several management writers and practitioners have argued for a paradigm shift in management. We should abandon management by rules and embrace management by ideas. However, in discussing the ways in which ideas and visions can be used to influence how employees understand their work, their arguments are typically in line with the rationalistic top-down principle. For example, Beckérus et al. claimed that, in a general sense, one could argue:

> that the managers' chief task, both in words and action, is to give the business enterprise a direction. It includes defining the situation of the company and its need for change, prescribing an action plan and gaining support for it. (1988: 86, translated from Swedish)

Hosking and Morley made a similar observation:

> On reading the literatures it is all too easy to form the impression that leaders manage meanings through relatively simple, one-directional, causal processes, in which they impose their (superior) vision and understanding. (1991: 252)

Within the literature on managing change researchers also typically follow the rationalistic top-down principle. For example, Kotter's (1995) well-known, eight-step process for managing change in business is in line with the rationalistic top-down principle: (1) create a sense of urgency, (2) form a powerful guiding coalition, (3) create a guiding vision, (4) communicate the vision, (5) empower others to act, (6) create small wins along the way, (7) consolidate improvements and create more change, (8) institutionalize the new culture. The model clearly identifies that key factors in the process are how employees view the competitive situation and the desired future of the company, and whether they trust the change efforts to be serious and productive in achieving a real change. It also makes clear that the change is dependent on local action that cannot be prescribed in detail. But when it comes to the implementation of the change efforts, the rationalistic top-down principle is particularly salient in the first four steps. Kotter argues that leaders should first establish a sense of urgency within the organization, that a change is needed. As a second step, he proposes that leaders form a powerful guiding coalition. Thereafter leaders should create a guiding vision as a way to provide a roadmap for more specific plans and directives and something compelling to strive for. When created, the vision must be communicated clearly. All of it is assumed to be achieved through strong decisions and actions from the part of the leader.

Also, in human resource management, most advocates of management by ideas fall back on the rationalistic top-down principle when describing *how* staff members' understanding can be influenced. For instance, this becomes evident in Berg's (1986) description of how the personnel managers one-sidedly transfer a desirable meaning of work to the employees. Such a one-sided imposition is also evident in Ogbonna's (1992) study on the use of the concept of culture in human resource management. Ogbonna's results showed that researchers who use the concept of culture in human resource management argued that the activities of training and development 'can be designed to inculcate in employees those attitudes which are "in tune" with the organizational culture' (1992: 81).

We can witness a similar one-sidedness when it comes to managing knowledge. As Newell et al. (2002) pointed out, the predominant way to manage knowledge has been through information and communication technologies (ICT). With the help of ICT, managers identify, store, retrieve and transmit knowledge throughout the organization. This way of managing knowledge has, however, proven to be problematic in many ways. For example, in an extensive investigation of 431 American and European companies by Ruggles (1998), it became evident that most companies were highly dissatisfied with their current ways of managing knowledge with the help of various ICT systems. More than 56 per cent of the companies experienced difficulties in influencing and changing workers' performance by creating and transmitting new knowledge to the employees. And only 13 per cent of the companies were able to transmit knowledge effectively between organizational units.

That managers to a large extent are still operating within the rationalistic management perspective is also apparent within leadership itself. As was described previously, there is a widespread recognition of the benefits in business of shifting from a hierarchical leadership to a more relational and dialogue-based leadership. However, as many researchers have noted, such as Fletcher and Käufer (2003) and Pearce and Conger (2003), most companies seem to have failed to implement a more relational leadership in practice. Fletcher and Käufer (2003) point out three central reasons for such a failure in terms of three paradoxes and contradictions in companies' attempts to adopt a more relational leadership: (1) hierarchical leaders are charged with creating less hierarchical organizations, (2) shared leadership practices 'get disappeared', and (3) the skills it takes to get the job are different from the skills it takes to do the job, or the 'that's not how I got here' paradox.

The first paradox, 'hierarchical leaders are charged with creating less hierarchical organizations', illustrates a deep contradiction in many organizations. Namely, that a strong 'hero' CEO is often seen as best equipped to manage an organizational change from a centralized and hierarchical organization towards a flatter organization and a more dialogue-based leadership. But as Fletcher

15

and Käufer and others point out, 'it is difficult to create less hierarchical systems by relying solely on better hierarchical leaders' (2003: 25).

The second paradox, 'shared leadership practices "get disappeared"', highlights how the idea of shared leadership disappears or gets overshadowed by the dominant image of leadership as heroic individualism. As Hiefitz and Laurie noted, despite all the strong signals and rhetoric about the need for a new leadership, 'manager and leaders rarely receive promotions for providing the leadership to do adaptive work' (1999: 65). Others, such as Hirschorn, (1990) and Meindl et al. (1985), claim that 'followers' also individualize leadership due to their strong need of heroes. Of particular importance are Fletcher's (1999, 2002) observations that central principles of relational leadership, such as 'taking time from one's own deliverables to share information, sending notes of appreciation, or asking for help, input or both, appeared so routine, mundane, and "non-heroic" in practice that they were hard to recognize as acts of leadership' (Fletcher and Käufer, 2003: 26).

Finally, the third paradox, 'that's not how I got here', points out that the training and development of managers in most organizations encourages intense competition between individuals. Individuals have to invest considerable energy to distinguish themselves from others. Promotion is thus very much organized around individual achievement rather than a shared or cooperative achievement. This means that those individuals who end up in influential management positions are often poorly equipped to adopt and implement a more dialogue-based leadership.

Fairhurst (2005) identified similar reasons why so many managers seem to fail to grasp what a more relational and dialogue-based leadership means in practice. In 1996 Fairhurst and Sarr published the rather well-known and influential book (particularly written for practising managers) *The Art of Framing: Managing the Language of Leadership*. Its main point was to describe and illustrate how leaders can manage understanding by framing the meaning of employees' reality in particular ways. They define framing as:

> the ability to shape the meaning of a subject, to judge its character and significance. To hold the frame of a subject is to choose one particular meaning (or set of meaning) over another. When we share our frames with others (the process of framing), we manage meaning because we assert that our interpretations should be taken as real over other possible interpretations. (Fairhurst and Sarr, 1996: 3)

Reflecting on the book a decade later, Fairhurst (2005) notes that while the book still receives high attention among managers, a large number of them struggle to comprehend what framing means in practice. Initially, she thought that the reason why so many managers struggled was related to where in the organizational hierarchy they were positioned. This was, however, refuted at an early stage. Upon further reflections and investigations, she pinpointed three main reasons why most managers fail to implement framing in their managerial practice.

One reason is that many managers experience insecurity about framing reality because it challenges the commonly held belief of an objective and stable reality. If managers adopt the idea of framing reality, it means that they become reality makers rather than reality discoverers (to discover how reality really is and act on the facts discovered). Due to the strong belief in an objective and stable reality, most managers feel highly insecure about abandonning their current role as reality discoverers and instead adopting the role of reality creators.

A second reason proposed by Fairhurst is that most managers embody a particular design logic in communication that hampers their framing ability. Based on O'Keefe's (1988, 1997) work, Fairhurst identifies three main design logics in communication: expressive, conventional and rhetorical design logic. Those who embody an expressive design logic regard communication primarily as a way to express their feeling about something. According to Fairhurst, those people often make blunt and inappropriate remarks, and when asked why they made that remark they often reply with 'because that was what I was thinking' (2005: 173). The individuals who embrace a conventional design logic regard communication as 'a cooperative game to be played premised upon socially conventional rules and procedures' (2005: 173). These individuals play the cooperative game by knowing what is appropriate and what is not appropriate to say in specific situations. Finally, the individuals who embody a rhetorical design logic do not primarily alter what they say in particular situations, but rather try to change the situation to fit what they want to achieve. According to Fairhurst, it is really only the rhetorical design logic that does not hamper managers' ability to manage meaning successfully. She notes, however, that in numerous tests, an overwhelming majority of managers fail to score higher than conventional design logic. This suggests that most managers are unable to put framing into practice due to their particular communicative design logic.

Finally, Fairhurst raises the issue of whether framing is a teachable skill. While research suggests that it is, there are, according to Fairhurst, four issues that hamper the teaching and learning of framing: arrogance, conduit thinking, authenticity concerns and lack of moral framework. Many leaders are arrogant and dismissive in their communication with others. Highly linked to arrogance is the strong view of communication as information transfer. As Fairhurst points out, we often encounter expressions in practice like 'getting one's thoughts across' and 'putting thoughts into words'. When reduced to transfer, the whole negotiation dimension of communication is overlooked.

17

Many people are also uncomfortable about losing authenticity when changing behaviour. As described above, when managers try to become reality creators, they not only challenge the basic assumption about an objective and stable reality, but they also lose a sense of authenticity of what they are doing. The framing logic also makes managers much more aware of their moral obligations. If they are framing the reality of others, the moral dimension of their actions comes to the fore. It requires that leaders take more responsibility for their actions.

A way to summarize the reasons provided by Fairhurst for why most managers fail to grasp what framing means in practice is because they still operate within a rationalistic perspective. This is particularly evident when it comes to feeling insecure and uncomfortable about leaving the assumption about an objective and stable reality behind and embracing the idea that reality, to a large extent, is socially constructed. The fact that a vast majority of managers only embody expressive and conventional design logic in communication also clearly highlights the rationalistic perspective. The difficulties involved in learning the art of framing due to arrogance, loss of authenticity, and conduit thinking further demonstrates that managers still operate within a rationalistic perspective on management.

The difficulty in breaking away from the rationalistic management perspective is not only evident in leadership but also in organizational forms. In an overview, Alvesson and Thomson conclude that despite the rhetoric about a shift towards post-bureaucracy (decentralized, non-hierarchical, flexible and fluid forms of organizations) 'empirical studies of changes reveal relatively modest changes in structural terms, and where change has taken place in some spheres, it is in the direction of more rules, hierarchy, and centralization. ... [P]ost-bureaucracy, for the moment, operates more as a means of legitimating change and marketing new ideas than as a solid empirical indicator of changing forms of work organization' (2005: 500–2).

How this book is organized

A central argument of this book is that the alleged paradigm shift has taken place at a rhetorical level but not at a practical level. Managers have not succeeded in realizing the paradigm shift because they have tried to do so using a rationalistic perspective. More specifically, since most current methods for managing understanding are based on the rationalistic principles, managers overlook the way employees' understanding of their own and the company's task influence their work performance. Without a deeper knowledge of how people's understanding of their work forms the basis for their performance, the possibility of influencing their understanding to achieve a certain performance is considerably limited.

In this book, we suggest an interpretative management perspective as an alternative to the rationalistic perspective. Such a shift in scientific perspective makes it possible to 'understand understanding' and to develop practical techniques for managing understanding in a way that will improve work performance.

Chapter 2 provides a basis for discussing the paradigm shift as a change from a rationalistic to an interpretative perspective on management. The rationalistic and interpretative perspectives are described in more detail. We also describe how many management researchers during the past three decades have gradually realized the significant role that people's understanding of their work plays on their work performance and, based on that realization, how they have adopted an interpretative perspective on management.

In Chapters 3–5 we describe and exemplify the main features of human understanding and how it forms the basis for people's work performance in organizations. To illustrate how understanding functions as the basis for individuals' work performance, we present in Chapter 3 Jörgen Sandberg's (1994, 2000) study about competence in a group of engineers developing new car engines. This study demonstrates how people's understanding of the same task differs and how the different ways of understanding the task form the basis for their work performance. Based on the same study, we continue in Chapter 4 to analyse the nature of human understanding by investigating how an understanding of work forms the basis for both how and what competence we develop at work. While in Chapters 3 and 4 we mainly focus on the characteristics of individuals' understanding of work and how it forms the basis for their work performance, in Chapter 5 we shift focus and discuss the nature of collective understanding and how it forms the basis for collective work performance and its competence. In Chapter 6 we summarize the main features of understanding developed in the previous chapters, and extend the discussion on core issues that are involved in transforming people's understanding of work. In Chapter 7 we review and evaluate the most common methods available for influencing human action, and discuss how they can be redesigned to enable managers to manage understanding more effectively. However, being able to manage understanding effectively is not just a question of redesigning available methods. It is also about redefining leadership and management as a whole in fundamental ways. That challenge will be further discussed in Chapter 8, along with an extended reflection on the paradigm shift in management and its possible obstacles and consequences for managing understanding in organizations.

Summary

The main thesis of this book can be summarized as follows:

> Managers have adopted ideas of a new management philosophy emphasizing knowledge, competence development and independent performance steered by ideas and visions. Managers know what they want to accomplish but do not really know what understanding is and, therefore, do not know how understanding can be developed and influenced effectively.

Why have traditional management problems been reproduced in management by ideas and visions? Managers have probably not fully realized all the consequences of what it means to manage by influencing people's understanding of their own and the company's task. Certainly, advocates of management by ideas have adopted the insight from interpretative research studies that understanding forms the basis of people's work performance. But when these advocates later describe how people's understanding can be influenced, they generally fall back into the traditional rationalistic principles of management.

We are convinced that people in management positions need to give more thought to what understanding is. Further, we believe that a deepened insight would lead to a more fruitful search for concrete ways to realize management by ideas. We hope that the rest of the book will contribute to this insight. The emphasis is on identifying problems and pointing out threats and opportunities. But we will also show where practical solutions may be found in the hope that this will encourage creative and forward-looking managers to experiment and try out new ways to manage and, thus, to achieve competitive advantage.

TWO The rise of an interpretative perspective on management

As described in the previous chapter, an alleged paradigm shift has taken place in management research, as well as in practice, concerning how to manage people's work performance: a shift from using rules and regulations to a leadership based upon visions and ideas. We, however, claimed that the alleged paradigm shift has mostly taken place at a rhetorical but not at a practical level. The main argument was that managers have failed to turn the paradigm shift into practice because they have continued to act within the rationalistic perspective. If the paradigm shift is to be materialized in practice, management needs to be understood in a different way.

Based on an increased amount of research that emphasizes understanding as the basis for human action, we argue in this chapter in favour of an interpretative perspective on management. We begin by outlining the main features of the rationalistic perspective and contrast them with the main features of the interpretative perspective. Thereafter, we portray the gradual realization among management researchers that an understanding of reality forms the basis for people's work performance, resulting in the emergence of an interpretative perspective on management.

Management has been dominated by a rationalistic perspective

Whether we live in a socialist or capitalist society, or in a mix of the two, some kind of management exists. Managers have the role of coordinating resources and human action in order to reach certain goals. Which goals should be given priority is of course a matter of debate in every society. In organizations that are part of traditional western market economies, we find goals formulated as shareholder value, corporate growth, competitive strength or increased productivity. The discussion about corporate goals is highly controversial and the whole idea of 'given organizational goals' has been disputed (Alvesson and Willmott, 1996). But on the whole, neither advocates of the rationalistic nor advocates of the interpretative perspective question the general principles of goal-directed action and the need for management. The dispute between the two perspectives concerns rather the question of *how* people's work performance can be coordinated in order to reach desired outcomes in a way that is effective and acceptable for society.

In the business world we often encounter the view that doing business is an art, based on skills such as business acumen and gut feelings. Such a view depicts business as something subjective and intuitive. There is also a tendency in the business world to emphasize the value of learning from experience, and having a hands-on and down-to-earth relation to business leadership. However, those involved in management research have had a completely different point of departure. Rooted in ideals from natural sciences, they have been searching for economic laws and general causal relations to better understand the nature of human action and how it can be influenced in a desirable way. They have adopted what is typically called a rationalistic perspective. This means that the predominant body of management knowledge that has been developed is saturated by a rationalistic view. The same can be said about the scientific tools and techniques that have been taught in business schools and used in companies for coordinating and managing human action to achieve desirable ends.

The rationalistic perspective and the body of management knowledge developed within that perspective are founded upon a set of basic assumptions that are typically taken for granted. To better understand the character of the rationalistic perspective, it is worth scrutinizing some of its central assumptions about the nature of human action and organizations, and how knowledge can be acquired about those phenomena.

Basic assumptions behind the rationalistic perspective

1 Subject and reality exist as two independent entities

One of the most basic assumptions underlying the rationalistic perspective is the idea that subject and world exist as two independent entities. This assumption implies a division of research objects into two main separate entities: a subject in itself and a world in itself. For example, corporate strategy is typically defined and described by seeing organization and environment as two independent entities. First, the inherent qualities of the organization, such as its strengths and weaknesses, are described, and then the inherent qualities of the environment, such as the threats and opportunities that it offers (Smircich and Stubbart, 1985). Similarly, within theories of competence in professional practice, competence is defined by looking at the worker and the work as two separate entities. Thereafter, an attempt is made to identify the specific attributes, such as knowledge and skills, that are inherent in the worker and what activities are inherent to the particular work he or she accomplishes (Sandberg, 1994, 2000).

2 There exists an objective world and by systematic observations we get closer to the truth

Another cornerstone in the rationalistic perspective is the presumed existence of an objective and stable reality beyond human consciousness. Reality is assumed to be objectively given and the qualities and meaning we experience are inherent to reality itself. Through systematic scientific observations and careful monitoring of the extent to which our theories and ideas correspond to the particular aspects of reality we are investigating, it is assumed that we will come closer to the true picture of reality. These premises are supposed to be valid for the scientist studying the inner structure of matter as well as for the market analyst studying customers' preferences for various product alternatives.

3 Language as a mirror of objective reality

The core idea behind this assumption is that language can represent or, as Rorty (1979) argued, 'mirror' reality in a true and objective fashion. The relationship between language and reality is thus seen as a relationship of correspondence. As it is assumed that language has the capacity to represent reality, it is treated as a representational system available to the researchers in their endeavour to describe reality objectively. Hence, while concepts certainly are formulated and defined by human beings, they are supposed to mirror specific aspects of objective reality.

4 Everything has an explanation

Another important assumption within the rationalistic perspective is the belief in causality. Everything that happens can be explained by causal factors. Scientific studies typically aim to identify the most influential causal relationships and laws that can explain regularities in human behaviour and activities. In practice, it might be very difficult to identify causal relationships, particularly when a large number of factors influence each other in a complicated pattern. Rationalistic management researchers have for a long period of time adopted a system approach. They do not search for one single cause, but presume that complex causal relations exist. But in essence, there is always a cause, even if it is difficult to isolate it within a complex pattern.

5 Human action can be explained by inherent characteristics of individuals and environment

Explaining human action is one of the most central challenges for both researchers and practitioners. In a rationalistic perspective, people are also part of objective reality. In the same way as physical reality is supposed to have certain objective and inherent characteristics, the human being is also assumed to have a set of characteristics that are given and independent of the situation at hand. For example, human action is often explained by specific attributes such as knowledge, personality characteristics and unique needs. If one could describe a certain situation with its specific characteristics and a human being with his or her specific characteristics, it should be possible to predict the performance of that person. Much effort has been spent on the identification and typifying of characteristics such as leadership styles or attitudes. Researchers have for a long time been searching for general relationships that could be used for predicting specific human actions, such as the impact that a particular leadership style may have on group performance or how the customers' personal characteristics influence their choice of certain brands.

6 The human being as a tool of necessity

The rationalistic perspective also builds upon the view that organized activities have goals that are more or less taken for granted. A company is a part of a larger economic system, and in order for the company to function successfully a number of activities and issues become *necessary*. Leaders become, as Willmott (1997) expressed it, executers of the necessity. They should analyse the environment in order to find out what is required for the company to remain competitive. They are then supposed to use their knowledge of causal relationships to identify the steps that need to be taken to continue to be competitive. In this view, the human being becomes a tool in a system of functional relationships and, thus, also released from a personal and moral responsibility for the actions being taken. The reason for the execution of the actions is not because the leaders want to – they just have to.

The cognitive approaches within the rationalistic perspective

Cognitive theory has made strong inroads into the management field in general and has been particularly dominant in the discussion on learning in organizations since the 1950s (Pawlowsky, 2001) and, more recently, in the discussion on managing knowledge in organizations (Newell et al., 2002). The cognitive approaches can be seen as a substantive modification of the rationalistic perspective. They advance the classic stimulus–response model (S–R) within the rationalistic perspective by introducing the human organism into the model: S–O–R. The 'O' in the model denotes an organism that selects and perceives stimuli and, based on that, responds in a particular way. In other words, within the cognitive approaches, the view of the human being changes from a black box without any significance for the relationship between stimuli and response to a more active creature who chooses and perceives the information he or she constantly encounters. While the cognitive field is highly diverse, it is possible to identify some basic assumptions underlying most cognitive approaches.

1 The objective reality and our knowledge about it

In line with the rationalistic perspective, most advocates of the cognitive approaches take for granted the existence of an objective reality. What the cognitivists add is the idea that human beings have the ability to cognitively *represent* objective reality in their minds. This means, as Semin and Gergen pointed out, that knowledge of reality is seen as carried within the cognitive system, 'and it is in the degree that this system is correspondent with the world that one can speak of a correct understanding or accurate knowledge' (1990: 3). For example, psychological studies of perception usually take their point of departure in a 'reality' that is as indisputable as possible, and then try to show how people, for various reasons, misjudge this true reality in their perception of it. They see, for example, two parallel lines that are in fact not parallel, to take a classic case. The view of knowledge as a (correct) cognitive representation of reality also plays a fundamental role in prevalent views of professional knowledge and knowledge management. The prototype of professional knowledge is scientific theory, justified through scientific reason, observation and experiment, and is seen as the highest form of knowledge. In this view, scientific knowledge forms the basis for professional knowledge. Skilful performance thus becomes very much applied scientific theory and techniques.

2 Cognitive maps and schemas

In order to make a large amount of new information manageable, people develop specific cognitive maps or schemas. Such cognitive structures describe how we collect, store and mentally represent aspects of the external environment. More specifically, we develop and use various forms of cognitive maps and schemas to sort and mentally represent the information already stored as well as to collect, sort and represent incoming information. These cognitive knowledge structures can be constructed by the individual him- or herself as well as be collected from others.

3 Emphasizing information processing

Cognitive approaches place a strong emphasis on the human being as an information-processing unit or computational device. We receive signals in various forms, process and represent and store part of them in our cognitive system. More recently, there has been an increased emphasis within cognitive theory that human beings do not only receive signals, which they represent

25

and categorize. In addition, the cognitive system influences which stimuli human beings pay attention to and which one's they ignore (Balota and Marsh, 2004). In practice, this means that large efforts have been made to study how information (words, figures, etc.) should be designed to make people perceive them correctly, that is according to the intentions of the information sender. How should an annual report, for example, be designed to make people 'understand' it, in the sense that they perceive the information in the correct way so that they do not acquire a faulty picture of the company.

4 Rational search

Human beings actively search for information when they have problems or face challenges. Cyert and March (1963) talk about 'problemistic search'. This means that learning is goal-oriented and functional, seen from a rational explanatory model. The search for information is a question of trying to formulate a correct representation of the new situation that has occurred and, based on that representation, take adequate action. Learning thus becomes a matter of cognitively representing the world as accurately as possible. One can, however, ask how rational the search is if one takes into account the idea of cognitive maps and schemas. As Semin and Gergen noted, the schema idea suggests that it is the particular schemas available that determine what is real. If this is the case, then it opens up an inherent problem within the cognitive approaches because 'if one understands reality through schemas, how can reality ever produce a schema?' (1990: 8).

The alternative: the interpretative perspective

Even if the rationalistic perspective has been dominating the past thrity years, interest in alternative perspectives based on the interpretative research tradition has steadily increased in management and organizational science (Alvesson and Sköldberg, 1999; Prasad and Prasad, 2002; Zald, 1996), as well as within social sciences more generally (Atkinson et al., 2003; Denzin and Lincoln, 1994, 2000; Flick, 2002; Lincoln and Denzin, 2003; Schwandt, 1994). The strong growth of interpretative perspectives mainly stems from a dissatisfaction with the methods and procedures for producing scientific knowledge within the rationalistic perspective. Advocates of interpretative perspectives claim that those methodological procedures and claims for objective knowledge have significant theoretical limitations for advancing our understanding of human and organizational phenomena (Alvesson and Sköldberg, 1999; Denzin and Lincoln, 1994, 2000; Lincoln and Denzin, 2003; Prasad and Prasad, 2002; Sandberg, 2001b). In particular, the rationalistic perspective has been subjected to increased criticism for being unable to advance adequately our knowledge of what constitutes human action and activities. The main criticism is that they fail to explain human action by overlooking people's understanding of reality and how it forms the basis for human action and activities in organizations and society at large. To overcome the shortcomings of the rationalistic perspective, most advocates of interpretative perspectives have followed ideas from philosophical phenomenology[1] most notably its emphasis on lived experience as the basis of human action and activities.

The development of the interpretative research tradition is often traced back to ideas from Weber (1964/1947) that subsequently have been developed by phenomenological sociologists such as Schutz (1945, 1953), Berger and Luckmann (1981/1966), Giddens (1984, 1993), and Bourdieu (1990). However, the roots of the interpretative research tradition are many and it is not a single, unified perspective. The more influential approaches are various forms of social constructionism (Berger and Luckmann, 1966; Bourdieu, 1990; Giddens, 1984, 1993), critical theory (Alvesson and Deetz, 2000; Habermas, 1972), ethnomethodology (Atkinson, 1988; Garfinkel, 1967; Heritage, 1984; Silverman, 1998), interpretative ethnography (Denzin, 1997; Geertz, 1973; Van Maanen, 1995), symbolic interactionism (Blumer, 1969; Mead, 1934; Prasad, 1993), discourse analysis (Alvesson and Kärreman, 2000; Foucault, 1972; Potter and Wetherell, 1987), deconstructionism (Derrida, 1981/1972; Kilduff, 1993), gender approaches (Calás and Smircich, 1996; Harding, 1986; Keller, 1985; Martin, 1994), institutional approaches (DiMaggio and Powell, 1983; Meyer and Rowan, 1977; Scott, 1995) and sense-making approaches (Weick, 1995).

Despite the great variety of perspectives, what unifies them is the phenomenological notion of life-world, which stipulates that person and world are inextricably related through lived experience of the world (Berger and Luckmann, 1966; Gadamer, 1994/1960; Heidegger, 1962/1927; Husserl, 1970/1900–01; Schutz, 1945, 1953).[2] Hence, within interpretative approaches, the human world is never a world in itself; it is always an experienced world, that is, a world that is always related to a conscious subject. This shift in the point of departure – from human being and environment as two separate entities to people's lived experience or understanding of reality – provides an alternative explanation or view of what constitutes human action and activities in organizations.

Central assumptions underlying the interpretative perspective

1 Life-world – the basis for the interpretative perspective
As was argued above, the basis for the interpretative perspective is the notion of life-world. The concept of life-world was first proposed by Husserl (1970/1936) but has been further developed by other phenomenologists, such

as Merleau-Ponty (1962/1945), Schutz (1967), Heidegger (1962/1927) and Gadamer (1994/1960, 1977). The idea of life-world expresses that person and world are inextricably related through the person's lived experience of the world. In particular, it highlights that we, as human beings, always live and act within our lived experience or understanding of the world, not above or outside it. It is within our lived experience of reality that we decide courses of action, make judgements and develop feelings and emotions (Deetz, 1992). Bengtsson captured the basic idea of life-world, that subject and world are inseparable through the subjects' experience of the world as follows:

> Even if the life-world is objective both in the sense that it is a shared world and in the sense that it transcends (exceeds) the subject, that is, its qualities are not qualities within the subject, it is likewise inseparable from a subject, namely, the subject who experiences it, lives and acts in it. The world is always there in the first person from the perspective of my space and time here and now. (1989: 72)

As Bengtsson points out, the life-world is the subjects' experience of reality, at the same time as it is objective in the sense that it is an intersubjective world. We share it with other subjects through our experience of it, and we are constantly involved in negotiations with other subjects about reality in terms of our intersubjective sense-making of it. Consequently, the agreed meaning constitutes the objective, intersubjective reality. Furthermore, the life-world is objective in the sense that it transcends the subject. This is because its qualities are not solely tied to the subjects' lived experience of it. At the same time, however, it is inseparable from the subjects through their experience of it. For example, most European countries have agreed to have daylight saving and move the clock one hour ahead for the period from March to October. Daylight saving thus becomes an objective fact through this intersubjective agreement. Even if some of us try to ignore the agreed daylight saving time, we encounter difficulty in doing so because its consequences extend beyond our subjective experience of clock time.

As became apparent in the above example, subjective and objective realities reflect each other. On the one hand, a basic condition for individuals to survive in society is that their subjective reality corresponds with objective reality. If my subjective understanding of clock time deviates considerably from the general understanding of clock time, I encounter difficulties in getting by. On the other hand, the construction of objective reality must correspond to the subjectively constructed reality. If not, a particular constructed reality will not achieve the status of objective reality. It is first when there exists a correspondence between a number of subjectively constructed realities, such as agreement among most countries in Europe concerning the introduction of daylight saving, that an objective reality can appear.

2 Our knowledge about reality is socially constructed

From the notion of life-world follows the assumption that our knowledge about reality is socially constructed. Does this means that there is no objective reality independent of human beings? We can leave the question of whether there exists a reality independent of us for the time being. It is more interesting to ask if the concepts that we are using to describe reality have some kind of genuine correspondence to objective reality. Most of us would consider it completely self-evident that buildings, stones and trees exist completely independently of how we look at them and the concepts we use to describe them. Concepts such as 'buildings', 'trees' and 'stones' are so naturally associated with our personal experience that we consider it rather stupid to question them. Yet, it might be worth thinking about the fact that Carolus Linnaeus, in the first version of his classification of all living beings, first published in 1738 in his book *Systema Naturae*, included stones. And even if mountains in our everyday understanding appear as extremely stable and static, from a geologist's perspective they are mobile and changing. In those cases it is obvious that what is true about reality is dependent upon which perspective we take.

It becomes even more interesting if we consider more abstract phenomena. What is truth when it comes to an economic crisis or the profit of a company? What is true love or genuine democracy? Is it really possible to talk about truth in such cases? Most of us would agree that it is not possible to talk about one given truth in the sense that all other views would be untrue. Instead, we would say that there is room for different interpretations.

From an interpretative perspective it can be argued that our *understanding of reality is created by ourselves and others* on the basis of our experiences and through communication and interaction with other people. When it comes to physical entities such as trees and stones, we have already during our childhood inherited ways of identifying and naming them. The concepts used to label physical entities such as trees and stones therefore feel natural and obvious in relation to our own experience. There has not been any need to question them. Here we can talk about firmly established conceptions of reality. But does that mean that they represent the 'truth'?

Even extremely stable conceptions of reality, such as those that we have inherited through generations, can later be questioned because we are confronted with new experiences or encounter new information from others. Our ancestors shared the view that the earth was flat, and that view did not violate their experience. In more modern times we have held the view that one will get a cold if one freezes – it is even evident in the saying – but today, due to new information, we have revised that view significantly.

Once again, the basic statement is that people's understanding of reality is based upon (1) their own experiences and the considerations and reflections they give rise to, and (2) other people's influence, either by uncritically adopting their views of reality, or by comparing one's own experiences with those of others and discussing how they should be interpreted. Through ordinary, everyday conversations, in which we talk about what we do, hear and see, we develop, without being aware of it, understandings of reality that are common among smaller or larger groups of people.

From this perspective, 'truths' are social conventions, stemming from shared experiences appropriated through a common upbringing and education within a particular culture. The conventions are developed through 'discourses', that is, conversations in various forms about what we do, hear and see. But for a particular individual the truth can be something different from the conventional truth. This is because a particular individual may have had experiences that point in a different direction from the existing convention. An individual can argue from absolute conviction that 'this treatment is really effective – I have used it myself, so I know what I am talking about'. For that individual, such a conviction represents the truth, regardless of what medical expertise says. This means that we can talk about *subjective as well as social truth* in the sense of certain ways of understanding reality that are based upon experience and created through interaction with other people.

3 People act according to their understanding of the world
From a rationalistic perspective, human beings are seen as basically passive and reactive. Their actions are regarded as primarily determined by the situation they are facing. From the interpretative perspective, human beings are seen as more active. Their actions are not primarily controlled by objective situational factors. Rather, they are controlled by their interpretation and understanding of the specific situation. This understanding covers the situation as a whole and includes:

- ideas about the factual character of the situation, what alternatives that are at hand, and what happens if you choose one or another path of action,
- ideas about other people involved in the situation – their feelings, intentions and expectations,
- ideas about what other people may expect in this situation and how they may react upon one's actions,
- one's own internalized ideas about what is right and what is wrong, what is considered appropriate in this situation, what duties one has, etc.

The different parts of this total picture are intertwined in a way that the individual is usually not aware of. Facts, feelings and values are not kept apart from each other, and we do not consciously differentiate between what is based upon our own experiences and what is a result of influence from others. Hence, from an interpretative perspective, individuals act in a way that makes sense to them. Based upon our understanding, we try to be rational and reasonable, to do what is socially acceptable, and act according to our own moral principles.

What is the practical relevance of having one perspective or the other?

At first sight it might appear that the discussion on different perspectives is foremost of philosophical interest. Does it have any impact upon how management questions are treated in practice? As a matter of fact it has a considerable impact.

Let us take recruitment as an example. A company is planning to hire a new marketing manager. The CEO takes help from a head-hunter. She starts out by analysing what the job involves, and what demands it places on the holder of the position. By using interviews and other material, the head-hunter generates a competency profile. It stipulates what specific knowledge, work experience and personal characteristics are required for a holder of the position.

The next step is to advertise the position. After a first rough selection a small group of candidates remain. The short-listed people now become the object to various tests and interviews. Based on the information generated from the tests and interviews, the head-hunter tries to evaluate the extent to which the candidates' specific knowledge, experience and personal characteristics match the characteristics specified in the competency profile. Finally the candidate whose qualifications and characteristics best match the profile is chosen for the job.

The example describes in a somewhat simplified fashion a rationalistic trait approach to recruitment, which is extensively used in companies. In such an approach it is assumed that a job can be described objectively and independently from the person who is supposed to accomplish it, and that it is possible to describe the knowledge, skills and personal characteristics that an individual possesses in an objective fashion. It also assumes that a human being possesses specific inherent characteristics that produce the same kind of behaviour independent of context.

The actual measurement of personal characteristics does not seem to be a major problem. There are many scientifically established tests available on the market. Yet, much recruitment that follows the procedure described above fail. Most head-hunters would argue that the failure is related to inaccuracy in the competency profile used in the selection of candidates. Follow-up studies tend to show that the hiring executives admit that the person recruited had exactly the characteristics specified in the profile, but despite that the outcome was not successful.

A person representing an interpretative approach would rather argue that the problem arises because of the use of a trait approach. In such approach, the way the chosen candidate behaves is supposed to be controlled by the specific knowledge, skills and personal characteristics possessed. If we instead assume that human beings act according to their understanding of the situation, it would be central to find out more about the following issues:

- The top executives certainly have some ideas about how the company should compete in order to gain advantage. Does the candidate share those views? Are they congruent with the candidate's general ideas about how to obtain success in marketing?
- What ideas and conceptions does the candidate have concerning potential ways of marketing the kinds of product found in the company, and what is the possible future for those products?
- How does the candidate consider her own coming role in the company and how is this role related to the view of the top management, co-workers and sales offices?
- Which of her own experiences does the candidate believe to be of most value for the intended work activities?

If we accept that human beings act according to their understanding of the world, it should be important to investigate, as far as possible, the candidate's worldview and particularly her way of understanding issues that are relevant to the particular task at hand. If the candidate gets the job, she would of course deepen and modify her understanding of the issues that are directly related to her particular job. But the experiences she will make in her new job will, over a longer period of time, be substantially shaped and guided by her past and more basic understanding of being a marketing manager.

From an interpretative perspective, it becomes clear that it is impossible to separate a job from the person doing the job. Even if managers and the head-hunter try to objectively define the characteristics of the job, it is in the end the appointed marketing manager herself who will create her understanding of what the job means and what the main challenges are. Her individually created understanding will constitute the basis for the new marketing manager's actions, and these actions constitute the job being done. Hence, from an interpretative perspective the key problem for managers is not to determine the job requirements objectively. Instead, the central issue is to have a thorough dialogue with the candidate about how markets can be interpreted, what marketing approaches can be chosen and what the main tasks of the position really are. Having such a dialogue enables the recruiting company to identify how the candidate sees the marketing job and how the candidate may act in that position. It also gives managers a sense of how deviant the candidate's understanding is from their own understanding of what the job is about. This is also true after the candidate has been appointed. It is now that the top management has the best opportunity to have an impact upon the learning process of the new manager.

The emphasis on people's understanding of their work and its context does not mean that we disregard knowledge, skills and personal characteristics as something irrelevant and insignificant for human action. It is of course possible that decisiveness and persistency, for example, are important for the manager's work performance. The two perspectives are not mutually exclusive. It is rather a matter of what we choose as our basic approach in our thinking, which in turn will determine what we are going to emphasize and consider as important.

Summarizing the main differences

The rationalistic perspective makes use of what has been called a dualistic view. It is assumed that reality and person can be kept apart and analysed separately. Since people in companies are characterized by a set of inherent and stable attributes, it is possible to influence their work performance by controlling the external conditions, such as changing rules and regulations, the organization structure or reward systems.

Management research from a rationalistic perspective often means searching for relationships between changes in conditions on the one hand and effects upon human behaviour on the other hand. Hence, while it is regarded as important to figure out what effects changed conditions have on human behaviour, how people understand the changed conditions is typically treated as a black box.

From an interpretative perspective we can argue as follows:

- People's actions are not controlled by external conditions *per se*.
- People's actions are controlled by their understanding of the external conditions.

In practice, this means that managers who want to have an impact upon people's performance in their company should not confine themselves to changing external conditions. They also have the option to influence people's understanding of what the changes in conditions mean and stand for. This means that it is possible to obtain behavioural effects without making formal or substantial changes in the external conditions, such as the introduction of a new reward system. Instead, it may be enough to influence people's understanding of the external conditions at hand.

A gradual shift of perspective in management research

In the previous section we described the basic characteristics of the rationalistic and the interpretative perspective. In this section we try to show how

33

management researchers gradually have gained interest into how human understanding forms the basis for action. A central thesis here is that the insight that people's understanding of work significantly influences their action was first developed by researchers within the rationalistic perspective. Therefore, management researchers were for a long period of time unable to identify and describe what constitutes people's understanding and how it forms the basis for their action in any deeper sense. It was only when management researchers started to adopt an interpretative perspective that it became possible to develop a deeper and more systematic knowledge about understanding and its role for action. In order to illustrate this realization, we describe below a few key studies that have contributed significantly to the insight that human action is based on people's understanding of work.

General economic theory

Attempts to explain what happens in business with regard to general economic theory has long been characterized by a tension between one view that emphasizes the situational circumstances and another that stresses the visions of the entrepreneurs. According to the first view, people react to changes in situational circumstances in a fairly rational manner at the same time as they try to maximize the benefits for themselves or for the interests they represent. In this perspective, the human being is reduced to an executor of necessity. The goals are given – even if conflicting goals sometimes exist that have to be balanced against each other in as rational a way as possible. The role of the individual is to be a rational information processing unit, which tries to detect the true reality as accurately as possible, then calculate the outcomes of possible action alternatives and, based on that, choose the alternative that best achieves the goals. The individual may have good or less good access to information, and be a good or bad calculator, but the human being behind the information processing is not of interest in this perspective. The model has strong deterministic tendencies.

A classical example of an economic theory that has influenced management thinking significantly is Michael Porter's (1980) analysis of conditions for competition and competitive strategies. He states that it is possible to distinguish five influencing factors, which constitute any competitive situation. Since each of the factors can vary independently of each other, we receive a large amount of possible competitive situations. These situations can, however, be grouped into a few categories, and for every specific category there is a 'natural' best business strategy, such as superior cost-effectiveness, differentiation of products and services, or focusing on specific customer categories.

In the second perspective, the unique and distinctive characteristics of human imagination and thinking are emphasized. Here, the entrepreneurs are honoured for their visions and ideas. Economic development is not merely seen to be the result of situational and factual circumstances. In order to achieve economic prosperity we need people with imagination and boldness who dare to act in a way that, given the circumstances, may look irrational and peculiar at the beginning but later on may turn out to be the origin of successful business concepts. Instead of determinism, this perspective stresses the importance of human creativity. A typical representative of this perspective is Joseph Schumpeter (1934), who has strongly advocated the importance of the entrepreneur.

The two perspectives do not necessarily need to be contradictory at a basic level. It is possible to consider the successful innovator and entrepreneur as a person who has been particularly skilful in reading the conditions and someone who has better access to information about the technical development and other important changes in the environment. On the other hand, one might argue that there is a crucial difference between regarding the decision maker as a 'victim of situational circumstances' or as an actor who is able to overcome the situational circumstances through human creativity.

We can see this ambivalence in management thinking from the beginning of 1900 up to 1960. While the creative and innovative entrepreneur is honoured, creative imagination is mainly reserved for people at the top management level. When it comes to organization and management for that period of time, the Tayloristic approach dominated the thinking, with its strongly functionalist and rationalist view.

The model of the human being as a rational economic decision maker was, however, questioned at a rather early stage in management research. The reason was the realization that complete rationality would require an ability to collect and process information that is beyond human capacity. Herbert Simon (1945) established a school of thought by introducing the concept of 'bounded rationality'. According to Simon, the human decision maker does not have the intention to reach the most optimal decision. Humans only process the information necessary to reach a satisfying decision, that is, a decision that, according to the individual's past experience, meets the expectations of information processing required by the particular situation. Simon's theory, however, still sees decision making as a rational and logical processing of information. In his later research he further refined his model to show how information processing takes place in decision making and problem solving (Newell and Simon, 1972), and the model has been advanced even further within the area of artificial intelligence (Dreyfus and Dreyfus, 1986).

The Hawthorne studies: the human being becomes a social creature

One of the earliest and most influential studies, which pointed out that the way people understand their situation influences their behaviour, were the Hawthorne studies carried out by Mayo (1933) and Roethlisberger and Dickson (1939). It started out as a traditional experiment in order to identify cause-and-effect relationships between the physical conditions at work and employee behaviour and work performance. However, the results from their experiments were confused and contradictory to the researchers' expectations. In particular, they were unable to explain a significant part of the employees' behaviour by their focus on the relationship between physical work conditions and work performance. Instead, work performance seemed to be influenced by social factors such as management style and the employees' attitudes towards their specific work situation. To better understand how social factors may influence work performance, they initiated a series of interviews with the employees. The findings from the interview studies further highlighted that social factors both inside and outside work had a major influence on the employees' work performance. Moreover, they also observed that individuals' attitudes or interpretation of their work situation seem to greatly influence their work performance. As Roethlisberger and Dickson noted:

> it is not possible to treat, as in the more abstract social sciences, material goods, physical events, wages, and hours of work as things in themselves, subject to their own laws. Instead, they must be interpreted as carriers of social value. For the employee in industry, the whole work environment must be looked upon as being permeated with social significance. Apart from the social values inherent in his [sic] environment the meaning to the employee of certain objects or events cannot be understood. (1939: 374)

However, while the Hawthorne researchers had recognized the importance of taking into account individuals' understanding of their work in order to more fully explain their work performance, they did not develop this insight further. According to Burrell and Morgan, it was instead 'largely buried under the deluge of empirical research generated by the study' (1979: 138). A more likely explanation is that they were unable to advance their insight because they were firmly rooted in the rationalistic research tradition. Nevertheless, their studies had opened the eyes of many researchers in that in order to explain human behaviour, not only physical but also social factors need to be taken into account, together with how people interpret the physical and social factors in their environment.

Theories of human nature and worldviews

Another early and influential representative for the view that understanding seems to be governing human action in organizations is Douglas McGregor. He claimed in 1960 that the ways of organizing and leading people in organizations should not be seen as rational responses to requirements emanating from external conditions. Rather, they should be seen as exponents of basic theories about human nature held by people in leading positions responsible for the design of organizations and their control systems. McGregor identified two main theories of what constitutes human nature, which he labelled theory X and theory Y. According to theory X, the human being was basically unwilling to work and avoided initiatives and participation in organizational change. In order to encourage people to contribute to organizations, managers must regulate this unwillingness with the help of specific rules and instructions together with various incentive systems. It was exactly this kind of theory that McGregor criticized. He claimed it to be the basis for the prevalent and Tayloristic-influenced management practice at the time. On the other hand, theory Y portrayed the human being as basically active, involved and curious. If organizations and management principles were developed based on such a view of human nature, people would respond and act according to those principles.

McGregor's thesis that leaders' choice of management principles primarily were guided by their understanding of human nature, of which they were mostly unaware, had a relatively strong impact upon management discussions in many countries in the industrialized world. It was also mainly the inspiration from McGregor that laid behind a growing uneasiness with the way management information systems were designed and applied during the early phases of the computerization of administrative work (Hedberg et al., 1971). We can note, however, that in most of the writings from the 1970s, knowledge is still seen as something objective and neutral, whereas many writers use the term *values* to designate something that varies among individuals and is a product of prior experience and social influence. Values interact with more objective observations, thus moulding people's actions, which then no longer are purely rational given the conditions. Gradually, researchers start to talk about managers' understanding as something that is intertwined with facts, experiences and values, forming a comprehensive picture. This picture is seen as having a major influence on what decisions managers take under complex circumstances.

In a widely acknowledged article from 1976, Bo Hedberg, Paul Nystrom and William Starbuck discuss the mechanisms behind the fact that certain companies enter into stagnation and seem to have great difficulties reforming themselves. The argument is that when times are favourable, companies expand and build structures (i.e. organizational routines, information systems, buildings, etc.) that become stiff and inflexible when external conditions call for change. Hedberg and Sjöstrand (1979) used the metaphors of 'palace' versus 'tent camp' to visualize the idea of a flexible and easily changeable structure that could be moved to new fields of action just as the camping sites of nomadic tribes are easily dismantled and moved to more favourable areas for hunting or grazing. The formal and physical structures have their equivalence in *mental structures* that are solidified in the same way and, thus, obstruct change. Mental inertia, resulting from what managers have in their heads, should be distinguished from action inertia that is caused by formal and physical constraints. Inability to renew companies should be blamed on the fact that key managers do not have the capacity to change their established views on markets, technologies or internal work processes, as much as blamed on external conditions and difficulties to change formal and physical structures.

Hedberg does not explain in detail how the mental structures and basic views of reality are constructed and developed. It is possible, however, to see from the text that what he has in mind is comprehensive conceptions of reality that integrate everyday experience and values similar to McGregor's theory X and theory Y. We receive a more elaborated picture of the theoretical foundations in Hedberg's article in *Handbook of Organization Design* (1981: 3–27). There it becomes visible that he is writing from a basically cognitive perspective. There is a 'true world' but as a consequence of our limited capacity to take in and process information, humans acquire a misleading view of the world, and this view is reinforced by social interaction where people having similar experiences contribute to the establishment of a collective misleading picture of the world.

At the same time we can identify a strong awareness that reality is ambiguous. Reality can be perceived and interpreted in many different ways (of which some are closer to the 'truth' than others) and the challenge is to break out of one's own established conceptions of reality, mainly by being exposed to information from new sources and by being confronted by people with alternative views. To get a reasonably true perception of reality people have to engage in active search and efficient evaluation and questioning of the information at hand. This is a task of managers and decision makers as well as for staff specialists who produce background material for decisions and for those who design information systems for the production of such material. Hedberg's practical recommendations point at increasing the degree of information diversity and questioning. The physical 'palace-type' organization can have its correspondence in carefully designed and adjusted information systems that streamline learning within a predictable framework. Hedberg and Jönsson (1978) recommended that 'semi-confusing systems' should be designed to offer surprising content and unexpected information and, thus, stimulate new paths of thinking.

The action frame of reference

The British researcher David Silverman made many management researchers increasingly aware of the importance of focusing on the actors of organizations and their particular views in order to explain human action and activities in organizations. In his book *The Theory of Organisations* (1970), Silverman claims that in order to understand what is going on in organizations it is not enough to ascribe various attributes to the organization, such as goals, motives and action. According to Silverman, the organization itself does not act, and the individuals within it are not neutral and powerless 'tools' who are victims of the necessity. Instead, if we want to understand organizations, we need to view people as actors who act according to their own motives and according to their particular understanding of the situation at hand. Actions have *meaning*, and different actions acquire their particular meaning through various collective processes that take place in organizations and society.

The above thesis becomes important primarily when practitioners or researchers study human action in organizations and try to find out why people act in the way they do. In the rationalistic tradition it was assumed that human action was guided by factors external to the individual, such as established goals, environmental conditions or reward systems. Silverman does not deny that this could be the case. A wise actor of course tries to be in alignment with the external conditions. But if we want to fully understand action, we must *get inside the actors' frame of reference* and identify the actors' motives, reasons and what meaning the action has from the actors' point of view. Silverman's theory opens up the possibility of regarding actions as culturally determined, an idea which has been discussed frequently by researchers during the two last decades. Human action does not need to be rationalistic in a functionalistic sense. It acquires meaning by being part of particular behavioural patterns that are seen as self-evident and natural within a specific culture.

It is interesting to notice that while Silverman certainly expressed a strong interpretative perspective on human action, his theoretical base was somewhat unclear (Burrell and Morgan, 1979). As he expressed it himself twenty years after the publication of *The Theory of Orginisations*: 'I refer many times

39

to Weber. I also refer to the phenomenologist Alfred Schutz and, in an unexplicated way, to ethnomethodology and Garfinkel. I wasn't altogether clear were I was coming from in that book' (Silverman, 1991: 6).

The enacted reality

Another driving force behind the development of an interpretative perspective in management research was the American researcher Karl Weick. While Weick initially embraced a strong cognitive approach, ever since his seminal work *The Social Psychology of Organizing* was first published in 1969 he has been developing a more interpretative perspective in management. A basic thesis throughout his work is that it is highly problematic to divide human beings and their environment into two separate entities, as is done within the rationalistic perspective. Weick argued that we are inextricably related to the world through our ongoing sense making of it. He used the term *enact* to capture this idea. He argued that this sense-making activity:

> is usually thought to involve activities of negotiation between people as to what is out there. Less prominent in these analyses is the idea that people, often alone, actively put things out there that they then perceive and negotiate about perceiving. It is this initial implanting of reality that is preserved by the word enactment. (1979: 165)

Hence, a key argument in Weick's work is that in order to understand human action we need to identify and describe the way in which people enact their reality, the initial process of knowing in which reality becomes a reality for them. As Weick expressed it, we put the enacted world out there as an external world, which we perceive and negotiate about. However, by transforming the enacted world to an external world, we overlook the process whereby the world becomes a meaningful world for us to perceive, negotiate about and act within. Hence, according to Weick, only when we begin to understand our ways of making sense of our environment – the ways in which we enact our environment – can we grasp what defines human action and activities in organizations. Weick published these ideas in his first book in 1969. Maybe it was too original and too radical to have a strong impact upon management thinking. It took more than twenty years and several more books before it became hot stuff for more practically oriented management writers.

The 'Business Idea'

Through his book *Skapande Företagsledning* (*Management for Growth*), Richard Normann (1975) was one of the first in Scandinavia to emphasize that the mindset of actors should be at the centre of thinking and learning about strategic leadership of organizations. Normann was, however, not influenced by Silverman or Weick. Instead, he brought his inspiration primarily from the British organizational sociologist Peter Selznick. In his work on corporate management, Selznick (1957) introduced the concept of 'mission', which was widely adopted among management, practitioners later on. He claimed that one key issue for top management is to formulate the main task of the corporation in a mission statement. When formulated, managers should make it explicit and meaningful to employees with the help of symbolic actions and manifestations, and by integrating it into the organizational structure such as its control and reward systems.

Similar ways of thinking can be found in Normann's book. A key argument in his book is that strategic leadership is not a rational, analytic process but a *creative* process. The key concept in Normann's theory is the *'Business Idea'* of the company. In Normann's thinking, the business idea can be identified at two different levels. It exists as constructions in the minds of significant actors, and is also manifested in formal policies, structures and systems. Normann accentuates this dualism very explicitly:

> What we have reacted against is first and foremost the naïve belief that it is possible to formulate a new 'business' for a company as a kind of intellectual exercise in an executive team. The 'definitions' that we now and then learn about have been comprehensive enough and often superficial, but it is striking how seldom they have had an impact on immediate operative actions and the structure of the company. The task of defining has most often been nothing else than a relaxed and nice, ritual game. (1975: 48, translated from Swedish)

Normann emphasizes that the business idea of a company can become a meaningful concept only when it captures both a thinking that is formulated in the mind of significant actors and materialized in their actual measures to create systems and structures. Understanding and action are tied together. Normann also stresses that the dominant ideas among significant actors about how a company can become competitive is the result of a learning process – or a knowledge development process, as Normann puts it – of dialectic character. Therefore, tensions arising from different experiences can be beneficial and be a breeding ground for development.

Normann's view of the nature of knowledge is not made explicit, but compared to, for example, Hedberg we can find a stronger element of constructionism in Normann's work. According to Normann, our view of reality is created through an interplay with real-life experience and discussions with other people. The idea of a true reality is thus played down in Normann's thinking and imagination is getting more space. In both Selznick and Normann's thinking there exists implicitly the view that mangers create their own ideas of what the company is supposed to do and how it is to be competitive. Managers then act according to their ideas and, by doing so, turn their ideas into organizational practice.

The book by Normann had a strong impact on Scandinavian management thinking. A contributing factor was that Normann was active in a large consultancy firm, SIAR (Swedish Institute of Administrative Research), where he and his colleagues practised a thinking based upon the theory of the business idea throughout the 1970s. The book by Normann was immediately translated and published in English (Normann, 1977), but it did not have any notable impact upon the international discussion on corporate strategy. Could it be that the book represented a thinking that was too deviant from the prevalent view in the management world, and that Normann's colleagues among international management consultants and management researchers simply did not understand the essence of his ideas?

Management of meaning

Another researcher who has played a key role in introducing the interpretative perspective to management research is Gareth Morgan. While researchers such as Silverman and Weick placed the interpretative perspective on the management agenda, one could claim that Morgan, through his work, more clearly identified and elaborated the interpretative perspective as a distinct paradigm within management research and how such a perspective could be used to advance our understanding of management practice. It was in their highly influential book *Sociological Paradigms and Organizational Analysis* (1979) that Morgan, together with Gibson Burrell, pointed out the interpretative perspective as a distinct paradigm within management and organization theory. Influenced by Kuhn's (1962) theory of scientific paradigm, Burrell and Morgan carried out a meta-theoretical analysis and identified and elaborated in a systematic fashion the main characteristics of the interpretative perspective that was evolving in management and organization theory. Such a systematic elaboration enabled management researchers to see more clearly what an interpretative perspective had to offer and how it could be applied to enhance our understanding of human action and activities in organizations.

A central result from Morgan's own adoption of an interpretative perspective is the thesis that leadership is primarily about managing meaning. The idea of the management of meaning was first coined in an article co-authored by Linda Smircich 1982. Based on their own empirical study and the findings of others (Peters, 1978; Pondy, 1978) about leadership, they argued that people:

emerge as leaders because their role in framing experience in a way that provides a viable basis for action, e.g., by mobilizing meaning, articulating and defining what has previously remained implicit or unsaid, by inventing images and meanings that provide a focus for new attention, and by consolidating, confronting or changing prevailing wisdom. Through these diverse means, individual actions can frame and change situations, and in so doing enact a system of shared meaning that provides a basis for organized action. (Smircich and Morgan, 1982: 258)

In the above and many other works, Morgan has demonstrated that human action is based on people's understanding of their reality – what their reality means to them. Therefore, according to Morgan, creating a shared system of meaning about what the company is supposed to do is essential for achieving high individual and collective work performance.

Through a range of work (1980, 1983a, 1983b, 1986, 1993) Morgan has developed the concept of metaphor as a key tool for managing meaning. In his research Morgan demonstrates that our understanding of reality is always directed and shaped by specific metaphors, which we take for granted most of the time. As he expressed it: 'The use of metaphor implies a way of thinking and a way of seeing that pervade how we understand our world generally' (1986: 4). In his book *Images of Organizations* (1986), he identified a range of metaphors that have had a profound impact on the way both practitioners and management researchers have come to understand organizations. The most dominating metaphors are the machine metaphor, the organism metaphor and the culture metaphor. Each of these metaphors provides distinctly different understanding of organization and management and, thus, directs and defines what research the management researcher will conduct and how leaders will manage organizations. In *Imaginization* (1993), Morgan has elaborated and popularized even further how managers can use metaphors as tools for managing meaning and thus human action.

So far we have described some studies that have played a key role in the gradual shift from a rationalistic to an interpretative perspective in management research. Below we continue to describe the shift by illustrating how it has taken place more generally in various management areas such as corporate culture, strategic management and knowledge management.

The corporate culture perspective

One important effect of the realization that understanding forms the basis for human action was a growing interest in corporate culture among both management researchers and practitioners. Among practitioners, the concept of corporate culture received dramatic attention as a result of two books published in 1982. The authors of the books were all related to the consulting firm McKinsey and Co. One was Peters and Waterman's book *In Search of Excellence*, and the other was *Corporate Cultures* by Deal and Kennedy. Both books drew attention to the importance of organizational phenomena that exist beyond formal structures and systems, such as competence and shared values. Among management practitioners, 'culture' became an expression for conceptions and values that were common among people in a specific company, which contributed to the development of the unique competitive capacity of the firm.

It was clear at an early stage in management discussions that certain corporate cultures played a pivotal role in the success of companies. At the same time, it was possible to distinguish corporate cultures that had once been highly valuable, but later on had been made obsolete due to changed business conditions and turned into a burden for the company. The conclusion was obvious. Corporate managers have the responsibility to develop and mould the corporate culture into a 'strong culture', which should have both a strong impact on human action and be congruent with the challenges the company is facing and thus have a supportive function.

Edgar Schein (1985) received much attention for his analysis of corporate culture as an instrument for integration and coordination of human actions and activities in organizations. The bureaucratic coordination was supposed to be de-emphasized for the benefit of cultural coordination, that is, a conscious creation of shared views and values, which in turn could be reinforced by the use of symbols and rituals.

Parallel to this management-oriented research focus, a more critically oriented management research emerged (Alvesson, 1993b). Instead of turning culture into a management tool, these researchers used the concept of culture to capture the often taken-for-granted and hidden premises that form the basis for organizations' way of operating. Since these taken-for-granted assumptions and behavioural patterns are typically shared by all organizational members, managers cannot really step outside the corporate culture and manage it.

From our point of view, the pattern is familiar. Researchers direct our attention towards new and interesting phenomena, such as culture. Leaders and consultants stick to the new ideas that they intuitively perceive as interesting and important. But when they set out to make use of the new ideas, they do it within their established understanding, and that typically means within a rationalistic perspective on management. Corporate culture becomes one area among others which must be monitored, administered and developed. It became an S among the six others in the famous 'Seven S model' from McKinsey. Confronted with the task of changing and modifying the corporate culture, 'internal marketing' becomes the tool available.

The development within strategic management

The development of the corporate strategy field can be used as one more illustration of the evolutionary pattern that we want to bring forward: the shift from a rationalistic to an interpretative perspective of management. As long as the discussion on strategies was based upon the 'machine' and the 'clockwork' metaphor of corporate reality, writers on strategy emphasized environmental analysis and long-range planning (Rumelt et al., 1994). Alfred Chandler's (1962) and Igor Ansoff's (1965) seminal work laid most of the foundation for the rationalistic framework embraced by early strategy researchers. These researchers held a highly mechanistic view of the management of organizations. The world was considered to be predictable, even though the relationships were very complex. Based upon environmental analyses and predictions related to the goals of the company, it was possible to analytically derive adequate strategies for the company. The role of leaders was to implement decisions in line with the strategies brought forward from the analysis. Kenneth Andrews (1971) takes Ansoff's argument further by stating that the analytical strategist must connect an analysis of the external conditions (opportunities and threats) with the internal capabilities (strengths and weaknesses). However, both the external and the internal conditions are seen as given in the situation at hand. They represent a 'true' reality that can be analysed by an observer who can step outside the particular situation at hand and analyse it objectively.

After the oil crisis in 1974, long-range planning and environmental analysis received an unfavourable reputation, and the interest among strategy researchers moved to the implementation of strategies. Not much is gained if managers formulate adequate strategies based on rational analysis and then cannot implement them. Consequently, Ansoff wrote a new book titled *Implanting Strategic Management* (1984).

Gradually the strategy researchers started to question the rationalistic perspective at a more principal level (Mintzberg, 1994). In particular, scholars started to look more closely at the social and subjective character of organizations (Whipp, 1996) as a way to better understand strategy. One stream of research started to examine corporate strategy by bringing theories of human cognition into the rationalist framework. A paradigmatic example is Miles and Snow's (1978) influential study. The main finding from their study was that the strategy for successful companies in one and the same industry varied because its managers had perceived the contingencies of the industry differently. Also other researchers such as Porac et al.'s (1989) study of Scottish knitwear manufacturers and Hellgren and Melin (1993) work on how managers' perceptions influence their strategic choices within the Swedish paper industry, highlighted that human subjectivity plays a significant role for what competitive strategy is chosen and developed.

Another stream of research, parallel to the above, was the so-called processual theorists, such as Pettigrew (1985a, 1985b) and Mintzberg (1994). They provided a more radical challenge to the predominant view of strategy as a basically rational process. As Knight and Morgan explained, by adopting an interpretative perspective they were able to highlight the socially constructed and 'thereby political character of strategic processes and the inability of rational models to account for the uncertain speed and direction of organizational change' (1991: 251–2). More specifically, their main findings were that strategy does not primarily emerge from a rational planning process but from 'political processes of negotiation (and sense making) within the organization and between the organization and different elements in its environment' (1991: 266). In other words, strategies are to a large extent emergent rather than a product of deliberate rational analysis.

During the 1980s the so-called resource-based view started its gradual breakthrough in strategy research (Hofer and Schendel, 1978; Snow and Hrebiniak, 1980; Wernerfelt, 1984). According to this view, the strategy of a company should be based on the conditions emanating from the unique resources of the company. In most cases the unique resources are equivalent to the *competence* of the company, that is the knowing of employees and their capacity to make use of this knowing in their interaction with other factors.

The strategic literature of the early 1990s clearly admits that 'core competencies' are a key factor for competitive success (Hamel and Prahalad, 1994). This is because they are most difficult for competitors to acquire and imitate. Strategic development is therefore very much seen as a learning process. But even if many writers emphasized the importance of competencies, the reader does not obtain much guidance concerning the task of developing core competencies and dealing with the learning processes that are obviously needed. When the task is being discussed, it is from a rationalistic approach and a top-down way of thinking.

The insight about the strategic value of competencies does not become fruitful until the writers abandon the rationalistic basis for their thinking and explore the potential of an interpretative conception of knowledge. Spender and Grant (1996: 5) express it in this way: 'But as we look over our entire field ... we see little attention to organizational or executive knowledge *per se*. The focus is on content, on what should be known rather than the manner of knowing or learning it.' They called for a more process-oriented view on learning, where not only explicit knowledge has legitimacy. Our conception of competence must also include tacit knowledge, and we must admit that human beings create a holistic understanding that does not lend itself to scrutiny and analysis based upon traditional cognitivistic approaches. They looked for a paradigmatic renewal of strategy research.

Von Krogh et al. (1994) have offered one example of such a new approach. They discuss strategic thinking and organizational competence from an approach that stresses the notion that human knowledge and understanding are created by ourselves in social interaction with our environment. They see human understanding of reality as social constructions, but the social interaction produces unique individual outcomes, because human conditions and earlier experiences differ. They strongly confirm the thesis that strategic thinking has shifted its focus towards competence and learning. This change, however, will not become truly fruitful until we are able to develop a new view on what constitutes knowledge, competence and understanding.

Knowledge management and knowledge work

The emergence of knowledge management can be seen as an attempt to better understand what constitutes knowledge and competence in organizations and how it can be managed. It also provides an additional illustration of the shift from a rationalistic to an interpretative perspective in management research. As described in Chapter 1, since the 1980s there has been an explosion of interest among researchers and practitioners in the role of knowledge within the society, the economy and organizations. This strong emphasis on knowledge has been accompanied by a greater dependency on professionals and so-called knowledge workers.

The work fields and the related academic disciplines of medicine, law, accounting and engineering arguably are exemplary of Novotony, Scott and Gibbons' proposition that 'society itself, and the institutions and organizations it comprises, are now organized around the availability and manipulation of "knowledge" (although this "knowledge" may not be precisely defined)' (2001: 11). The strong emphasis on knowledge as the key resource for growth and wealth creation has led researchers to seek to understand more comprehensively the nature of knowledge and how people and organizations create, absorb, develop and appropriate knowledge.

As within other areas, the rationalistic perspective has been dominating the research on knowledge and its management. Within this perspective knowledge is primarily seen as a specific entity separated from people's work, which can be codified into symbolic forms and transmitted digitally. For example, competence in professional practices such as medicine, engineering, architecture and business, but also in more recent professions and knowledge work, is typically portrayed as a distinct body of formalized scientific-based knowledge that they apply in their work (Alvesson, 2004; Dall'Alba and Sandberg, 1996; Freidson, 2001; Fuller, 2002; Lave, 1993; Newell et al., 2002; Schön, 1983).

The view of knowledge as something that can be formalized and codified has also been strongly encouraged by technological developments in the information and communication technology (ICT) industry. The ICT-industry has developed a range of electronic media (e.g. internet, email and relational databases) to store, retrieve and transmit scientific knowledge. For instance, access to legal databases via the internet has enabled corporate lawyers to speed up their work substantially (Susskind, 1996). The use of ICT has also been a major way to manage knowledge and knowledge workers. However, this way of managing knowledge has proven to be problematic in many ways. As was shown in Chapter 1, a majority of companies in Ruggles's (1998) study experienced difficulties in influencing and changing workers' performance by creating and transmitting new knowledge to them.

Given the problems experienced when using ICT for managing knowledge, researchers have gradually started to question the rationalistic view of knowledge. For example, a large body of research from several disciplines, such as anthropology (Lave, 1993), artificial intelligence (Dreyfus and Dreyfus, 1986; Winograd and Flores, 1986), education (Schön, 1983; Wenger, 1998), sociology (Atkinson, 1988; Fielding, 1988a, 1988b; Garfinkel, 1986; Kusterer, 1978; Livingston, 1987), and management and organization (Barley, 1996; Baumard, 1999; Brown and Duguid, 1991; Sandberg, 2000; Tsoukas, 1996), found that a substantial part of the knowledge used at work is tacit, which cannot be fully articulated and described. As Giddens noted, work performance is 'largely carried out in practical consciousness. Practical consciousness consists of all the things which actors know tacitly about how to "go on" in the context of social life without being able to give them direct discursive expression' (1984: xxiii). What they essentially say is that the knowledge codified into symbolic forms within the rationalistic perspective is only the top of the iceberg. There is a strong subjective dimension of knowledge that is hard to formalize. Polanyi's (1958) bike-riding example is paradigmatic for this view. He points out that an experienced bike rider cannot formulate everything she knows about bike-riding into explicit rules because a substantive part of her bike riding knowledge has been bodily acquired. She knows bodily how to ride a bike but she cannot fully articulate that knowledge.

More recently, a range of other researchers, like Lave and Wenger (1991), Cook and Brown (1999) and Gherardi (2000), have more forcefully demonstrated how the rationalistic perspective on knowledge overlooks the subjective and contextual nature of knowledge at work. They claim that knowledge is more relational than an entity possessed. As Lave expressed it, in this view, professional knowledge cannot be pinned down to the head or the bodies of the individual or to 'assigned tasks or to external tools or to the environment, but lie instead in the relations among them' (1993: 9). As we can see, knowledge is seen as socially constructed within a practice. Regarding knowledge as embodied and contextual has major implications for how to manage it.

Research paradigms control the content of knowledge

What becomes apparent from the analysis of early management research is that an interest in what we call understanding is by no means anything new. Researchers who were active in the 1970s were fully aware of the existence of basic patterns in people's thinking, and that those patterns had a decisive importance for decision and action in organizations. But since they, broadly speaking, worked within a rationalistic perspective, the nature of human understanding remained hidden in a 'black box'. It was possible, as in the case of strategy research, to observe that competence in the sense of knowledge and ways of thinking was crucial for a company's innovative capacity and competitive strength. It was conceivable to say that 'the culture of this company is too production-oriented' and to plead for a different thinking. But no one delved deeper into what actually constitutes human understanding. To put it differently, within the rationalistic perspective it was easy to observe the importance of something resembling what we call understanding. But within that perspective it was not possible to fully grasp the nature of human understanding. It remained in the black box.

To be able to open the black box a new paradigm was needed within management research. When phenomenology and interpretative perspectives became part of the researchers' methodological repertoire, together with a view on knowledge as socially constructed, it became possible to search more thoroughly for an answer to the questions of what understanding is, how it develops and how it guides human action. Presumably, it was not until this paradigm shift took place in management research that the researchers themselves understood the problems involved in the task of clarifying what constitutes understanding.

During the 1990s numerous studies in different fields were carried out within an interpretative perspective, and understanding is now less obscure for management researchers. Through the gradual adoption of an interpretative perspective by management researchers, it can be argued that the paradigm, shift in management research has moved from the level of rhetoric to the level of practice. Following a new paradigm, researchers redefine their role as management researchers. They identify new problems, and new kinds of observation and discussion become meaningful. Finally it has become possible to 'understand understanding'.

But an equivalent process remains to take place among the practitioners. In order to conduct daring experiments and a search for good practical methods for developing and changing understanding among employees, we need practitioners who are themselves clear about what understanding is. Here, as writers and teachers, we have a big challenge, and it is to this that we hope to provide a contribution.

Notes

1 When referring to philosophical phenomenology, we do not primarily mean Husserl's (1962/1931) descriptive phenomenology and his idea about a transcendental subject as the foundation of all knowledge, but rather the *interpretative* phenomenology developed after Husserl. More specifically, if we look at how the various forms of modern phenomenology have been developed since Husserl, not even his closest colleagues accepted a pure and transcendental ego as the foundation of all knowledge (Spiegelberg, 1976). It was primarily through Heidegger's work, *Being and Time* (1962/1927), that Husserl's transcendental subject was rejected by most advocates of phenomenology. Heidegger's work demonstrated, above all, that (a) a pure transcendental subject standing above reality cannot exist because subjects are always situated in a specific culture, historical time and language which mediate reality and that (b) it is not possible to produce objective descriptions of reality because the descriptions are always constituted by the researcher's pre-understanding of the particular aspect of reality under investigation. In other words, researchers' descriptions of reality are always based on their interpretation of the reality described. Moreover, since both Gadamer and Derrida are profoundly influenced by Heidegger's thinking (Bernstein, 2002: 276), it can also be appropriate to see hermeneutics and deconstruction as part of the ongoing development of philosophical phenomenology (Moran 2000: 436). Although Husserl's transcendental philosophy has been heavily criticized, modern philosophers such as Mohanty (1989) and social scientists such as Giorgi (1992) have established a descriptive phenomenology closely based on Husserl's work.

2 Given the great variety of research perspectives related to the interpretative research tradition, there are naturally not only unifying themes but also significant differences and tensions between the different approaches. See for instance Sandberg (2001b) and Schwandt (2003).

THREE Human competence at work: a question of understanding

In the previous chapter we discussed the interpretative management tradition and its development in contrast to the prevalent rationalistic management tradition. In particular, we discussed how the insight that human action is based on people's understanding of their specific work has been developed within management research. The insight emerged initially within the rationalistic perspective, but it was not until management researchers adopted an interpretative perspective that it became possible to grasp more fully the nature of human understanding and how it forms the basis for work performance. The purpose of the next three chapters is to spell out in more detail the main characteristics of understanding and how it forms the basis for work performance in organizations. In Chapters 3 and 4 we mainly discuss what characterizes individuals' understanding of work, while in Chapter 5 we focus on what characterizes collectives' understanding of work and how it forms the basis for their work performance.

In order to illustrate in more detail how understanding functions as the basis for action, we present in this chapter Jörgen Sandberg's (1994, 2000) interpretative study of what constitutes competence at work. It demonstrates how people's understanding of the same task differs and how the different ways of understanding the task form the basis for their work performance. More specifically, it shows how people's ways of understanding work make up, form and organize their knowledge and skills into distinctive competence in performing their work.

We have chosen human competence as an empirical illustration of the simple reason that a company's success ultimately depends on people's competence at work. Without competence there is no performance, at least not an acceptable performance. As was described in both Chapters 1 and 2, the importance of understanding competence has also increased substantially during the last decade, due to the strong emphasis on knowledge for effective work performance. This is particularly so because it is professionals like engineers, lawyers, accountants and other knowledge workers who routinely create, develop and appropriate knowledge to improve work performance. Understanding human competence is thus particularly important for being able to manage and organize professionals and their work effectively.

Human competence: the basis for all enterprises

As we described in the previous chapters, competence development has to a large degree come to be seen as crucial for organizational effectiveness and competitive advantage. In particular, the increased dependency on human competence has resulted in requirements for new and more effective ways to manage and organize the development of competence within organizations. Perhaps the most fundamental problem for all forms of competence development is what constitutes competence in particular work performance and how it can be identified and described. Without an adequate understanding of what competence is, it is impossible to pursue an effective development of competence. It becomes even more difficult to find new and more effective ways to manage competence development. Therefore, there is a good reason to more closely examine existing theories and models of competence to see how they characterize competence and what methods they use to identify and describe it.

If we look at the literature within management and human resource management, it is primarily during the last two decades that the concept of competence has been used most frequently. As we described in the first chapter, the main reason for the increased interest in competence is that industry is becoming more knowledge-intensive and service-based in conjunction with rapid technological development. The concept of competence that is used within industry today refers primarily to the stock of knowledge and skills that are required to achieve growth and renewal within organizations.

There are, however, many other concepts referring to knowledge and skills at work which conceivably could be used. The advantage in using the concept of competence is its focus on the relation between worker and work. As Morgan (1988) argued, the concept of competence encourages us not only to think about knowledge itself, but also to think in terms of knowledge that is required for effectiveness in performing particular work. Hence, the expression 'human competence at work' that is used in this chapter does not refer to all knowledge and skills but to those that are strictly work-related. In other words, human competence refers to those knowledge and skills *people use when working*.

Identifying competence at work: a classic management problem

In a general sense, the question of what constitutes competence at work can be worded as follows: why do some people perform a job better than others? In other words, what characterizes those people who perform a job better than others, and what characterizes those who perform it less well? An answer to that question will enable us to know *what to focus on* and *what to do* when developing competence at work. Consequently, it is necessary to answer that question if the effectiveness of organizations is to be improved by developing competence at work.

Even if the question of what constitutes competence and how it can be identified and described has been accentuated during more recent years, in particular through the emergence of knowledge management, it is not a new management problem. Looking historically, Socrates was one of the first to explicitly raise the question of what constitutes competence at work in his description of the ideal state in the fifth century BC (Primoff and Sidney, 1988). In particular, Socrates described how to select and train workers to acquire the specific competence needed to accomplish particular work in society. In modern times, Frederick W. Taylor was one of the first to identify competence as a managerial problem. In his famous book *The Principle of Scientific Management* (1911), he strongly criticized the managers of the time because they left the training and development of competence to the workers themselves in the different trades within the firms. Within each trade, knowledge and skills were developed and transferred by word of mouth or were learned more or less unconsciously by personal observation. According to Taylor, the main reason for the inefficiency that was apparent in many organizations at that time was that the development of competence had been handed over to the workers themselves. Therefore, managers had never been able to find out what constituted the workers' competence. In that way, managers' ability to influence the effectiveness of organizations was highly limited. In other words, the potential for increased effectiveness was more in the hands of the employees rather than in the hands of the managers.

In order to find a remedy for these circumstances, Taylor argued for a management based on scientific principles from the rationalistic research tradition, the Scientific Management, as he called it. Based on such principles Taylor developed his well-known time and motion studies as a way to identify competence. Using such descriptions of competence as a basis, Taylor showed that managers could design systematic training and development activities that resulted in substantial improvement of the employees' competence, which in turn gave rise to increased effectiveness and productivity within organizations.

Rationalistic approaches to competence

Even if the prevalent approaches to competence today do not consist of time and motion studies, they are to a large degree based on the scientific principles from the rationalistic research tradition. Three main approaches can be distinguished: the worker-oriented, the work-oriented and the multimethod-oriented approaches. Despite the variation, these approaches do not differ concerning the view of competence. They all regard competence as an attribute-based phenomenon. More precisely, according to them, competence consists of a specific set of attributes, such as knowledge and skills, that are used in the performance of work. One of the most common definitions of competence within the rationalistic approaches is KSA. The K stands for knowledge, the S stands for skills and the A stands for ability. Often personal traits are added to the KSA definition of competence. However, what distinguishes these approaches is the ways of identifying and describing competence.

Worker-oriented approaches

The most dominating rationalistic approaches are *the worker-oriented approaches*. Advocates of these take their point of departure in the attributes a person possesses in relation to his or her work. A commonly used worker-oriented approach is the so-called job element method (Veres et al., 1990). It consists of the following six categories for identifying competence: knowledge, skills, ability, willingness, interest and personal characteristics. In order to identify the competence within a certain task, a group of experts such as job incumbents and supervisors is often used. These experts are asked to identify the attributes of the workers who are regarded as most competent. These attributes are then organized with the help of the six categories above. Finally, the experts rate the workers' attributes to be able to measure the correlation between success in the performance of the task and the possession of the identified attributes.

Even if the worker-oriented approaches traditionally have emphasized KSA and personal traits, during the last decade there has been an upsurge in the use of the term 'competencies' (Armstrong, 1991; Boyatzis, 1982; McClelland, 1973; Morgan, 1988; Spencer and Spencer, 1993; Woodruffe, 1990). Advocates of competencies emphasize the importance of focusing on those attributes that are strictly work-related. For example, in an extensive study about competence in leadership, Boyatzis (1982) found that leadership competence consists of 12 specific competencies such as efficiency orientation, proactivity and oral presentations. Boyatzis' study has also had a strong impact on practice as it has been used to establish so-called competence-based assessment centres in the USA and in Europe. Companies send their staff to these centres in order to find out the extent to which they possess competence in leadership in terms of the 12 competencies Boyatzis identified. More recently, Spencer and Spencer (1993) have confirmed and extended Boyatzis' findings. Their investigation into which competencies superior performers were using in more than 200 different jobs show that superior performance at work is usually a result of specific sets of competencies combined in a particular way.

The worker-oriented approaches have, however, been criticized for producing too a general description of competence. For example, Jacobs (1989) questioned Boyatzis' general description of what competencies characterize a competent manager. Within a British study of more than 500 organizations, Jacobs came to the conclusion that different forms of management tasks required different types of competency. The difference was particularly evident among managers from different lines of business.

Work-oriented approaches

To a large extent, advocates of *the work-oriented approaches* overcome the problem of producing too general a description of competence. Instead of the person, they take the work as the point of departure for identifying competence. Based on the identified work activities, they try to deduce the attributes that are central in the work performance. The range of the work-oriented approaches is based on the so-called critical incident technique. The aim is to identify incidents that are crucial in the performance of work. A critical incident is a specific action that indicates either a good or a bad performance of some aspect of work. The number of incidents that needs to be identified depends on the character of the work. In order to identify competence in simpler work it is enough to identify about 100 incidents. In more advanced work, such as management, up to 4,000 incidents need to be identified.

One basic criticism of the work-oriented approaches is that descriptions of work activities are difficult to transform into attributes. According to Raven (1984), for example, there are few indicators in a list of work activities that demonstrate the attributes required to accomplish those activities efficiently. Instead, Raven argued, the focus should be 'on the people who perform well in many situations and not on the task to be done: the latter is too transient and too unstable' (1984: 27). As we saw previously, however, it is difficult to identify competence in more general terms as, for example,

Boyatzis did concerning management competence: different management tasks require different management competence.

Multimethod-oriented approaches

Those who advocate the *multimethod-oriented approaches* try to avoid the criticism that has been directed to both the worker and the work-oriented approaches by using a combination of those approaches. An example of such an approach is Veres et al.'s (1990) study about what constitutes competence in policing. Their analysis resulted in a list of 46 different forms of knowledge, skills and abilities related to 23 specific police activities.

A critical evaluation of the rationalistic approaches to competence

Looking historically, despite the highlighted limitations, Taylor's introduction of a management system based on the rationalistic research tradition greatly improved managers' ability to manage people's competence in organizations. Through the rationalistic approaches managers accessed methods to systematically identify employees' competence of their work performance. With these descriptions as a basis, it became possible to improve the training and development of the employees' competence considerably. The large numbers of rationalistic approaches that have been developed since Taylor's time have continued to refine the ways in which competence can be identified and described.

However, there are several problems within the rationalistic approaches that severely limit their ability to identify and make explicit the most fundamental aspects of what constitutes competence. One such problem is that they often produce fragmentary and atomistic descriptions of competence. These descriptions give rise to diffuse guidelines for managers in developing competence. For example, Veres et al.'s (1990) description of competence in policing, consisting of 46 worker attributes, offers little assistance to managers in deciding which attributes should be developed to improve work performance. Another problem is that the rationalistic approaches predefine competence through models such as KSA (knowledge, skills and ability). If we define competence in advance, there is an overwhelming risk that we confirm our own model of competence rather than make a particular competence at work explicit.

The most fundamental problem, however, is that even a fine-meshed net of categories developed by advocates of the rationalistic approaches, will generate indirect rather than *direct* descriptions of competence. A list of attributes related to work activities does not make competence at work visible. At best, these lists indicate prerequisites for being able to accomplish the specified work competently. They do not demonstrate what is competence *in* work performance. Describing competence as a set of attributes related to a list of work activities does not demonstrate whether the workers use the prerequisite attributes, or in what way they use them in accomplishing the work. For example, two persons can possess identical attributes but perform the same task differently depending on which attributes they use and how they use them.

That the rationalistic approaches are only able to generate indirect descriptions of competence presents us with a range of problems for developing competence. For example, when translating work activities there is a risk of misjudging what constitutes competence in performing that work. A possible consequence is that the desired development of competence will not take place. In addition, if we use indirect descriptions of competence as a basis for developing competence, it can lead to the development of a less effective competence than the work requires. The most serious problem with indirect descriptions is that they limit our ability to find new and more effective ways to develop competence. This is because the better we know what constitutes competence, the more likely it is that we are able to improve our methods for developing competence. It is only when we understand what competence at work is that we will be able to progress in developing competence more effectively in our organizations.

Why is it, then, that advocates of the rationalistic approaches do not seem to be able to generate direct descriptions of competence? The reasons for this are not completely apparent either in the rationalistic models of competence such as KSA, or in their different methods of identifying competence. The reasons why they generate indirect descriptions become more evident when we examine the assumptions underlying the rationalistic approaches about what constitutes competence and how it can be studied.

As we described in Chapter 2, all production of knowledge rests on basic assumptions about the reality we study and how we can acquire knowledge about that reality. These assumptions are often so incorporated in our ways of thinking about and looking upon our reality that we often do not even reflect on them when we try to gain knowledge about some specific aspect of reality. In that sense, they become treacherous as it is possible to produce knowledge about something without being aware of the assumptions that underlie the produced knowledge.

As was pointed out in Chapter 2, the rationalistic research tradition is based on a dualistic view of reality and an objective view of knowledge. The dualistic view of reality implies an assumption that people and reality exist as two independent entities. This means that one thinks that it is possible to study people and reality independently of each other and then how they are related in a particular activity such as work performance. An objective view of knowledge, on the other hand, means that one assumes that an objective reality exists beyond human consciousness.

The underlying dualistic view of reality and the objective view of knowledge within the rationalistic approaches to competence seem to give rise to indirect descriptions of competence. First, the dualistic assumption underlies a division of competence into two separate entities, the worker and the work. Secondly, the objective assumption has lead to describing work activities independently from the workers who accomplish them. From this objective vantage point, in combination with the dualistic perspective, it follows that advocates of the rationalistic approaches identify and describe competence as consisting of two independent entities, a list of attributes possessed by the worker related to a list of work activities.

Given the problems that exist within the rationalistic approaches, it is reasonable to assume that we cannot continue to rely on the rationalistic research tradition for improving our ways of identifying what constitutes competence at work. In particular, it is necessary to overcome the problem with the indirect description of competence. There is a need for a shift in scientific perspective to one that is not based on a dualistic view of reality and an objective view of knowledge. Instead, we need a scientific approach that enables us to identify and describe competence in a direct way, as it is manifest in the work performance.

Towards an interpretative approach to competence

The interpretative research tradition can provide an alternative approach to competence that overcomes the problems within the rationalistic approaches. As was described in Chapter 2, the main features of the interpretative research tradition are its phenomenological assumptions that it is not possible to separate the person and his or her world, and that the basis for human knowledge is our experience of our world. It is, above all, during the last twenty years that we have started to use interpretative approaches within organization and management. Even if interpretative approaches have been used more frequently within organization and management, few studies have used interpretative approaches when identifying and describing what constitutes competence at work. Interpretative approaches to competence have more commonly been employed in fields such as artificial intelligence, nursing and education. Some of these studies will be explored further to see what they say about competence.[1]

Within artificial intelligence (AI) Dreyfus and Dreyfus (1986) studied, for example, how different professional groups, such as pilots, chess players and car drivers, developed competence. They identified different stages in their development of competence: beginner, advanced beginner, competent, proficient and expert. What became evident in their study was that the knowledge and skills that people develop are not isolated from people's understanding of their specific tasks, as assumed within the rationalistic approaches. Instead, their results show that independently of the level of competence, people develop knowledge and skills that are bounded to their understanding of their specific tasks. That the competence that people develop is strongly bounded to their understanding of work became even more apparent in Benner's (1984) study about what constitutes competence in nursing. By comparing how a beginner and an expert nurse understood the same nursing situation, Benner demonstrated that the beginner and the expert nurse understood and dealt with that 'same' situation differently.

A range of other interpretative studies has reached similar conclusions. For example, in his study about what constitutes competence in policing, Fielding (1988a) found that skills such as 'observing' and 'negotiating' tend to vary in meaning or significance depending on which ways the police understand a particular work situation. Moreover, in a comprehensive study of professionals such as architects, psychotherapists, engineers, urban planners and managers, Schön (1983) come to the conclusion that it is not possible to separate the person from the work when studying competence. His study showed that people never perform an 'objective' work but always an 'understood' work. That work is never objective but understood means that our knowledge and skills are always related to work through our understanding of it.

Establishing an interpretative approach to competence

What the findings from the interpretative approaches suggest is that a person's attributes at work, such as knowledge and skills, do not exist independently of their understanding of work. Instead, the attributes appear to be bounded to work through people's understanding of it. Thus, in an interpretative approach to competence the vital point is to come as close as possible to people's own understanding of their work. The more precisely we can describe people's understanding of their work, the more likely we are to identify what constitutes competence at work.

However, even if the interpretative approaches seem to overcome the problem of indirect descriptions of competence, there are a number of problems that make it difficult to identify and describe competence at work. One such problem is that such approaches are unable to provide a more integrated description of what constitutes competence at work. Another problem is that their descriptions do not seem to capture the variation in competence that may exist among a group of people who perform the same work. In 1911 Taylor had already noted a considerable difference among employees in terms of their competence in performing the same work. The studies discussed above capture a variation in competence in terms of different levels of competence acquisition, but not the variation that may exist at a particular level, such as among advanced beginners.

Phenomenography as an interpretative approach to competence

Phenomenography is an approach that can provide a potential solution to the limitations of current interpretative approaches to competence. It was originally developed as an approach for describing qualitative variations in people's ways of understanding their reality, and was used as a basis for development activities in formal education (Marton and Booth, 1997; Marton et al., 1977). According to the phenomenographic approach, understanding is not an attribute. Instead, understanding signifies our inextricable relation to our world. More precisely, understanding signifies the particular meaning that an aspect of reality has for us. In order to capture understanding one has to investigate the ongoing process in which reality receives a specific meaning and significance for us.

A common expression is that there are as many ways to understand a particular aspect of reality as there are people. A central conclusion from the phenomenographic studies disputes that idea. Instead, their results suggest that there is only a limited number of ways to understand the same aspect of reality among a certain group of people – often between two and six different ways. It can be everything from understanding why a particular item costs a certain amount of money to understanding death (Marton and Booth, 1997).

Another central conclusion from phenomenographic studies is that people's ways of understanding a specific subject or a specific learning task govern their ways of acting. For example, phenomenographic studies have shown that children's ways of understanding numbers govern their way of solving mathematical problems (Neuman, 1987). Moreover, in another study it was found that compulsory school students accomplished a range of natural science tasks in different ways, according to what they considered the task to be about. The outcome they achieved varied depending on their ways of understanding those tasks (Dall'Alba, 1987).

There are primarily three reasons why phenomenography is a more promising interpretative approach for identifying what constitutes competence at work. One reason is its focus on describing the person and the work as an indissoluble relationship. As Marton and Svensson argued, 'Instead of two independent descriptions (of the student on the one hand and of his [sic] world on the other) and an assumed relation between the two, we have one description which is of a relational character' (1979: 472). A second reason is that, in contrast to the rationalistic description of competence as a list of separate attributes, the phenomenographic approach strives to describe people's understanding of reality in an integrated way. By doing so it has the potential to describe competence in a less fragmented way than previous interpretative approaches. A third reason is that the focus on the variation captures a whole range of competence within a group of people, from the least to the most efficient.

Development of phenomenography as an interpretative approach

A phenomenographic approach to competence was developed and tested empirically by Sandberg (1994, 2000). Sandberg developed phenomenography as an interpretative approach to competence by deepening and clarifying the concept of understanding with the help of the phenomenological notion of life-world. As we described above, within phenomenography, understanding refers to the meaning a particular situation receives through our specific way of understanding it.

As pointed out in Chapter 2, the phenomenological notion of life-world highlights that we as human beings always live and act within our understanding of reality and not above or outside it. Figure 3.1. can help us to illuminate the principle of life-world as the basis for all human action.

What appears when we experience the object in Figure 3.1? The object may appear as an umbrella. We can now begin to explore the umbrella and develop our knowledge about it. For example, we can compare it with other umbrellas and identify similarities and differences. However, if we 'bracket' the umbrella and look at the object a little longer, the object may become something else. Perhaps a three-dimensional cube appears from the same object as the umbrella. The object has now received a new meaning for us and we can begin to explore the appearing cube and develop our knowledge about it. What the example illustrates is that the meaning of the object that appears in our understanding of it precedes our knowledge about it and our

61

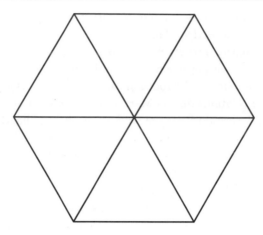

Figure 3.1   The experienced object

skills in mastering it. If we understand the object as an umbrella, we will develop knowledge about umbrellas and skills to master it. If, on the other hand, we understand the object as a three-dimensional cube, we develop knowledge about three-dimensional cubes and the skills to handle those.

A practical example: competence in engine optimization

The phenomenographic approach to competence was tested empirically on á group of engineers, called engine optimizers, at Volvo Car Corporation in Sweden. The primary task of the optimizers is to develop car engines for new car models. They develop these engines by optimizing a range of qualities such as driveability, fuel consumption, emissions, and engine power (performance). These qualities are optimized by adjusting different parameters within the electronic monitoring systems for fuel and ignition. They should be optimized in such a way that an engine works smoothly. An approved car (one that meets the Volvo Corporation's requirements) should be able to be driven by almost any driver, in almost all conditions. There are several interest groups that set specific requirements for what makes a good car engine, and these requirements have to be met by the car makers. The optimization process is not made any easier by the fact that some of the requirements are contradictory. The complex and contradictory nature of the requirements creates uncertainty and ambiguity in the optimizers' performance. So how can the engine optimizers refine an engine according to the stipulated requirements? In other words, *what is competence in engine optimization?*

Three different ways of understanding engine optimization are evident among the optimizers investigated.

1   Optimizing separate qualities
2   Optimizing interacting qualities
3   Optimizing from the customers' perspective.

The optimizers within each understanding differ from each other through their way of delimiting and organizing the optimization work in three qualitatively different ways. Within each understanding, it is also possible to distinguish a number of essential attributes of competence. More specifically, each understanding is characterized by a specific structure of attributes which emerge as the optimizers accomplish the optimization. Thus, the particular way of understanding the optimization work delimits certain attributes as essential and organizes them into a distinctive structure of competence in engine optimization. Hence, the optimizers' ways of understanding the optimization work constitute their competence in engine optimization. Let us explore in more detail how each understanding and its attributes form a distinctive structure of competence in engine optimization.

Understanding 1: Optimizing separate qualities

The most characteristic feature of this understanding is that the optimizers who express it delimit and organize the optimization work in terms of a number of separate optimizing steps, focusing on the relationship between the monitoring parameters and each single quality of the engine. Within each step, they test various adjustments of the parameters to optimize a single engine quality, for example, driveability or fuel consumption, according to stipulated requirements. The optimizers optimize one single quality at a time until all qualities meet the requirements. The following discussion between the interviewer (I) and an optimizer (O), which developed out of the key question 'What is a competent optimizer for you?', illustrates this view:

I: What do you use these (measurement results) for?

O: You get measurement results about how much hydrocarbon and NOX [nitrous oxide] and CO [carbon monoxide] the engine leaves and fuel consumption. You do a whole series of tests and it [the measurement] will change a little bit. Then you take a mean value for it and the result should be under a particular value and when it does that, it's okay.

I: What do you do when you have reached it?

O: Well, then one says it's okay and begins to concentrate on other qualities.

Their focus on the relationship between monitoring parameters and a single engine quality implies that all their key attributes are centred around that relationship, forming a distinctive structure of competence in engine optimization. By focusing on the relationship between monitoring parameters and each single engine quality, these optimizers reduce the complexity and uncertainty within engine optimization. When they have identified a specific quality of the engine, they test various adjustments of the parameters to optimize the quality according to the stipulated requirements. The optimizers must be able to analyse and interpret the measurement results generated from tests – determining what a certain discrepancy from the expected result can depend upon – and then judge which parameters should be adjusted to achieve an optimum of the quality in question.

Therefore, being able *to analyse and interpret how one or several monitoring parameters have influenced the quality* is one of the most fundamental attributes that appear within this understanding. It is through this attribute that the optimizers evaluate each single optimization.

I: Yeah, but those diagrams, why are they important?

O: Well, from them we should be able to read and judge what we should change and if the results are bad we have to fix them. ... If we are dealing with emission tests and you start to drive a car that has been standing at a temperature of +25 degrees (Celsius) ... you run a test and it isn't acceptable. Well, then you may reduce it [the emissions], you look at those curves and at the monitoring parameters. Yeah, it has decreased, it has gone down so much, but at the same time another gas, that is, nitrogen oxide, has gone up instead. Here it's a question of being able to read the diagrams correctly, both the measurement results, diagrams and monitoring system.

Despite the fact that the optimizers reduce the complexity and uncertainty in their work by delimiting and organizing it into separate steps, some uncertainties remain. This uncertainty becomes evident when one examines the tolerances of the measurement instruments in various testing rooms and the test drivers' different ways of driving. The optimizers control this uncertainty and build up their understanding of analysing and interpreting the particular optimization through the attribute *to be accurate and methodical in the optimization*. When optimizing a specific quality, these optimizers change one monitoring parameter at a time, analyse the influence it has on the current quality, make a note of it, choose a new parameter and change it, investigate the influence on the quality and so on:

O: There are many optimizers who have been here for a long while but, despite that, they have to do ten tests in order to reach the same result that X [name of colleague] maybe will see from two or three tests.

I: What do you think that depends on?

O: A great sense of being methodical and systematic in the work. You are changing one thing each time and you don't change ten things because then you don't know which one was the cause of this change or the result of the change.

This attribute enables the optimizers to speed up their work of analysing and interpreting which parameters need to be adjusted in order to reach the desired optimum of the particular engine quality. This attribute also interacts with the attribute *to understand how the qualities of the engine react to changes in the parameter*:

O: You need to have this knowledge, [to] know how emissions are influenced by the amount of fuel and air, how air pressure and temperature may have an influence on emissions and driveability.

This is the kind of knowledge that the optimizers build up around the qualities of the engine so that they can judge which parameter should be adjusted and by how much in order to reach the desired requirement. This attribute is closely connected to the attribute *to understand which monitoring parameters have an influence on a specific quality of the engine and how they do so*. Together, these two latter attributes form two poles of the focused relationship between the parameter and engine quality. This allows the optimizers to analyse and interpret the results from the tests and then adjust the relevant parameter so that the optimum value of the quality in question will be reached in each separate optimization step.

Understanding 2: Optimizing interacting qualities

The optimizers who expressed understanding 2 also regard the optimization work as consisting of different optimization steps. But in contrast to the previous optimizers, they do not delimit and organize the optimization in separate steps, but in several interacting steps in which each engine quality is optimized in relation to each other. Delimiting and organizing the optimization work in interacting steps shifts the focus from the relationship between monitoring parameters and a single engine quality to the relationships between the qualities of the engine. These optimizers take all optimizing steps into consideration at each single step: if we optimize a specific quality, what will happen to the remaining engine qualities that will subsequently be optimized? Hence, for these optimizers, the primary aim in each step is to optimize a single quality so that it will interact with the remaining qualities to ultimately produce an approved engine:

I: What is a competent engine optimizer for you?

O: It's someone who has an idea about ... someone who can see into this crystal ball, in this engine's future, yeah, into the future of my work. The further you are able to understand the future, the better I think it is. We have to make modifications to certain things to be able to achieve other things later on. So to be able to understand how ... a certain optimization influences other qualities. It's not so simple that if I optimize x, then all other qualities are independent, because they aren't. The link between these qualities, I think, is important and you learn them through experience. That's what I'm talking about, being able to understand things, understand the links, because if you understand the links you can more easily look into the future and judge what will happen.

This change in focus implies that the attributes within this understanding appear from the relationship between the qualities of the engine, forming a distinctively different structure of competence in engine optimization. As the qualities of the engine interact with each other, the optimizers must understand in which order and how accurately the qualities should be optimized in each optimization situation. Therefore the attribute *to optimize the qualities of the engine in the right order and to be accurate* is of fundamental importance for these optimizers:

O: The most important thing is to be extremely accurate.

I: In what?

O: Well in your work, to know exactly what you're doing and to know which step you should take. ... You have to know the order to take this [work] in. You shouldn't sit in FB [function testing room] and do tests until you have it [the optimization] exact for each point. ... It's not certain that it's optimal. Perhaps it's optimal, but it's the wrong tactics. You ought to get it to tolerable as fast as possible, then when I see that the car can be driven, take it in on the emission rolls, then you have to make these rounds again, because everything influences something else. The worse the emission value you have, the better the driveability often, that is, it runs smoothly and evenly.

It is of interest to note that accuracy means different things to the optimizers expressing this understanding compared with those expressing the former understanding. The optimizers in the former understanding take one thing at a time, recording it and so on, to achieve a desired optimum for a certain quality in a specific optimization step. On the other hand, optimizers with this understanding attempt to optimize a quality as accurately as possible within a specific step, without negatively influencing the remaining qualities. It is through the attribute to see *links between the qualities of the engine* that these optimizers are able to establish the right order of the steps and to judge the degree of accuracy within the optimization:

I: So what is a competent engine optimizer for you?

O: Well, to have perspective on everything he's doing. I think that's very important. But when I say perspective on everything he's doing, then he must have a good grasp of what the component activities mean and that implies ... yes, well if I'm not using the word competent ... it means that he has an understanding of how the parameters interact.

I: Do you mean emissions, driveability?

O: Emissions, driveability, fuel consumption ... he must have that in each situation. Competence is being able to link a measurement to a subjective judgement of a quality which, in fact, you don't have in front of you.

Like the optimizers expressing understanding 1, these optimizers also point out the attribute *to understand and develop monitoring systems* as central in the optimization work. However, while knowledge of monitoring systems for the previous optimizers means being able to influence a single engine quality in a desired way, knowledge of monitoring systems for these optimizers means being able to reach the desired interaction among the qualities of the engine:

O: So you have to have a certain basic education in maths, at least high school level, in order to grasp those functions, those algorithms that are in the monitoring system. You have to see that if you increase

67

by a factor of 2, then that [factor] is an integral part of an equation for fuel injection.

In the statement about the equation, it becomes apparent that adjusting one parameter may affect other phases of optimization as the parameter is an integral part of a system, an equation. In order to develop new monitoring functions but, above all, to build up knowledge about the links between qualities of the engine, the attribute *interest in engines and self-learning* appears:

I: Why is self-learning important?

O: Well, if you're curious and ask yourself some questions ... there are always people who wonder why it [the optimization result] is like this and then they continue to think until they have figured out why and such people educate themselves much faster than if you do something and ... look that's the result ... and then you accept it, but you may not wonder why it is so. ... Curiosity, to be able to see why you got that result. ... It's some kind of self-education that such people are giving themselves.

However, in advancing the work the task is not only to learn for oneself. It is also a matter of communicating with others. Here, the attribute *to cooperate with the other people involved and communicate to them how the engine ought to be optimized* is central:

O: The task is about pushing something forward and not only educating yourself. So that's what you need to do, yes, to communicate and tell others how it should be.

These optimizers not only develop their own knowledge but also include other optimizers in the learning process, so a shared understanding is built up about the ongoing optimization work. By doing so, others involved in the optimization become more motivated and efficient in their work.

Understanding 3: Optimizing from the customers' perspective

Optimizers who express this understanding also take account of all the stages at each single optimization step. However, these optimizers focus on the relation between the optimized engine and the customers' experience of driving. Wherever these optimizers are optimizing the engine, be it in the testing room or on the road, they drive the car as an ordinary customer would. As illustrated by a response to a follow-up question to the key question 'What is a competent optimizer for you?', the optimizers relate the single optimization situation to the approved car and, in so doing, they try to incorporate the customers' requirements at each step of the process:

> O: The reality is in fact that you should be like, yeah like any one of the customers. You should be able to take a young boy's perspective on a car, and an older person, how he wants to experience the car. Then if your car works, hopefully in both ways, then they'll both be satisfied. This is what I think is the role of the optimizer, it's to be able to drive a car as you think people want to experience the car.

The attributes that emerge within this understanding are all centred around the relationship between specific qualities of the engine and the customers' requirements, forming a distinctively different structure of competence in comparison with the first and second understandings. The most essential attribute for these optimizers is *a practical sense of the engine*. It is through this attribute that they are able to evaluate the interaction of the qualities of the engine and the customers' perspective. The attribute consists of knowing the customers' requirements of what a good car should be. At the same time, the optimizers also need to understand how optimizing a particular quality influences the end result of the optimization. Of greatest importance is knowledge of the relationship between the customers' requirements and the optimization of particular qualities in producing the end product – if I change this particular quality, then the other engine qualities will react in this way but, above all, the customers will experience it like this:

> I: So it's a different requirement then?

> O: Yes, it's fuel consumption and emissions, then there are other requirements such as performance or driveability. In this [optimization] point you may have the lowest asphyxiate emissions but then the car may run very badly. You may not be able to drive with that ignition position because then the customer feels it directly, that it feels odd and then you have to choose another ignition position which is not optimal from the point of view of asphyxiate, maybe not optimal from the point of view of fuel, but somewhere in between. You have to make compromises between them.

Although the attribute *to understand and develop monitoring systems* is also essential for these optimizers, its meaning differs compared with that given by the optimizers who expressed the first and second understanding:

O: And there are thousands of functions in such a monitoring system
that should allow for all different driving situations. For instance,
take such a simple thing as the air conditioning function. ... When
the AC starts it puts a load on the engine. The engine can't then go
and stall or something but we have to make sure it runs right.

As the quote illustrates, there is an enormous range of situations in which the
customers drive the car. These optimizers have to be able to allow for all
these, by adjusting suitable parameters and by developing new operations
within the monitoring system which are better suited to meeting a particular
customer requirement. Also, the attributes *interest in engines and self-learning
and to cooperate and have relevant contacts* appear to be central for these optimizers as they are for the optimizers expressing the second understanding.
However, in contrast to these optimizers, who in their self-learning increase
their knowledge about the relationships among the engine qualities, the optimizers expressing the third understanding build up knowledge about the
relationship between the customers' wishes and the approved engine.
Therefore, collaboration with the department for complete vehicle testing,
which tests the car from the customers' requirements, is of particular importance for these optimizers:

O: That's what I see as the most important feedback. We don't build
cars for ourselves, we build cars for customers. They should be satisfied with it and it should meet all these legal requirements in different markets, not only when the car is new but also when it has
gone a number of miles. But then there are always in-house experts ...
and they look at the total picture maybe more than we do. That's
the closest check or judges you have who can give feedback.

These statements emphasize the importance of cooperating with the
department for complete vehicle testing. Here the attribute *practical sense of
the engine* becomes clear. The most important transformation is the knowledge about the relationship between the character of the engine and the customers' requirements.

A hierarchy of competence in engine optimization

As was described in the previous section, the optimizers' understanding of
work constitutes their competence at work. More specifically, the different
ways of understanding optimization work constitute three distinctive forms
of competence in engine optimization. However, their ways of understanding

constitute and give rise to not only a variation in competence, but also to a hierarchy of competence. More specifically, a hierarchy of competence in engine optimization is established in terms of an increasing comprehensiveness of ways of understanding. In the first understanding (optimizing separate qualities), the optimization work is delimited as several separate steps, with the relationship between the parameter and the single quality of the engine in focus. In the second understanding (optimizing interacting qualities), the optimization work is expanded so that it not only includes separate steps but also the relationship between the qualities of the engine in each step. In the third understanding (optimizing from the customers' perspective), the optimization work is expanded still further so that it consists not only of separate steps and interaction between qualities but also of the relationship between the optimized engine and customers' requirements.

The hierarchy of competence in terms of an increasing comprehensiveness of ways of understanding is still more evident through the attributes within each understanding of engine optimization. For instance, the attribute *knowledge of the engine* was expressed by all the optimizers as essential to engine optimization. However, the meaning of this attribute varies depending on in which particular understanding it appears. In the first understanding (optimizing separate qualities), knowledge of the engine means knowledge about how the qualities of the engine react to changes in the monitoring parameters. The second understanding (optimizing interacting qualities) also includes knowledge of how the various qualities react to different influences from the parameters. However, this knowledge of the engine is inadequate for the second understanding. In order to optimize interacting qualities, it is also necessary to see links between the engine qualities. Within the third understanding (optimizing from the customers' perspective), knowledge about how the qualities of the engine interact is important but insufficient. Of greater importance is a practical sense of the engine, as the focus for these optimizers is the relationship between the engine qualities and the customers' requirements. Hence, the hierarchy of competence has the following character: the first understanding is least comprehensive, the second is more comprehensive than the first, while the third understanding is most comprehensive.

Understanding: the basis for human competence at work

The question we have tried to answer in this chapter is what constitutes competence at work and how can this competence be identified and described? According to the rationalistic approaches to competence developed since the time of Taylor, competence is constituted by a specific set of knowledge,

71

skills and other attributes that a person possesses in relation to a particular type of work. The empirical results generated by phenomenography as an interpretative approach to competence challenge the descriptions of competence produced by the dominant rationalistic approaches. In particular, the usefulness of these descriptions as a starting point for training and development activities becomes highly questionable. We will give two examples of why this is the case. In the examples, we adopt a rationalistic approach to competence in engine optimization and compare it with the findings generated by the phenomenographic approach.

First, if we adopt a rationalistic approach to the optimizers' competence, we would regard the essential aspects of their competence in engine optimization as a specific set of attributes related to the optimization work. Accordingly, competence in engine optimization would be described as the total number of attributes identified in engine optimization: the greater the number of these that the optimizers possess, the more competent they would be. In the light of the findings from this study, such a description of the optimizers' competence is misleading.

A severe implication of describing competence as consisting of a set of attributes is that the attributes identified would be treated as though they belong to one and the same understanding of engine optimization. By doing so, we would be unable to discern that the attribute *to optimize the qualities of the engine in the right order and to be accurate* is part of understanding 1 but not of understanding 2 and 3. Moreover, we would be unable to see that *to be accurate and methodical in the optimization* only appears in understanding 2 and that the attribute *a practical sense of the engine* only appears in understanding 3.

Second, if we adopt a rationalistic approach to the optimizers' competence, it appears that each attribute in engine optimization has the same meaning, irrespective of the optimizer who has expressed it. From the perspective of the findings generated by the phenomenographic approach, this is directly misleading. The study has shown that the attributes have different meanings, depending on which understanding they are a part of. For instance, all the optimizers expressed the importance of knowledge about the engine. From a rationalistic approach, 'knowledge about the engine' would be regarded as having the same meaning for all of them. If we turn to the findings from this study, we discover that the meaning of this attribute varies depending on the particular understanding in which it appears. In understanding 1, knowledge about the engine means *understanding how the qualities of the engine react to changes in the parameters*. In understanding 2, knowledge about the engine means *seeing links between the qualities of the engine* and, finally, in understanding 3 knowledge about the engine means *a practical sense of the engine*. The variation in meaning also occurs for the other attributes expressed by the optimizers.

Above all, what the findings from the phenomenographic study show is that competence is not primarily constituted by a specific set of attributes a person possesses. Instead, persons' knowledge, skills and other attributes used in accomplishing the work are *preceded* by and based upon their understanding of the work. As became apparent in the description of what constitutes competence in engine optimization and in the examples above, it is through our particular ways of understanding it that our work receives a specific meaning, that is, what it is about. The presented results suggest that it is the understood meaning of work that forms the basis for the development and maintenance of competence at work. In other words, it is people's ways of understanding their work that form and organize their knowledge and skills into a distinctive competence in their work performance.

From the above conclusions it follows that the main reason why the dominant rationalistic approaches are unable to identify and describe competence satisfactorily is related to the basic assumptions underlying those approaches. In particular, the fallacy relates to the dualistic separation of human competence into separate entities: on the one hand, a person who possesses a number of attributes and, on the other hand, a task consisting of a number of work activities. This dualistic separation leads advocates of the rationalistic approaches to overlook that the basis for competence is our understanding of work. In other words, they are unable to see that person and work constitute an inextricable relationship in terms of the person's understanding of his or her work. As the two examples above illustrate, advocates of the rationalistic approaches are unable to identify the specific knowledge and skills that appear within a particular understanding of work. In that sense, the rationalistic descriptions of competence are incomplete and, consequently, misleading as a starting point for competence development.

Concluding remarks

In conclusion, these results not only present a strong challenge to the rationalistic approaches, but also imply *an extension and a specification* of the interpretative management perspective. In line with findings from other studies using interpretative approaches, this study suggests that human action is based on our ways of understanding work. However, what has not previously been made explicit within the interpretative management tradition is that the meanings that appear in our understanding of work are not only the basis for our work performance but also *the basis for the competence we develop and use in accomplishing our work*. This insight has far-reaching implications not only for competence development but also for management in general.

Traditionally competence development has been limited to specific training and development activities. But from the above insight it follows that development of competence is an inevitable part of all forms of management. This is because when managers influence staff members' ways of understanding their work, they also influence the competence employees use in accomplishing their work.

Note

1 For a more extensive and detailed description of interpretative approaches to competence, see Sandberg (2000), Sandberg and Pinnington (forthcoming) and Dall'Alba and Sandberg (in press).

FOUR Understanding: the basis for competence development

An important insight from the previous chapter was that understanding of work does not only function as a basis for human action but also for the competence we use in accomplishing our work. This chapter aims to analyse further the nature of human understanding by investigating in more detail how understanding forms the basis for both what competence we develop and how we develop competence at work.

As was pointed out in the previous chapter, competence in workplaces has been regarded as an attribute-based phenomenon: a set of knowledge, skills and attitudes possessed by a person in relation to a particular type of work. From the above view of competence follows a corresponding view of its development: competence development is regarded as the acquisition of a specific set of knowledge and skills that constitutes a particular competence. Within such a view, the overriding principle for development of competence becomes transmitting such attributes to those people who not possess them. A range of activities, such as general communication, classroom teaching, on-the-job training and job rotation, are used to transmit the attributes.

However, as was demonstrated in the previous chapter, competence is not primarily constituted by a specific set of specific attributes such as knowledge and the skills a person possesses in relation to his or her work. Instead, the study about competence in engine optimization showed that a person's knowledge and skills are preceded by and are based on the person's understanding of his or her work. It was the optimizers' ways of understanding engine optimization that formed, organized and developed their knowledge and skills to a specific and distinct competence in engine optimization. These findings have also been confirmed in more recent empirical studies on competence, such as Dall'Alba, 2002; Dall'Alba and Sandberg, in press; Sandberg, 2001a; Sandberg and Pinnington, forthcoming; Stålsby-Lundborg et al., 1999).

Understanding as the basis for *what* competence we develop at work

If understanding of work is the basis for what constitutes competence at work, then this understanding is also arguably the basis for developing competence since the way we understand work stipulates *what* competence we develop at work. That this is the case can be illustrated through an attempt that was made to find out who was the most competent engine optimizer. The interviewed optimizers were asked to point out a person whom they thought was particularly skilled. Optimizers who had demonstrated understanding 3 were judged by the interviewees to be most the competent optimizers. For example, one optimizer demonstrating understanding 1 named a colleague who had demonstrated understanding 3 as being among the most competent optimizers in the department:

I: What's a competent engine optimizer for you?

O: Ability to analyse, that you can do a couple of tests and look at the curves and see that all the curves don't look similar but you have to understand why they look different ... that you have to have a feel for, if you do this then that should happen. It's a kind of sixth sense then, but it is probably based on knowledge.

I: Is there anyone you think has such ability?

O: XX [a colleague with understanding 3]

I: Yes, how does he accomplish this optimization, when he sees it [the test result]?

O: I really don't know how he accomplishes it but when you ask him he always knows why [the curves appear as they do] and the reason for it.

I: But what is it that is so special about XX?

O: Perhaps there are people who have the same amount of knowledge as XX but despite that don't achieve a desirable result. I don't know why that is.

I: Don't you have any ideas about that? What do you mean when you say that some of the optimizers have the same amount of knowledge as XX?

O: There are a number of optimizers who have been here for a long time but despite that, they have to carry out ten tests in order to get the same result that XX might see from one or two tests.

I: So you mean the fact that they have many years of experience doesn't mean everything?

O: No.

I: But what do you think is the reason for that?

O: A great sense of being methodical and systematic in your work. You change one thing at a time and you don't change ten things because then you don't know which one was the cause of the change or the result of the change.

What is interesting to note is that when the optimizer is asked what distinguishes the colleague holding understanding 3 from a less competent colleague, he claims that the most competent colleague hold the same competence as himself but has more of it. In particular, this optimizer claimed that his competent colleague had 'more' of the most basic attribute of understanding 1, namely, *to be accurate and methodical in the optimization work*. The same pattern was also evident among the optimizers who expressed understanding 2. Although they were unable to describe understanding 3, they pointed out their colleagues with understanding 3 as the most competent optimizers. When they tried to describe the competence of those whom they regarded as most competent, they claimed that these optimizers had more of the attributes of understanding 2.

Hence, the optimizers develop and maintain a specific competence which is based on their understanding of engine optimization. This becomes even more evident if we look more closely at the specific attributes which appeared in their work. For example, all the optimizers expressed knowledge of the engine as being crucial for optimizing competently. However, depending on whether they understood engine optimization as (1) optimizing separate qualities, (2) optimizing interacting qualities or, (3) optimizing from the customers' perspective, they developed specific forms of knowledge of the engine. The optimizers who expressed understanding 1 developed knowledge of the engine in terms of how the engine qualities react to changes in the adjusting parameters. The optimizers with understanding 2 developed knowledge of the engine in terms of seeing links between the qualities of the engine, and the optimizers with understanding 3 developed knowledge of the engine in terms of a practical sense of the engine.

If the basis for competence development is understanding of work, the most fundamental form of competence development would require one *to be able to understand the 'same' work in a qualitatively different way* (Sandberg, 1994, 2000). For instance, if optimizers with understanding 2 should develop understanding 3, they have to change their understanding from 'optimizing interacting qualities' to 'optimizing from the customers' perspective'.

77

However, competence development does not normally consist of such changes in understanding but of ongoing refinement of the present understanding of work. The fact that competence development mainly occurs within the present understanding of work can be regarded as ineffective for the optimizers who have expressed understanding 1 and 2. They appear to strive to be as competent as the optimizers with understanding 3, while maintaining their present understanding of engine optimization. This means that they will not develop understanding 3, but rather render it more difficult to make such a change. In other words, the more they develop their present understanding of work, the more automatic and taken-for-granted their way of accomplishing the optimization work will become. 'This is the way you optimize car engines!'

Understanding as the basis for *how* we develop competence at work

In the previous section, it was argued that understanding of work stipulates what competence we develop at work. However, our understanding of work does not only determine what competence we develop, but also *how* we develop that competence. As we have pointed out and elaborated elsewhere (e.g. Sandberg and Targama, 1998), the way in which the optimizers understood their work not only stipulated what competence they developed (the three forms of competence described previously), but also the particular way they engaged in developing that competence. For instance, the particular way in which the optimizers 1 understand engine optimization gives rise to a specific way to engage in developing competence in engine optimization, namely by delimiting and organizing optimization work into a number of separate steps, and within each step optimizing a single quality of the engine according to requirements. This specific way to engage in developing competence simultaneously gives rise to a specific competence in engine optimization: competence in engine optimization as 'optimizing separate qualities'. That the way to engage in developing competence, and what competence is developed, from an inextricable relationship through understanding of work is also evident among the optimizers in understanding 2 and 3. The way in which optimizers 2 understand their work gives rise to a specific way to engage in developing competence, which means that they develop their competence by delimiting and organizing the optimization work into a number of interacting steps and by optimizing within each step the single qualities of the engine in relation to each other. The specific way of developing competence results in a particular optimization competence, namely 'optimizing interacting qualities'.

Similar to the optimizers expressing understanding 2, optimizers holding understanding 3 develop their competence by delimiting and organizing the optimization work in such a way that every single optimization step is related to the remaining steps in the optimization process. However, the optimizers with understanding 3 differ from the optimizers with understanding 2 in that their particular way of understanding engine optimization means that they develop their competence by also relating every single optimization step to the customers' requirements. The specific way to engage in developing competence in understanding 3 means that these optimizers develop the competence in engine optimization of 'optimizing from customers' perspective'.

The discussion above suggests that the ways individuals understand their work form the basis for both the particular way they engage in developing competence and what specific competence they develop at work. In other words, the specific way to engage in developing competence and the competence that is developed at work form an indissoluble unit through individuals' ways of understanding work. That understanding of work constitutes an inextricable relationship between the way of engaging in competence development and the outcome of that development has also been empirically demonstrated in formal education (Marton and Booth, 1997; Svensson, 1976, 1977).

Of particular interest is Dall'Alba's longitudinal study of aspiring doctors (Dall'Alba and Sandberg, in press). By following medical students over a five-year period she was able to demonstrate empirically that understanding of work forms the basis for what specific body of scientific knowledge aspiring professionals acquire in professional education. On the first day of their medical programme she identified specific ways of understanding medical practice among the medical students. Over time the aspiring doctors gradually developed a stipulated body of scientific theory and technique in parallel with a greater fluency and confidence in various routines and procedures relating to medical practice. However, the specific body of knowledge they developed and used varied according to their specific understanding of medical practice. In particular, to a large extent the development of their professional knowledge took its point of departure, and was limited by, the students' understanding when they commenced on the medical programme. In addition, Dall'Alba's study demonstrated a variation in the understanding of professional practice within a single skill level, both at the beginning and at the end of the medical programme.

In conclusion, the insight that developing understanding of work constitutes competence development suggests that the development of competence to large extent is *circular* rather than linear. The circular nature becomes most apparent in terms of competence development as an ongoing refinement of a present understanding of work. Every time the optimizers encounter their work they typically understand it in a similar way as they did before. For example, every time optimizers 1 encounter optimization work, they understand it as optimizing separate qualities, and every time optimizers 3 encounter optimization work, they understand it as optimizing from the customers' perspective. This means that their previous understanding of engine optimization is largely reproduced in each new encounter of it. In other words, the circular nature of competence development seems to be due to the fact that their previous understanding of optimization work stipulates in advance how they understand what their work is about in every new encounter of it and, thus, *how* they develop their competence and *what* competence they develop in engine optimization.

How does understanding operate?

If understanding of work constitutes both how we develop competence and what competence we develop, then the question of what it takes to understand something is fundamental. Within the interpretative research tradition, advocates of hermeneutics have provided one of the most comprehensive theories of how understanding operates. What makes the hermeneutic theory of understanding of particular interest here is its emphasis on the circular nature of understanding.

The origin of the word 'hermeneutics' is Hermes, the Greek god who was a 'messenger-god' between the gods and people. Hermes was known for this power to make messages from the gods understandable to people. The Greek verb *hermeneuin* and the noun *hermeneia*, generally translated as 'to interpret' and 'interpretatation', refer to the interpretative process of making something foreign and unfamiliar understandable.

According to Palmer (1969), it is possible to distinguish two central hermeneutic problems: (1) the problem of understanding the meaning of human work and activities; and (2) the problem of understanding itself, that is, what it takes to understand something. The hermeneutic problem of understanding the meaning of work can be seen as a specific event of understanding. The more fundamental hermeneutic question of how understanding takes place relates to every act of understanding. Although developing competence at work can be seen as a specific event of understanding, the focus here is on the question of understanding itself because to illuminate the basic conditions for competence development, we need to examine how understanding operates. In particular, the aim here is to explore what is regarded in hermeneutics as the most fundamental principle of how understanding operates, namely the hermeneutic circle.

The circular nature of understanding

Friedrich Ast (1778–1841) is often considered to be the first to introduce the idea of the hermeneutic circle as the basic principle of how understanding operates. According to Ast, understanding something such as a text means to grasp its inherent meaning structure in terms of its parts and whole. However, rather than seeing understanding as something achieved by proceeding in a progressive manner from simple parts to a complex whole, Ast regarded it as a simultaneous interaction between parts and whole. This means that developing understanding of something does not simply involve adding new parts. For example, when reading a sentence we do not understand it by adding the words one by one. Instead, we understand it by a simultaneous interaction between the words and the sentence as a whole. This is because the meaning of the words is achieved through their relationship to the whole sentence, and the meaning of the sentence is achieved with reference to the words that comprise it. This means that understanding:

> is a basically referential operation; we understand something by comparing it to something we already know. What we understand forms itself into systematic units, or circles made up of parts. The circle as a whole defines the individual parts and the parts together form the circle. ... By dialectical interaction between the whole and the part, each gives the other meaning; understanding is circular, then. Because within the 'circle' the meaning comes to stand, we call this the hermeneutic circle. (Schleiermacher, quoted in Palmer, 1969: 87)

Hence, when we understand our work, we do so through the circular relationship between its whole and parts. For example, the 'whole' of understanding 1 in engine optimization is engine optimization as optimizing separate steps. The meaning of this whole is achieved through its parts, such as to analyse and interpret how one or several monitoring parameters influence the quality and to be accurate and methodical, while the meaning of the parts is achieved with reference to the whole.

Understanding as intrinsically historical

Although Dilthey (1833–1911) agrees that understanding is circular, he claims that it is also intrinsically *historical*. Seeing the circular nature of understanding as intrinsically historical gives rise to a more fundamental circle than that suggested by Ast and Schleiermacher. This is because the circle is: 'a relationship of whole to parts seen by us from a given standpoint, at a given time, for a given combination of parts. It [understanding] is not something above or outside history but a part of a hermeneutic circle always historically defined' (Dilthey in Palmer, 1969: 118). Consequently, understanding is not primarily seen as a timeless entity located in the work itself, but as a temporal relationship between us and our work. This temporal circularity of understanding between us and work was indicated in the empirical illustration of how competence development took place within engine optimization. That is, the optimizers' historical understanding of engine optimization seemed to stipulate in advance how they interpreted their work the next time they encountered it. For example, the optimizers demonstrating understanding 2 were striving to be as competent as the optimizers with understanding 3. But every time they encountered their work they interpreted it in accordance with their historical understanding of work, namely, engine optimization as optimizing interacting steps. The specific historical understanding of engine optimization which these optimizers are part of, reproduces engine optimization as optimizing interacting steps in their accomplishment of it. The historical stipulation of understanding was also empirically evident in Dall'Alba's longitudinal study of aspiring doctors.

Understanding: a fundamental dimension in human existence

In Heidegger's (1962/1927) *Being and Time,* the circularity of understanding is not only seen as being historical, but also as ontologically defined. For Heidegger, understanding is not primarily a cognitive attribute we possess. Instead, it is a basic dimension of human existence in terms of something we *do* and at the same time *are.* In Heidegger's own words: 'We sometimes use the expression "understanding something" with the signification of "being able to manage something", "being a match for it", "being competent to do something". In understanding, as an *existentiale,* that which we have such competence over is not a "what", but Being as existing' (Heidegger, 1962/1927: 183).

Moreover, seeing understanding as a basic form of human existence means that it not only defines what and how we do things and who we are, but also our possibilities of doing and being something at all. But why does understanding, as Heidegger asks, 'always press forward into possibilities? It is because the understanding has in itself the existential structure which we call *projection'* (1962/1927: 217). Projection does not mean we are directed to a specific goal or are following a particular plan. Instead, projection refers more to our habitual and taken-for-granted ways of doing and being in different situations. For example, when an optimizer who expresses understanding 1 encounters a specific optimization situation, his particular understanding of engine optimization provides him with certain possibilities of optimizing engines and to be an engine optimizer.

If understanding enables and constrains our doing and being, then how does understanding develop? According to Heidegger, we develop our understanding through *interpretation*. Although we develop our understanding through interpretation, Heidegger claims that 'in interpretation, understanding does not become something different. It becomes itself' (1962/1927: 221). Moreover, interpretation is not 'the acquiring of information about what is understood; it is rather the working out of possibilities projected in understanding' (1962/1927: 221). Hence, according to Heidegger, interpretation is not something separate from understanding but, rather, a particular mode of understanding, which clarifies what we already have understood in advance: 'Interpretation always only takes care of bringing out what is disclosed as a cultivation of the possibilities inherent in an understanding' (1992: 260).

This means that when the optimizers interpret their work, they do so within their specific understanding of it. For example, optimizers 1 interpret their work within their understanding of it as optimizing separate steps. Through those interpretations, their understanding of work is developed continuously as these interpretations gradually disclose and clarify further aspects of their understanding of work.

Hence, while the most primordial form of understanding means being and doing something such as teacher-teaching, parent-parenting, driver-driving, plumber-plumbing and reader-reading, interpretation means we start to see what we are doing *as something*. The interpretation 'brings to prominence *"as what"* the encountered thing can be taken, how it is to be understood. The primary form of all interpretation as the cultivation of understanding *is the consideration of something as something in terms of its "as what" considering something as something'* (Heidegger, 1992: 261, italics in original).

However, interpretation does not mean that we first encounter something unintelligible and then later on interpret this unintelligible thing as something. Instead, as the optimization example showed, what we encounter is already understood in advance, but in our interpretation we make it explicit *as* something. Thus, when we interpret something as something, we do not, as Heidegger expressed it, attach a specific value to it. Instead, 'when something within-the-world is encountered as such, the thing in question already has an involvement which is disclosed in our understanding of the world, and this involvement is one which gets laid out by the interpretation' (Heidegger, 1962/1927: 223). For instance, the optimizers do not encounter engine optimization as an isolated issue but as something which is already part of their understanding of the world in which they live and act. Cars are central in the human world and engine optimization is related to the practice of developing and producing cars.

Thus, in order to develop our understanding we must have something to interpret and this something is already understood in terms of an 'involvement whole', of which we are an inextricable part. The involvement whole provides both something to interpret and an inevitable background to which it always refers and belongs. The involvement whole is the world in which we live and act and which we have internalized through socialization. For example, the use of cars and car manufacturing in our world can be seen as the involvement whole for the optimizers. It provides both engine optimization as a phenomenon to interpret and an inevitable background to which engine optimization refers and belongs. In other words, the understood world of which we are an inextricable part is what every interpretation presupposes, and that gives rise to an inevitable circularity in developing understanding, and therefore in developing competence. Heidegger called the basis for this circular process 'pre-understanding'. It consists of a threefold structure in terms of a fore-having, a fore-sight and a fore-conception.

The most basic dimension is *fore-having*. It can be seen as the totality of the social action context (Kögler, 1999) in which we are constantly involved and within which our interpretation always takes place. The social action context is made up of all our practical relations through which we live our lives, and provides the inevitable background context for our interpretation of something as something. For example, Volvo Car Corporation can be seen as one central aspect of the optimizers' specific social action context. It delimits what makes sense and what does not make sense in engine optimization, and thus, which competence is considered relevant to develop. However, the social action context of engine optimization is not limited to Volvo. It also includes the car industry in general, the use and purpose of the car in society and how it impacts on our way of life, for example, through its effects on the environment. Hence, the optimizers' social action context provides them with the inevitable background context of how to understand engine optimization, and thus also which competence they develop and possibly can develop.

Even if the fore-having provides the total context in which something becomes possible to interpret as something, our interpretation is always guided by some particular standpoint which more specifically defines in advance what has been understood and, thus, how it can possibly be interpreted. Heidegger called this standpoint *fore-sight*. It can be seen as a more specific constituent of the circularity of understanding. This is because it '"takes the first cut" out of what has been taken into our fore-having, and it does so with a definite way in which this can be interpreted' (Heidegger, 1962/1927: 223). As the fore-sight of understanding 'takes the first cut', it further delimits and specifies in advance what is understood, and thus what can possibly be interpreted as something. The three ways of understanding engine optimization – optimizing separate qualities, optimizing interacting qualities and optimizing from the customers' perspective – can be seen as three specific fore-sights of understanding engine optimization. Each of these fore-sights further delimits and specifies in advance how engine optimization is interpreted, and thus which specific competence can be developed. For example, the fore-sight of understanding 1 delimits and organizes the optimization work in terms of separate optimization steps, focusing on the relationship between monitoring parameters and each single quality of the engine. As illustrated previously, this way of delimiting and specifying engine optimization stipulates the way these optimizers interpret engine optimization and therefore which specific competence they develop.

Finally, the *fore-conception* is the most specific constituent of the circularity of understanding. It specifies even further in advance what has been understood through fore-having and fore-sight. Fore-conception points to the way in which we conceptualize something. It can be seen as a specific conceptual framework which guides our interpretations by conceptualizing what we have already understood in advance. As Heidegger argued, 'the interpretation has already decided for a definite way of conceiving it (the thing to be interpreted), either with finality or with reservations; it is grounded in *something we grasp in advance* – in a *fore-conception*' (1962/1927: 223, italics in original).

Hence, fore-conception stipulates that what is to be interpreted is already understood from within a conceptual framework which entails certain conceptual possibilities and confinements for the interpreting subject. For instance, central concepts within the specific fore-conception of engine optimization, such as 'driveability', 'fuel consumption', 'emissions' and 'engine power', specifies even further the way the optimizers interpret engine optimization, and therefore which competence they develop. Moreover, the particular concepts used within each specific fore-sight direct their interpretations and their competence development in even more detail.

Pre-understanding: the basis for competence development

From the above analysis it follows that pre-understanding constitutes an inevitable circularity in all interpretations, and thus in the development of understanding. As developing understanding of work is the basis for competence development, the pre-understanding of work must also operate as an inevitable circularity in all forms of competence development. More specifically, our fore-having of understanding work provides an inevitable starting point for developing competence in terms of a social action context in which the work is accomplished. What competence we develop is therefore stipulated in advance by the specific action context in which we stand and in which we are meant to serve. While fore-having provides the basic starting point, our fore-sight of understanding work provides an inevitable direction for the development of competence at work. It does so by providing a specific perspective on work which delimits and organizes in advance how we interpret our work. Finally, our fore-conception of understanding work constitutes even further how competence development takes place. It does so by providing a conceptual framework which directs our interpretations of work by conceptualizing that which has been understood in advance through the fore-having and the fore-sight of understanding work.

Reflection: a basic condition for developing competence

As argued above, understanding operates principally in a circular manner because developing understanding of something is always based on pre-understanding. Developing competence at work operates as an inevitable, unfolding circularity since it begins from our pre-understanding of work (Dall'Alba and Sandberg, in press; Sandberg, 2001c). Without this circularity of understanding, competence development would not occur at all.

How can competence be developed if understanding is circular? When competence development is seen as developing understanding, two primary forms emerge. These are the development of competence within the present understanding of work and through transforming understanding of work. More specifically, if the purpose of development activities is to reinforce particular competence at work, then these activities should be directed to maintaining the current circularity in our understanding of work. On the other hand, if their purpose is to renew competence, the activities should be designed to 'break' the current circularity in our understanding of work and redirect it to an alternative circularity of understanding.

Whether the aim is refinement or renewal of competence, some form of *reflection* is crucial to enhancing our awareness of the specific pre-understanding from which our competence develops. Without such awareness, we are unable to question our current circularity of understanding. Furthermore, we cannot question the competence we develop and the way in which we develop that competence.

Although central to competence development, reflection is not a typical state in work performance. When we work, our attention is directed to performing the work, not reflecting upon it. It is not until our work performance is interrupted, either voluntarily or involuntarily, that we are able to reflect upon it. Involuntary reflection is usually triggered by an unexpected disturbance in work performance. Such disturbances can vary from minor distractions to major disruptions that make it impossible to continue performing our work in an acceptable manner. We then need to reflect on the work in order to resolve the disturbance. Voluntary reflections, on the other hand, are deliberate and typically seek to understand or improve work performance. These reflections can involve activities such as self-reflection, critical discussions among colleagues, and undertaking a programme of training or education.

Using reflection as a means of developing competence requires distancing ourselves from our work in order to increase our awareness of the way we understand the work. Creating a distance to our work is a prerequisite for more clearly seeing our pre-understanding of work and the way in which it defines our work performance and competence development.

Since reflection is an important vehicle for developing competence, we need to specify its meaning further. Although the literature on reflection is vast, two basic meanings can be distinguished: reflection as (a) becoming aware of oneself, and (b) systematic thinking about or considering something in the world. From an etymological point of view, the former meaning is closer to the original meaning of the word 'reflection'. Etymologically, reflection derives from the Latin word 'reflectere', which means 'bending or turning backwards'. In order to become aware of ourselves in our work activities, we need to direct our attention away from being oriented to performing work and towards our way of understanding the work.

When using reflection as a vehicle for increasing awareness of our pre-understanding of work, reflection in the form of self-discovery is more crucial than reflection as systematic consideration. This is because when we systematically consider an aspect of our work, we typically seek to deepen our knowledge about the work in itself. We can consider what our work involves many times without becoming aware of ourselves in this process. The more we direct our attention to work activities, either when performing them or through systematic consideration, the less likely we will be to discover ourselves in the work. However, as Bengtsson (1995) pointed out, the two meanings for reflection can be seen as complementary. This is because when we discover ourselves through reflection, we must sustain the discovery as we engage in systematic consideration in order to gain deeper knowledge about ourselves.

Based on the two meanings outlined above, reflection can take an enormous range of different forms (Moon, 1999). Three basic forms are self-reflection, reflective dialogue, and research (Bengtsson, 1993). *Self-reflection* means we 'step out' from our work performance and reflect upon it. Through reflecting on our understanding of work, we can become more aware of the way in which this understanding governs our work performance and competence development. Although self-reflection can generate knowledge about

87

how we understand work, it is often difficult to become aware of our own understanding without being exposed to other ways of seeing the work. *Research about work practices* can therefore function to create further distance, enabling deeper reflection on our understanding of work.

Different forms of *reflective dialogue* with others can also increase awareness of our understanding of work. It is primarily through exposure to others' understanding that we become more fully aware of our own understanding as one among many (Kögler, 1999). Considering our own understanding in the light of others' understanding makes it possible to clarify what is specific about our understanding of work.

In sum, becoming aware of our pre-understanding is essential to challenging the ongoing circularity of understanding our work. Reflection and dialogue can provide a means of increasing such awareness. More specifically, a general principle arising from the alternative framework for competence development proposed here is that the point of departure for development activities should be pre-understanding of work. Ways in which competence can be developed in this manner will be explored in more detail in Chapter 7.

FIVE Shared understanding: the basis for collective competence and its development

Within the two previous chapters we discussed and analysed the main features of individuals' understanding of work and how it forms the basis not only for human action but also for the competence we use and develop in accomplishing our work. However, while an individual's competence is central for an organization's work performance, it is only when individuals start to interact with each other that an organization's task can be performed in an acceptable manner. In other words, it is first and foremost collective competence that determines the extent to which a particular organization can achieve effective work performance. The purpose of this chapter is to discuss and analyse the main characteristics of collective understanding of work and how it might constitute collective competence and its development.[1]

Collective versus individual competence

Collective competence means that a group of individuals interact in performing a specific task that it is impossible for a single individual to carry out alone. When individuals accomplish a particular task together, each of them contributes with a specific competence. However, it is only when they interact that a collective competence is developed and established. Hence, collective competence is first and foremost characterized by an interaction between several individuals in performing a specific task.

An example that nicely illustrates the distinctive feature of collective competence in contrast to individual competence is Hutchin's (1993) description of how a group of people navigate a warship. The navigators' collective competence becomes particularly salient when the team navigates in narrow water, such as in and out of harbours. There are, above all, two questions that are central in such a situation: where are we now, and where will we be when we have sailed a certain distance? The first question must be answered to be able to answer the second. This is particularly true with regard to big vessels due to their limited manoeuvrability space. When the vessel is supposed to turn, it is not enough to know that one has reached the turning place. If it has not commenced turning before it has reached the turning place, the vessel will pass that place due to the time delay between the turning manoeuvre and the vessel's reaction on that manoeuvre.

In order to keep the right course it is necessary to position the vessel continuously, both where it is now and where it will be within a certain time given its current speed and course. This positioning is called the fixation cycle and is performed at frequent intervals. On such occasions, specific bearing takers provide new information concerning the location of the vessel. They search for different landmarks close to the vessel and measure its bearing with particular instruments. The bearing takers report their results via telephone to the log keeper, who stands inside the steering cabin and keeps track of all the bearings in a logbook. The bearing-time recorder of the team records all the bearings that the log keeper has received. When the bearing-time recorder has found the exact bearing of the vessel, he calculates where the vessel will be in the next coming fixed observation points. In order to do this he needs to know both the course and the speed of the vessel, which he receives by reading the logbook.

When the bearing of the vessel has been found, the bearing-time recorder discusses with the position marker in order to decide a suitable position for the next fixation cycle. Thereafter, the bearing-time recorder contacts the bearing takers via telephone to inform them about the chosen land marks for the next fixation cycle. He maintains the telephone contact with the bearing takers and when he says, 'stand-by to mark' the bearing takers should identify the chosen landmarks and measure the bearing of the vessel. At the same time as the bearing-time recorder gives the bearing takers a signal to 'stand-by to mark,' he also stands in contact with the echo-sounder operator, who reports the water depth under the vessel at the same time as the bearing takers report its bearing.

Within the navigation example it becomes apparent that collective competence cannot be related to a single individual. Certainly, each person of the navigation team contributes with a specific competence, such as bearing takers, the bearing-time recorder and the log keeper. Each person's competence is, however, insufficient in navigating the vessel effectively. It is only when they interact with one another that a collective competence in navigation is established. The example also highlights that it is highly problematic to treat individual competence in isolation. This is because individual competence receives its specific meaning from the role it plays in the collective's work performance. As Tsoukas (1996) argued, individual competence is possible precisely because of the social practice within which the individual engages.

Hence, a general characteristic of collective competence is that it belongs to a group of individuals who interact in performing a specific task and not to any single individual. However, in order to interact, the member of a collective must have some form of *shared understanding* of their work. For instance, to navigate the vessel adequately, the navigation team must have a reasonable level of shared understanding of navigating vessels. Without a shared understanding, no meaningful interaction will emerge and, by then, no collective competence will appear in their work performance. Expressed differently, if the foundation of an individual's competence is his or her specific understanding of work, then the basis for collective competence must be a group's shared understanding of its work. However, before discussing more specifically how understanding also forms the basis for collective competence it is necessary to elaborate further the social nature of human understanding.

The social nature of understanding

When, in the previous chapter, we discussed how understanding operates, the focus was primarily on the individual's understanding of reality, and how it forms the basis for his or her actions and activities. However, while we always live and embody an understanding of reality, we are not born with such an understanding but are socialized into it. That this is the case became particularly clear in our discussion about how our individual understanding originates in the social action context in which we are constantly embedded. This context is our shared world, the world into which we have been born and socialized through our upbringing, education, work and leisure. Through socialization we develop an understanding of the world in which we live and act which we hold in common with our fellow human beings. This internalized, shared understanding of our world becomes the basic framework for making sense of our actions and activities. Hence, our understanding of reality is not something we first develop ourselves, but is something we take over by being socialized into society, its various social practices, and specific organizations like hospitals, schools, restaurants and IT firms.

Understanding as a dialectics between subjective and objective reality

How understanding is socially defined but simultaneously operates at an individual level can be further elaborated with the help of the social phenomenological theory of the social construction of reality developed by Berger

91

and Luckmann (1981/1966). They have offered a comprehensive account of the simultaneity of individual and social understanding of reality in terms of a dialectic construction of subjective and objective reality. According to Berger and Luckmann, there is, in the social construction of reality, an ongoing dialectical process between subjective and objective reality, which can be described in terms of *externalization, objectivation and internalization.*

Externalization means that we produce our reality through our activities, such as talking, thinking, building, managing, curing, eating, writing and driving. The agreement of daylight saving time exemplified in Chapter 2 is an externalization of human activities. Objectivation means that we experience our activities as having an objective existence independent of ourselves as individual subjects. For instance, the agreed upon change in time is experienced as objective because it influences our daily life in different ways. Internalization refers to the socialization process whereby we become part of the reality we have produced. For example, we internalize the daylight saving time by living and acting according to that time. These three dialectical moments do not occur sequentially, but simultaneously. At the same time as we act in accordance to the stipulated daylight saving time, we externalize, objectify and internalize it. More precisely, by following this time, we reproduce it, and by doing so, daylight saving time achieves the status of objective reality, which we internalize by being socialized into daylight saving time.

Socialization: from subjective to objective construction of reality

Although we participate simultaneously in the societal dialectics between the subjective and objective construction of reality, there is often a sequential time span in which each of us becomes part of these societal dialectics. The starting point for this is the internalization process, the immediate experience of an activity that expresses meaning, that is, as a manifestation of someone else's subjective processes that become subjectively meaningful to me. Through the externalization, this person's subjectivity becomes objectively available to me, and thus also meaningful to me independently if my interpretation is in line with his or her intention.

There are two central processes by which an individual internalizes society: primary and secondary socialization. Primary socialization is the first and most fundamental step in the internalization of the construction of objective reality. In primary socialization we internalize the most basic constructions of reality, such as 'language', 'greetings', 'mother', 'father' and 'gender', which regulate the most common activities and interactions among people. Secondary socialization is any of the subsequent socialization processes by which individuals internalize central aspects of reality, such as 'professions', and institutions such as 'money', 'banks' and 'tax authorities'.

A central feature in both primary and secondary socialization is that the internalization of roles and attitudes from significant others, such as parents, relatives, friends, teachers and colleagues, becomes progressively abstracted to roles and attitudes in general. When the generalized other has been incorporated into consciousness, a symmetrical relation between objective and subjective reality is established. As Berger and Luckmann expressed it: 'What is real "outside" corresponds with what is real "within"' (1981/1966: 153).

From the above description, it may appear as though the interaction between subjects in the process of constructing reality is primarily harmonious and symmetrical. This is, however, not always the case. As was pointed out earlier, the symmetry between subjective and objective reality can never be complete because there is always 'more' objective reality available than subjective. In addition, the interaction is to a large extent asymmetrical, both in terms of knowledge and power (Foucault, 1972). This asymmetry is obvious between parents and children and teachers and pupils, but also particularly salient in leadership. In Berger and Luckmann's words:

> He [sic] who has the largest stick has the better chance of imposing his definitions of reality. This is a rather safe assumption to make with regard to any larger collectivity, although there is always the possibility of politically disinterested theoreticians convincing each other without recourse to the cruder means of persuasion. (1981/1966: 127)

In sum, the theory of social constructionism suggests that human understanding is constituted by a simultaneous dialectics between subjective and objective construction of reality. However, the social dimension of understanding is more basic because as soon as we are born we become part of objective reality in the sense of particular social practices such as eating, cleaning, car driving and various professional practices. These practices always already contain a specific understanding of reality, which we gradually take over by becoming socialized into those practices and, thus, begin to share the particular understanding with people already part of the particular practice in question.

The same is true for organizations. Every kind of organization, such as health care providers, airline companies, accounting firms, schools and car manufacturers, require that their employees hold a similar understanding about what their work is about and how to accomplish it. The employees' shared understanding is developed and maintained through the circular dialectics between the subjective and objective construction of reality, and forms the basis for the competence developed and used within the particular organization in question. As Wenger expressed it, the members of a collective 'are bound together by their collectively developed understanding of what their community is about, and they hold each other accountable to this sense of *joint enterprise*. To be competent is to understand the enterprise well enough and contribute to it' (2003: 80, italics in original).

Shared understanding of flute manufacturing

Cook and Yanow's (1993) description of flute manufacturing illustrates how a collective's shared understanding of its work forms the basis for its specific competence. Cook and Yanow identify three flute manufacturers – Haynes, Powell and Brannen Brother – as among the most outstanding in the world. These are all located around Boston, Massachusetts in the USA. The three companies are all organized in a similar manner. They are small. The number of employees is about 25 in each company. Except for a few who work in administration, all employees, including the owners, are directly involved in the production. The companies also follow similar procedures in the manufacturing process.

The pipe that makes up the flute body is manufactured outside these companies according to their specific requirements. This is also true for other parts, such as screws and metal poles. When the flute parts have been delivered they are thoroughly inspected and are given a first refinement. Thereafter, the flute body is refined in more detail. Tone holes are drilled and the tangent mechanism is assembled and its tangents are adjusted to manage incredibly fine tunes. Meanwhile, the main flute body is connected to its mouthpiece. Finally, the flute is polished and packed ready to be sent to its new owner.

For Powell, as Cook and Yanow describe in more detail, it takes about two weeks to complete a flute. The production consists of a number of iterative steps. Each flutemaker has developed a specific competence in certain aspects of the flute production. This means that each flutemaker only accomplishes a specific aspect of the flute production. When a flutemaker has completed her specific tasks, she hands over the flute to the next flutemaker in the manufacturing process. This means that the second flutemaker's work is based on that of the previous flutemaker. Each time the second flutemaker experiences something not completely right, he takes the flute back to the previous flutemaker in order to get it reworked. That the flute needs to be reworked is often expressed in vague terms such as 'It doesn't feel right' or 'This piece doesn't look quite right' (1993: 380). The first flutemaker then investigates why the flute 'doesn't feel right'. When she thinks she has found the 'error' and corrected it, she checks whether the flute still 'doesn't feel right' to the second flutemaker. This interaction continues until both are satisfied with the result of the reworked flute.

Cook and Yanow observe that why the language in such interactions is vague depends to a large extent on the fact that several qualities of the flute have never been made explicit. The extreme standards on which each flute's specific style and quality are based have, however, been maintained by these flutemakers' reciprocal judgements through hand and eye. Since the flutes are primarily produced by hand by several craftspersons, no Powell flute is exactly the same. Each has its own personality. Despite the difference between each Powell flute, Cook and Yanow remark that:

> a knowledgeable fluteplayer would never fail to recognize a Powell by the way it feels and plays, nor would she confuse a Powell with a Haynes or a Brannen Brothers. Each Powell flute, although unique, shares an unambiguous family resemblance with all other Powells. This family resemblance is the essence of Powell style and quality. And although each Powell has its own personality and aspects of the flute's physical design have been changed from time to time, the Powell style has been maintained. In this sense, a Powell flute made 50 years ago plays and feels the same as one made recently.
>
> This principle is equally true of Haynes and Brannen Brothers flutes. Each company has developed a distinctly recognizable product, transcending individual variations among flutes and design changes over time. Further, this constancy of style and quality has been maintained over years, even though each instrument has typically been the product of several flutemakers and the workshops have passed through several generations of flutemakers. (1993: 380-1)

Cook and Yanow's observation that the flutemakers have manufactured a flute with a recognizable style and quality for fifty years indicates that the company's collective's competence transcends both the single flutemaker as well as earlier generations of flutemakers. More specifically, Powell's ability to produce a flute with a recognizable style and quality over time is based on an institutionalized shared understanding of how a Powell should play and feel. In each sub-moment of the manufacturing process the shared understanding is actualized in the judgement of the flutemaker in the sense that the members of the group come to an agreement about the extent to which the flute has reached the Powell criteria.

In the two previous chapters we could see that individuals' ways of understanding their work develop, form and organize their knowledge and skills into a specific competence in their work performance. If the basis for collective competence is the members' shared understanding of their work, it would in a similar way develop, form and organize collectively relevant knowledge and skills into a specific competence in work performance. Subsequently, the collective competence manifested through Powell's shared understanding of its work is different from the collective competence at Haynes and Brannen Brothers. The collective competence at Powell generates Powell flutes with a specific style and quality, and Haynes's collective competence generates flutes with a qualitatively different style and quality.

This means that Powell cannot start to produce Haynes flutes even if it would like to do so. It also implies that a single flutemaker from Haynes cannot start to perform a specific moment in the flute manufacturing at Powells, despite the fact that she has performed an identical moment at Haynes. Cook and Yanow also point out that many flutemakers have moved between the three companies. At each such move, the flutemakers have been forced to develop their competence, even if they have performed identical work in the other companies. According to Cook and Yanow, these flutemakers are forced 'to learn a new "feeling", a different way to deal with the flute parts' (1993: 381). In other words, this new competence can only be acquired by being socialized into the new company's shared understanding of flute manufacturing.

Development of collective competence through socialization

However, socialization involves not only the individual's development and maintenance of a specific understanding, but, above all, the collective's development and maintenance of a specific understanding of its work. According to Cook and Yanow, when a new member is:

> socialised or acculturated into the organisation, learning by the organisation takes place: the organisation learns how to maintain the style and quality of its flutes through the particular skills, character and quirks of the new individual. The organisation engages in a dynamic process of maintaining the norms and practices that assure the constancy of the product. ... It is an active reaffirmation of maintenance of the know-how that the organisation already possesses. (1993: 381–2)

According to Cook and Yanow, apprenticeship is the most common form of socialization at Powell and the other companies. Usually, the apprentice is trained by working at different stages of the flute manufacturing process at a time, in the same way as the other members of the collective. When the learner has finished his task, he goes to the master who judges that work in the same way as she judges the others' work. If the work 'doesn't feel right' or 'doesn't look right', she hands it back to the apprentice for reworking. Finally, when the apprentice is seen as capable of judging his own and others' work according to the specific Powell criteria, he becomes a fully fledged member of Powell.

Through this socialization process, the apprentice develops a specific competence in the manufacturing of Powell flutes, at the same time as he becomes an active part in Powell's collective competence. By the end of the apprenticeship the new member has developed an ability to judge and control the extent to which the flutes produced have reached the Powell criteria. This means that socialization involves both an individual and a collective learning. The individual develops and maintains a specific competence in flute manufacturing at the same time as Powell as a collective develops and maintains its specific competence in flute manufacturing.

If the members' shared understanding of their work is the basis for collective competence, the process that constitutes the shared understanding becomes crucial for how collective competence is developed and maintained. The members' shared understanding is primarily developed and formed through the *sense-making process* concerning the meaning of their work, of which they are inevitably part. As was shown by the Powell example, the members of the collective are constantly involved in negotiating the meaning of their work – what their work is about, and what it means to manufacture Powell flutes.

Above all, it is in the interaction between the group members, as the ongoing sense-making process develops, reproduces and reshapes the group members' shared understanding of their work, that constitutes the basis for collective competence. It is within the collective's understanding of its work that each single member understands his or her part of the collective's work in a particular way. People from outside are socialized into the collective by being engaged in the ongoing sense-making process within the collective. The shared understanding that forms the basis for collective competence is thus something that is cultivated, refined and maintained by the group members' ongoing sense making of their work.

Collective competence as culture

Adopting a cultural perspective offers a way of further exploring how collective understanding is developed and maintained within a collective's sense making of its work. Culture comes from the Latin word 'cultura', which means refinement and cultivation. Within a general anthropological perspective, culture refers to a humanly developed and maintained shared meaning and system of signification, which provide order and direction in human lives. According to Hannertz et al., regarding a specific group of people and their actions and activities from a cultural perspective is:

> a question of a specific emphasis, an emphasis on the collective's consciousness and the forms of communications that carry it. Thus, culture includes shared knowledge, values, experiences and connected patterns of thoughts. But it does not only exist inside people's heads. The consciousness becomes shared only by communicating, sharing a language, understanding codes and messages, seeing the whole environment as loaded with meaning in a way that is reasonably similar to all – or at least to most people. (1982: 40, translated from Swedish)

The perhaps most important insight from the above quote is that central aspects of collective competence are not just in the minds of its members. These aspects are first shared by communicating with each other, sharing a language. Everyone in the interaction understands the norms, rules and orientations that form the basis of the work performance. It is in communication with others that a shared understanding is created, and thus communication is the basis for the distinctive competence that a collective develops and maintains in its work. As the socialization example at Powell illustrated, it is through communication with the master and other flutemakers that the apprentice gradually becomes part of Powell's shared understanding of flutemaking and, by so doing, also becomes part of its distinctive competence in flutemaking.

Communication does not only imply oral and written activities. We also communicate with others through our bodies, for example with poses, gestures and facial expressions. Bourdieu provides an informative illustration of how non-verbal communication takes place:

> A whole group and a whole symbolically structured environment ... exerts an anonymous, pervasive pedagogic action. ... The essential part of the *modus operandi* which defines practical mastery is transmitted in practice, in its practical state, without attaining the level of discourse. The child imitates not 'models' but other people's actions. Body *hexis* speaks directly to the motor function, in the form of a pattern of postures that is both individual and systematic, because linked to a whole system of techniques involving the body and tools, and charged with a host of social meanings and values: in all societies, children are particularly attentive to the gestures and postures which, in their eyes, express everything that goes to make an accomplished adult – a way of walking, a tilt of the head, facial expressions, ways of sitting and of using implements, always associated with a tone of voice, a style of speech, and (how could it be otherwise?) a certain subjective experience. (1977: 87)

As was discussed earlier, Powell's specific criteria for style and quality are primarily not maintained through oral and written communication but through its members' reciprocal judgements by hand and eye. Non-verbal communication is particularly apparent in professional practices that use the body as a means of expression, for example dancers. When dancing, the dancers communicate with each other via poses, gestures and facial expressions. The dancers have to 'read' each other's movements continuously in order to see where in the dance they are and when they themselves should be part of a particular combination of movements. In team sports such as soccer and basketball, communication via poses, gestures and facial expressions is also important. For example, a soccer player who has the ball and is planning to pass it on to another team player must, in order for the pass to be successful, know what the team player has in mind by reading his movements. Even in groups, were the body is less significant, body language is a central component in creating a shared understanding of work. For instance, being able to read subtle poses and gestures is often crucial if you want to be a successful negotiator.

Current organizational and management research reveals a number of different cultural perspectives on organizations (for an overview see, for instance, Alvesson, 1993b; 2002, Alvesson and Berg, 1992; Frost, 1985; Martin, 2002). The symbolic cultural perspective is closely related to the interpretative perspective on management that we are trying to develop in this book. Alvesson and Björkman characterize the symbolic cultural perspective as focusing:

> on what is common for a certain group: understanding those patterns of interpretations and decipherments which help individuals to relate to an intersubjective world, that is, a social reality which, to a considerable extent, is experienced in a similiar way. Shared symbols are important here: material things, patterns of actions, specific events and language use which denote distinctive views and significations and which give guidelines for orientation in life. (1992: 21, translated from Swedish)

From a symbolic cultural perspective, collective competence can be regarded as a system of shared symbols that signifies central aspects of the collective's work performance. A company's product is one example of a shared symbol which denotes a core aspect of collective competence. For instance, the Powell flute means something specific to those craftspersons who manufacture them. At a certain stage in the manufacturing process the flute reaches the benchmark standards of style and quality that define Powell flutes. Only then does it pass on to the next stage in the production process.

The physical layout of the work design is another example of a cultural symbol. It is an expression of a specific workflow in the production system, which symbolizes a core aspect of the collective competence in flutemaking. Moreover, symbols such as organizational stories express criteria, norms and procedures on how to perform the work and therefore also represent core aspects of collective competence. For instance, stories can be about 'what one does here' at this particular stage in the flute production process. The rites and rituals, ceremonies and celebrations that belong to a collective also help its members to formulate, develop and maintain a shared understanding of their work. For instance, at Powell, the purchasing procedures of the flute body and employees' interactions with the customers can be seen as specific rituals. These rituals symbolize important aspects of Powell's competence in flute manufacturing.

These shared symbols are developed, sustained and changed through communication between the members of the collective. Orr's (1996) description of Xerox service technicians learning at work, reported by Brown and Duguid (1991), can be used to illustrate more specifically how collective competence is developed and sustained in terms of a storytelling. On one occasion a service technician received a phone call from a machine operator who was complaining about a troublesome machine. The technician tried to solve the machine problem both by following formal problem-solving procedures and by using his own tricks of the trade, but without success. He called in a specialist but the specialist was also unable to repair the machine. In an attempt to make sense of the problem, the technician and the specialist started to tell stories about the machine fault. The stories were invented as they tried to remember earlier occasions when they encountered similar symptoms. Each story generated one possible explanation of the machine's fault which could be tested at the same time as new insights were produced. In that way the technician and the specialist could generate several new tests and stories. Gradually, their stories made up a more coherent explanation of the machine's fault. After about five hours they had created a story that generated a 'sufficient interplay among memories, tests, the machine's responses, and the ensuing insights to lead to diagnosis and repair' (Brown and Duguid, 1991: 44). Through the process of storytelling, the service technician and the specialist had created a shared understanding of the previously incomprehensible machine error. Through that understanding they developed both their own competence and the service technicians' collective competence. Moreover, this story became an integrated part of the service technicians' collective competence. A few months later, Orr reported that he heard an identical version of this story told in the service technicians' lunchroom.

Seeing shared symbols as constituents for collective competence provides one explanation of why a company such as Powell is able to manufacture flutes with a recognizable style and quality year after year even though several generations of flutemakers have come and gone. In order for the symbols to be shared, they have to be handed over from the more experienced flutemakers to the newcomers. In other words, in order to be able to participate in Powell's flute manufacturing, newcomers have to grasp the shared symbols that denote Powell's competence in flute manufacturing. The apprentices are not regarded as fully-fledged members of Powell until they have embodied the meaning of the shared symbols that denote Powell's distinctive competence in flutemaking. The extent to which new and other members act according to the shared symbols of their work is continuously maintained in the interaction between the members.

Thus, the symbols can be seen as shaping and maintaining the development of Powell's distinctive collective competence in flutemaking. More specifically, the symbols which denote the flutemakers' shared understanding of their work, are embedded in their daily practice. The symbols create a feeling of security and identity in their work performance. They tell the flutemakers how to act and who they are: we manufacture flutes in this way and we manufacture

Powell flutes. The longer the flutemakers are involved in manufacturing flutes, the more they take these symbols for granted. The flutemakers only need to look at a piece of work in order to understand each other. It is only when a new member enters the collective that the other flutemakers have to articulate consciously why a piece of work 'doesn't feel right'.

Formation of collective competence through symbols

As the shared symbols denote a collective's specific understanding of its work, they can be seen as *forming* the collective's distinctive competence. The specific formation of shared symbols functions as a basis for and gives direction to the members in developing and maintaining a distinctive collective competence. IKEA, the Swedish furniture company, is a good example of how collective competence is formed through shared symbols. The most basic shared symbols at IKEA are the nine propositions formulated by Ingvar Kamprad, the founder of IKEA, in *A Furniture Trader's code* (1976):

- The assortment – our identity
- The IKEA spirit – a strong and viable reality
- Profit gives us resources
- Reaching good results through small means
- Simplicity is a virtue
- Being different
- Make a vigorous effort – important for our success
- Take responsibility – a benefit
- Most work is undone – a wonderful future.

The code is accompanied with a general description of how IKEA understands the furniture business, namely it aims 'to create a better everyday life for many people'. IKEA employees see their work as being to develop functional and beautiful furniture that most people can afford to buy. This general description symbolizes a certain understanding of the furniture business and also provides a specific basis for the development and maintenance of a distinctive competence. The distinctive character in IKEA's competence is that the workers should be able to develop functional and beautiful furniture but also that most people should be able to afford this furniture. Kamprad's propositions concretize IKEA's distinctive competence formation by symbolizing central aspects of IKEA's understanding of the furniture business.

The first proposition, 'the assortment – our identity', is fundamental in IKEA's competence in the furniture business. It symbolizes that IKEA should provide a wide assortment of beautiful and functional home furnishings at prices most people can afford. IKEA should strive to provide an assortment that can be used to furnish every space at home, inside as well as outside. Moreover, the assortment should have a distinct IKEA profile characterized by simplicity and should be durable and easy to appreciate. Further, the assortment should appeal to every age. Its functionality and technical quality should be of a high standard. The quality should, however, not be an end in itself but be adjusted to customers' needs. The basic intention is to strive for a low price without reducing the functionality and technical quality of the assortment. This proposition is also sometimes labelled 'flat pack – low price'. Flat pack have been an IKEA symbol, denoting that IKEA shares the furniture business with the customer. IKEA provides, in flat pack, prefabricated furniture which consumers assemble themselves. Thus, the proposition 'the assortment – our identity' symbolizes some of the most basic aspects of IKEA's distinctive competence in the furniture business. It expresses a specific competence in designing functional and beautiful furniture at a low price. Moreover, it expresses a specific competence in designing furniture that is easy to assemble. The thesis also expresses a specific competence in storage and logistics within IKEA.

The second proposition, 'the IKEA spirit – a strong and viable reality', expresses primarily a number of norms that constitutes core aspects of IKEA's competence in the furniture business. IKEA's workers should demonstrate a willingness to continuous renewal, have an awareness of costs in all situations, show a willingness to take responsibility and help out, be humble towards their task, and strive for simplicity and straightforwardness both in developing products and in their interaction with people. The meaning of these norms is developed and deepened through the other propositions.

The proposition 'profit gives us resources' refers above all to the idea of being aware of costs. It stipulates that profit should be achieved by keeping the lowest price in combination with high quality. 'If we ask for too much payment we don't keep the lowest price and if we ask for too little payment we don't get resources. A wonderful problem that forces us to develop our products more economically, to purchase goods better and to stubbornly reduce all costs. This is our secret. The basis to our success' (Kamprad, 1976: 3).

The proposition 'reaching good results through small means' stipulates in more detail what cost awareness means in IKEA's competence in the furniture business. Kamprad writes, for example, that the 'waste of resources within IKEA is a deadly sin. All architects can design a writing desk that is allowed to cost 5.000 SEK. But only the most skilful are able to design a functional writing desk of high quality that is allowed to cost 100 SEK' (1976: 4). Again, a specific design competence that can unify functionality and a low price is emerging as a core aspect of IKEA's competence in the furniture business.

The proposition 'simplicity is a virtue' refers primarily to the competence of striving for simplicity and straightforwardness both in the product development and in interaction with customers. It symbolizes IKEA's drive to simplify its business. IKEA's products should be as simple and functional as possible. IKEA also strives for simplicity in the planning and implementation of its business. This proposition also symbolizes the core aspect of cost awareness. Complicated products lead to unnecessary costs and if planning and implementation are complicated they also give rise to unnecessary costs which make it more difficult to operate the furniture business in an IKEA manner.

The Proposition, 'being different', expresses the core aspect of a willingness to continually improve IKEA's competence. It emphasizes the importance of continuously trying to think in new ways, always asking the question 'why are we doing it like this?' The idea is to find new and better ways to carry out the furniture business in an IKEA manner. The seventh proposition, 'make a vigorous effort – important for our success', not only stipulates that employees should be thinking in new ways, but also that they should always be willing to go the extra mile in whatever they do.

The eighth proposition, 'to take responsibility – a benefit', expresses a willingness to ensure that the furniture business is moving on and is developing in an IKEA manner. Here, responsibility has nothing to do with a degree of education or position, but is about the importance of always paying attention to those problems and requirements that come up in the business and trying to solve them in the best possible way according to the IKEA standards.

Finally, the proposition, 'most work is undone – a wonderful future', reinforces the core aspect of continuously asking the question 'how can members of IKEA improve their performance in the furniture business, and by so doing their competence?' The basic idea is that the only way to make progress is to 'ask ourselves how can what we are doing today be improved tomorrow?'

How these shared symbols demonstrate IKEA's competence in the furniture business becomes clear when a new furniture store is established outside Sweden. Establishing a new furniture store means that a completely new group of people has to develop the distinctive IKEA competence. Salzer's (1994) study about IKEA's culture demonstrates that the informal network of Swedish managers and decorators is the most important ingredient in establishing a new furniture store. The Swedish managers and decorators build up the new furniture store and train the new personnel. In most cases a Swedish manager runs the store for up to a year before the business is handed over to a local manager.

IKEA always uses a group of Swedes to establish a new furniture store because they are carriers of IKEA's specific culture – they are able to form IKEA's distinctive competence in the furniture business through a shared set of symbols. Through speech and action this group communicates a set of basic shared symbols that express IKEA's understanding of, and distinctive competence in, the furniture business. The fact that IKEA has been able to establish more than 100 similar stores in more than 20 different countries has largely to do with the formation of IKEA's competence through a clear set of shared symbols.

In conclusion, then, a collective's shared understanding of work is the most basic characteristic of collective competence. This shared understanding is constituted through members' ongoing sense making of their work. Through ongoing sense making of work, a shared understanding is gradually instituted and embodied in the constitution of a distinctive competence in work performance. Furthermore, as with interpretative studies of individual competence, the interpretative inquiry of what constitutes collective competence provides insights into why some companies perform a particular type of work, such as transporatation or education for example, better than others. Within the rationalistic perspective, companies performing a particular type of work better than others are seen as possessing a superior set of shared attributes, such as knowledge and skills in that work. However, according to the interpretative perspective developed here, variation in work performance is not primarily related to a specific set of shared attributes possessed by those companies that are seen as most superior or successful. Rather, superior company performance is linked to the variation in ways of understanding that work. Powell's success is related to its workers' shared understanding of flute manufacturing, which constitutes a unique and distinctive competence in flute manufacturing. The reason why IKEA is so successful in the furniture business is related to its workers' shared understanding of the furniture business.

Developing collective competence by changing shared understanding

Up to now we have primarily discussed how a collective develops and maintains a distinctive competence within its present understanding of work. Powell developed and maintained a distinctive competence in flute manufacturing within its present understanding of flute manufacturing. IKEA developed and maintained a distinctive competence in the furniture business within its present understanding of the furniture business. Within their respective understanding, Powell and IKEA have both been profitable for several years.

Some situations, however, cannot be dealt with by developing competence within the present understanding of work. Such situations emerge, for instance, when collective competence is questioned because it does not generate the expected result. A crucial condition for a collective to develop a new distinctive competence in such a situation is that they change their present shared understanding of their work to a qualitatively different understanding. Edström et al.'s (1989) study about Scandinavian Airline Systems (SAS) and its change from being an airline company to becoming a travel company illustrates how a new distinctive competence can be developed by changing a collective's understanding of its work.

SAS's understanding of itself as an airline company had developed and been maintained since the company's inception in 1946. A number of central shared symbols had been established which formed SAS's distinctive competence in the airline business. The general focus was highly production-oriented. The technical production of air travel was placed at the centre in SAS. The aircraft, their technical quality and safety were the most central symbols forming SAS's distinctive competence in the airline business. The overarching motto was continuously to improve the production of air travel by maintaining a high standard of quality and safety. They also invested heavily in new, more technically advanced and safer aircrafts, and in advanced equipment for maintenance.

SAS's understanding of itself as a production-oriented airline was successful while the market continued to grow. During the 1970s, however, SAS became less successful as the competition among the airlines intensified and the market began to reach saturation point. The company entered a downward spiral. Less and less profit was generated and, during the financial year 1979–80, SAS made a loss for the first time in 17 years. More and more people within SAS started to doubt whether it was possible to continue to run the airline business as they had been doing. However, since management to a large extent embodied SAS's current understanding of the airline business, they had difficulty in seeing how SAS could run the airline business in a different way. Instead, they tried to stop the accelerating losses by cost rationalizations. What was rationalized most, however, was not the technical production of air travel but the already neglected customer service dimension. Those reductions generated even more dissatisfied customers, a deteriorating internal climate and further financial problems. In the end, the general management of SAS had reached a situation which they could not master. A new CEO, Jan Carlzon, entered the scene and began the work of changing SAS from an airline company into a travel company.

One central phase in such a change process is to formulate an alternative understanding of the airline business. Since a collective's understanding is materialized in routines and systems, it is often taken for granted: 'This is the way we do it here!' Thus, without an alternative understanding it is difficult for those who are acting within a certain understanding to be aware of the way in which they understand their work. The old managers who lived and acted in an understanding of SAS as an aircraft company were unable to see the airline business in a new way. The same was true for the remaining employees within SAS. Therefore, it was crucial that the new management was able to understand the airline business in an alternative way.

One central reason why Jan Carlzon and the other new managers were able to create an alternative understanding of the airline business was that they both had different work experience and different educational background than the previous leadership. Jan Carlzon and other new managers had an educational background in business, whereas the previous managers all had technical expertise. Carlzon and many of the other new managers also had work experience from travel agencies and other customer-related companies and, as a consequence, they began understanding the SAS airline business as a travel company.

This new understanding of SAS as a travel company came to form the basis for developing a qualitatively different competence in the airline business. Whereas the aircraft were the main focus in SAS's old understanding, the customer became the centre of attention in the new SAS understanding of the airline business. When the customer is placed at the centre, the customer relationship is no longer seen as a single relationship. Instead, the relationship with the customer is seen as a whole chain of relations, from ticket purchase, check in, and service in the aircraft to punctuality and baggage handling. All these links in the chain influence how customers experience travel with SAS.

The new leadership tried to make the meaning of SAS as a travel company visible through a new set of symbols. The most basic were summarized by the new leadership in six propositions, described by Edström et al. (1989):

- The customer is the basis of SAS business
- Customer service must be adjusted to different customers' and to the competitors' behaviour
- The customers must judge the whole service chain as positive
- Each customer should be treated individually
- Networking with other airlines will develop attractive travel routes
- The creation of a more flexible organization is necessary in a dynamic and competitive environment.

Through an intensive communication programme of this system of symbols, most SAS employees became involved in an intensive meaning making of their work and thus developed a new distinctive competence in the airline business. The first step in this meaning-making process was to involve top management and, subsequently, middle management and remaining employees. One way to communicate with all employees was to present the new SAS direction in a pamphlet called 'Carlzon's little red book'. This expressed the central theses described above. The new understanding was also embodied in a number of local change programmes initiated throughout the company. Their purpose was to develop the new understanding in routines and systems.

When the first stage of the change process was completed, Jan Carlzon and the other new mangers tried to format the new SAS direction in a set of new symbols:

> In April 1983, SAS presented its new corporate identity in a hangar at Kastrup's airport to represen-
> tatives of the owners, authorities, media, employees and specially invited guests. ... In his speech Jan
> Carlzon emphasized that the new identity reflected important internal changes. There was no partic-
> ular difference between the picture of the company that was presented externally through new uni-
> forms, newly painted aircraft, signs and logo, and the internal practice that customers encountered
> in terms of a willingness to provide service, time tables, punctuality, security and sensitivity for new
> demands. The symbols represented something real and not just a beautiful appearance. Despite this,
> the external image was important. The personnel's clothes should be both practical and appealing,
> and the aircraft safe, comfortable and attractive. The personnel should be both service-minded
> and skilful. In this way, the symbols, the picture and the design received a particular value. They [the
> symbols] were able to make explicit, beautify and dramatize the internal change. (Edström et al.,
> 1989: 10–11, translated from Swedish)

A second stage then took place in the change process. The main purpose was to develop further the new understanding of SAS as a travel company at the local level. A range of local change projects was initiated with the intention to concretize the new understanding in different routines and systems. It was a demanding task to change well-established routines and systems that were based on the old understanding of SAS as an aircraft company. To manage the change process, SAS's top managers worked hard to develop a more active and dialogue-based leadership among SAS's 200 middle managers. For example, one aim for the middle managers was to start up local study circles and engage the employees in actively reflecting on what SAS as a travel company would mean for them and their specific work. The study circles generated a number of concrete suggestions of how local activities such as routines and systems could be developed. These suggestions were, to a large extent, implemented as a way of gradually changing SAS from an airline company to a travel company. In other words, a new distinctive competence in airline business was developed.

The SAS example shows that it is not possible to develop a new collective competence within the present way of understanding work. It is only when the collective starts to understand its work in a qualitatively different way that a new collective competence can be developed. What also became evident in the SAS example is that management was not placed above, but formed a central part of SAS's collective competence. This was particularly apparent when SAS's old management was unable to adapt to SAS's new understanding of the airline business. The same was true for other employees. It was only when the old management had been replaced that an alternative collective understanding of SAS business could be developed, and a new collective competence achieved. The SAS example also shows that: (a) one of the most central leadership tasks in developing collective competence is to initiate and involve staff in an active reflection on their work; and (b) leaders continuously need to formulate the shared understanding that arises from an active reflection among co-workers clearly in a set of specific symbols. As the SAS example demonstrates, a system of symbols that highlights a shared understanding of work guides members of the collective in their development of a new distinct competence in their business.

What also became apparent from the SAS example is that the collective's understanding of its work is the basis not only for its competence but also for its identity. SAS's understanding of itself as an airline company meant that it identified itself as an airline company. This was a basic characteristic of the old SAS. The identity as an airline company gave rise to the existential crisis at SAS when it went into decline. The SAS collective then started to question its identity as an airline company. The existential crisis that SAS had ended up in was gradually overcome by the fact that the employees began to understand SAS business as a travel company, which also resulted in a new identity as a travel company.

Note

1 While extensively modified, some of the material used in this chapter first appeared in Sandberg, J. (2000) 'Competence: the basis for a smart workforce', in R. Gerber and C. Lankshear (eds), *Training for a Smart Workforce*. London: Routledge.

SIX Understanding and its transformation

In Chapters 2–5 we described and exemplified the main features of human understanding and how it forms the basis for work performance in organizations. An important insight from those chapters was that an understanding of work functions as a basis for not only work performance but also for the competence people develop and use in accomplishing their work. The purpose of this chapter is to summarize the main features of understanding developed in the previous chapters and to extend the discussion to the issues that are involved in transforming understanding. In Chapter 7 we will outline a range of methods for managing understanding and set out guidelines for how these methods can be redesigned to enable managers to manage understanding more effectively.

Once again – what is understanding?

As we have seen in the previous chapters, it is not easy to provide a simple answer to the question of what defines understanding. Many would probably like a short and succinct definition of understanding, but we do not believe that a definition – whatever formulation it may have – would present an adequate answer to the question. Instead, we have, through lengthy reasoning and examples, tried to show what constitutes understanding and how it determines work performance and the competence used in accomplishing our work. What we have tried to provide is therefore not really a theory of understanding in a traditional sense, but rather what Shotter (1993) called an 'instructive account' of what constitutes understanding. In other words, we have provided a range of instructive examples and statements that show what understanding is and how it forms the basis for work performance and competence at work. Below we summarize what we regard as the main features of understanding.

One of its central features is that every human *creates and develops his or her own understanding*. It never comes to us in a ready-made fashion. Its creation is stimulated by all kinds of impressions and experiences, but the main stimulation comes from our interaction with other people. Since we always develop our own understanding, it forms a significant part of ourselves. It is therefore not something we can keep at distance and observe from the outside. An observer may be able to analyse the understanding of others and conclude that there are different forms of understanding among these people concerning some part of reality. But for myself, my own understanding of the world is not simply one way of understanding the world among others. It is basically my own reality. My understanding is my relationship with reality. It provides me with answers to questions such as: What is it? What's going on? How does it work? Why is it so? How does it concern me?

A second important feature is its *social nature*. As was described in Chapter 5, while we always embody an understanding of reality, we are not born with such an understanding but are socialized into it. Our understanding of reality is thus not something we first develop ourselves, but is something we learn from others by being socialized into society, its various social practices, and specific organizations. For example, an optimizer expressing a particular understanding of engine optimization, such as 'optimizing interactive qualities', has not developed that understanding himself. Instead, he has been socialized into it by practising engine optimization. However, while understanding is social in origin, it is personal in the sense that a person like the optimizer described above at the same time embodies that understanding. The same can be said about collective understanding. While Powell's collective understanding of flute manufacturing is socially defined through the interaction of its staff members, it is simultaneously personal by their embodiment of it.

A third key feature is that understanding is not static but is always *in process* and under continuous development. It is possible to distinguish two ways in which understanding can be transformed:

- Refining an existing understanding of reality
- Changing the understanding of reality.

An example of how understanding develops through refinement is demonstrated by the optimizers (described in Chapter 3). They refine their understanding through every new encounter of engine optimization. Every time optimizers who embody the understanding 'optimizing separate qualities' encounter an optimization situation, they will refine and deepening their existing understanding of engine optimization in some way or another. The more optimization situations they encounter, the more nuanced their understanding of engine optimization as optimizing separate qualities becomes. An example of how understanding develops through change is when an optimizer moves from the understanding 'optimizing separate qualities' to the understanding 'optimizing interacting qualities'. Such a development of understanding means that the optimization work takes on a different meaning for the optimizer in question. Optimization is no longer about 'optimizing separate qualities' but about 'optimizing interactive qualities'.

The two basic forms of transformation also apply to collective understanding. The ongoing sense making among the flutemakers at Powells (see Chapter 5) can be seen as an example of how collective understanding is transformed through refinement. We saw from the description of Powells that its members were continuously involved in an ongoing sense making about what makes a Powell flute. Their ongoing sense making enabled them to continuously refine their understanding of what makes a Powell flute at the same time as it enabled them to produce Powell flutes with an identical style and character. The development within SAS from understanding the corporation as an 'airline' to seeing it as a 'travel business' represents how collective understanding can develop through change. The changed understanding led SAS to make new and different interpretations of its business activities and to shift its judgements and priorities.

A fourth feature is that the development of understanding unfolds in *a circular* rather than in a linear manner. Understanding is circular in character (see Chapter 4) in the sense that 'developing understanding presupposes and elaborates something already understood' (Dall'Alba and Sandberg, in press: 16–17). This means that people's way of interpreting and making sense of their work follows a pattern that has been established and will be reproduced as long as their experiences do not draw into question the established circularity. For instance, every time the optimizers who understand engine optimization as 'optimizing interacting qualities' encounter an optimization task, they will interpret and make sense of it as 'optimizing interacting qualities'. However, its development is not completely circular but is also open in character. The circularity can be disrupted for various reasons and can lead either to a refinement or a change of existing understanding.

To conclude this section we can note that:

1 Employees as well as managers all have an understanding of their specific company's specific tasks, business, market, competitors, and so on.
2 Employees as well as managers act in line with their understanding, which also forms the basis for their work performance and the competence they develop and use in accomplishing their work.
3 This means that when people change their understanding they will also change their competence and work performance.

111

Given that understanding forms the basis for both people's work performance and the competence they develop and use in accomplishing their
work, it should be of significant interest from a management point of view
to be able to manage people's understanding. We argued in Chapter 1 that
most efforts to influence people's understanding of work have not delivered
expected outcomes. Our explanation of that failure was that managers do not
know what constitutes understanding and how it forms the basis for work
performance and the competence used in accomplishing work. If managers
begin to understand what understanding is and how it works, they may be
more successful in their efforts to influence employees' work performance.
However, influencing employees' understanding in a deliberate way cannot
be done on command or through top management decisions and directives.
The first characteristic of understanding mentioned above was that people
develop and create their own understanding. It therefore cannot be delivered
ready-made. This is why the task of developing employees' understanding in
a desired way provides such a challenge for managers. In the section below
we will analyse in more detail the main issues involved in transforming
understanding.

Issues involved in transforming understanding

How understanding unfolds

In discussions with practitioners we often found the view that if management
provides more explicit knowledge to employees about a task, they will
develop a 'better understanding' of it (that is, more in line with the manger's
intentions). Behind such a view we can trace an assumption that explicit
knowledge is an independent entity that can be used to transform people's
understanding in a desirable direction. But as was pointed out in Chapter 4,
people always have a pre-understanding, which is inevitably already operating when the explicit knowledge is made available to them, and this pre-
understanding will impact on how they make sense of the explicit knowledge.
In the circular process of understanding, with its simultaneous interaction
between parts and whole, people try to fit new partial elements into their
established understanding, and when this does not seem possible, the preferred alternative is to disregard these elements. In some cases, however, new
elements might evoke a questioning of the whole, which may lead to a
change in the pattern of understanding.

From the perspective presented here it is not surprising that two persons,
who have acquired the same amount of explicit knowledge regarding an

issue, can still understand it in very different ways. Therefore, the mere quantity and richness of factual knowledge does not automatically lead to the development of a given way of understanding a particular issue. An interesting illustration of this can be found in the interpretations and reactions that accompanied the development of the personal computer during the 1980s. The computer specialists, who were educated within the field of 'Electronic Data Processing (EDP)' and worked within computer departments and in software companies, were without doubt the most able to pass judgement on what the PC was in the first place and what it offered for the future. This was precisely why they often came to the conclusion that the PC would never really pose a threat to the mainframes and the mini-computers. At best the PC could function as a toy or as a simple office tool, such as a more advanced typewriter or calculator.

The computer specialists followed the developments of the PC but frequently noted that it was inadequate for handling the operating systems required by more advanced administrative applications. Why devote a large amount of effort and time to learn the PC language and its technology, which in any case will never become important within the context of EDP business?

Not surprisingly, the PC-dependent IT-sector became dominated by young people who had developed their understanding of the PC and its possibilities by spending part of their childhood playing with the PC that their clairvoyant – or maybe simply enthusiastic – parents had brought home. Others received hands-on experience from the new technology at schools and universities. By experimenting with its capacity and testing the limits of its performance, a younger generation developed a totally different understanding of what a PC was, what could be done with it, and what future potential it had compared to the already experienced computer specialists.

When people learn something new through their daily work activities they already have a more or less well-developed understanding of their work. This is the case in everyday work as well as in education, as was shown by Dall'Alba and Sandberg (in press). What is learned is interpreted and becomes meaningful within the confines of their existing understanding of it. Therefore, learning something new at work means, in most instances, that the new elements are made sense of and integrated into one's established understanding of work. By gaining new information and experience that are interpreted within our existing understanding, our competence becomes richer, our understanding is developed further but remains unchanged and may even be further entrenched through its refinement. Once again, we receive confirmation that the world is comprehensible and manageable. The

113

EDP specialists, who during the 1980s tried out the first personal computers, received confirmation of their existing understanding – this toy does not fit into the context within which mini-computers and mainframe computer systems are employed. If there is an established shared understanding of something, the social interaction within the group can further reinforce an interpretation that confirms and justifies the established understanding.

However, sometimes we cannot interpret new impressions and experiences within our existing understanding. In most such cases we try to get rid of these experiences by viewing them as temporary and inexplicable phenomena. If somebody presents ideas, theories or observations that stand in conflict with our existing understanding we tend to view them simply as being incorrect: 'This is not true. We do not believe in this.' However, the computer specialists referred to above have surely changed their understanding about the PC since the beginning of the 1980s. Eventually, the new impulses became so strong that they could not discard them easily. They started to question the premises of their understanding and began to search for new ways of interpreting the reality that they had to manage. As we mentioned in Chapter 4, the most fundamental form of learning is the one that occurs when people *change their understanding of something*.

Changing understanding: what is known about it?

It is possible to identify two different processes by which people change their understanding, or, to be more correct, there are two poles on a continuum that may lead to a change in understanding.

1   Where an individual experiences something, tries to make sense of it and so changes his or her understanding in some fundamental sense.
2   Where somebody more or less subconsciously internalizes views and behaviours that are established in a social community by simply imitating others without conscious reflective inquiry.

Most cases of changing understanding represent a mix between the two processes. When individuals experience something unique, it is possible to reflect upon these specific experiences individually – that is a conscious reflection will inevitably make use of concepts, ideas or explanations that are products of earlier social influence. Most often, however, an individual's experiences are also subject to reflections that are carried out with other people. As we pointed out in Chapter 5, the creation of understanding has by necessity a social dimension. The typical situation in organizations also seems to be the one where people experience things that are more or less shared with others and where one's own and others' experiences are continuously intertwined with reflections and discussions. On the other pole of the continuum we have the case of socialization, where people who are newcomers in a certain social context learn the ways of thinking, talking and behaving that are established in the community. They become meaningful just because they are considered natural and are taken for granted by the other members.

But how do we *change* an established understanding? According to Weick (1995), sense making is an ongoing activity, but this ongoing sense making will most often confirm and refine existing understanding, which means that the changes are non-existent or marginal. As was stated in Chapter 4, changing the circularity of existing understanding requires that we become aware of that circularity, which normally happens when something unexpected occurs or when the outcome of our actions is surprising. Such events will trigger reflection and inquiry, which sometimes can bring about changes in understanding.

In a classical social psychology experiment, Janis and King (1954) asked students to deliver an improvised speech to some fellow students concerning a controversial issue at that time, namely the probable effect of television upon cinemas. The researchers showed the speakers a rough outline of the speech which stipulated that television would have a lower impact than was usually assumed, and offered a number of possible arguments for that position. However, the students were asked to formulate the speech in their own words. An identical outline was shown to the listeners in advance. Some time before the experiment all the students had been asked to estimate TV's impact on cinemas. When the same measurement was made after the speeches, it turned out that a higher proportion of the speakers had changed their pre-experimental view towards a position closer to that of the outline of the speech than the students who had been passively listening. Results from this and similar experiments indicate that action has an impact upon how people judge and evaluate their world.

Festinger (1957) described a similar mechanism in his classical studies of 'cognitive dissonance'. According to Festinger, people strive towards achieving congruence between their attitudes, cognitive frames and their behaviour. If there is a lack of correspondence, the individual will feel discomfort and try to adjust one of the factors in order to achieve congruence. This also means that when individuals have achieved a satisfactory correspondence, they will subconsciously be inclined to defend it by finding excuses to support their own observations or actions, sometimes even to the extent that these excuses appear exaggerated or distorted by people in the environment.

115

Kuhn (1962) described how new scientific paradigms arise within the world of research. Some patterns within such change processes may also apply to how people change understandings in other social settings.

1 Researchers within a scientific community, who have acquired a certain paradigm and have learned to categorize their observations and control their thoughts in congruence with it, tend to defend their existing paradigm. If they are confronted with observations and information that seem to contradict the existing paradigm, the researchers will work hard to invalidate these observations.
2 Only when the researchers have been confronted with various or strong signals ('anomalies') which contradict the existing paradigm are they inclined to question it and even abandon it.
3 A paradigm shift can sometimes take place in a dramatic fashion. Often, however, it occurs over a long period of time, where different paradigms coexist and compete for the researchers' trust. During this time researchers often feel somewhat insecure and caught between the frontlines.

While Kuhn discusses how changes take place in scientific paradigms within large collectives, we can see similar patterns when individuals change their fundamental understanding of their work. People defend their existing understandings, and strong impulses are needed in order to bring about a questioning of them. The change process tends to stretch over a considerable period of time. The questioning is often a process that unfolds during times of uncertainty, and it may be impossible for a person to identify exactly when in time a shift in understanding actually occurs.

Since individuals act within their understanding, action is always preceded by understanding but, at the same time, every action questions the relevance and plausibility of that understanding. Every action has adherent expectations concerning its outcome, and these expectations are in line with the understanding that precedes the action. Therefore, action leads in most cases to a confirmation of existing understanding and, according to Kuhn, there are strong social pressures to keep it intact. However, unexpected outcomes or surprises can trigger intensive reflection. Such reflections can enable people to become aware of their own understanding, particularly if there are other people who can pinpoint the contradictions and help them to visualize alternative ways of understanding the course of events.

Understanding is tied to identity

As was described in Chapter 4 with reference to Heidegger, understanding is not only something we do, but is also something we are. It therefore forms a fundamental part of our whole way of being. This means that our identity is intimately related to how we understand phenomena in the world. For instance, if we experience something that is unexpected and surprising, and is not consistent with our existing understanding, it will evoke not only a questioning of our existing understanding of how to handle the situation, but also of our personal identity. Such questioning can arouse anxiety that leads to a willingness to find excuses or explanations that can disarm the conflict between the unexpected experiences and an established personal identity. This in itself is a mechanism that provides a defence for existing understandings in a similar way as in Festinger's theory of cognitive dissonance.

For instance, let us imagine an open-minded and curious natural scientist who of course has an understanding of the physical world that is based upon the standard paradigm of natural science. In that kind of understanding there is no room for divine forces acting upon the physical world or of strange energies such as those advocated by the New Age movement. If the scientist accepted an opportunity to try a dowsing rod (used to find water in the ground or a suitable place for a well), and suddenly felt that the rod was moving (indicating that water is present), what would be the reaction? The scientist may be puzzled, but we can also be sure that her first reaction will not be to immediately abandon her natural science-based view of the earth. To accept the observation as a true movement of the rod, caused by something other than the person holding it, would threaten her identity as a natural scientist. It is highly likely that she would search for alternative explanations, such as psychological factors, to remove any state of uncertainty and anxiety.

In a similar way, an organization's identity is also tied to a collective's particular understanding of work. In Chapter 5 we referred to Cook and Yanow's (1993) study of how the flutemakers at Powell's used various activities in the factory to maintain the specific style and character of the Powell flute. Cook and Yanow also described how a new 'scale' (designing and combining the holes in the flute that determine the level of the tone) was developed in England, the 'Cooper scale'. The professional flutists who had the opportunity to try a Cooper flute (originally handmade in very few numbers) considered the innovation to be an improvement. Consequently, Powell had to decide whether it should adopt the innovation, and if it could be done without harming the specific style and character of the Powell flute. The flutemakers' first reaction was that this was 'totally unthinkable'. The new scale was considered to threaten the identity of the company and themselves as flutemakers. After a considerable period of debate and procrastination they decided to adopt the new scale, but only for customers who requested it. The traditional flutes would continue to be produced. It soon became apparent however, that a vast majority of its customers preferred the Powell flute with the Cooper scale, and gradually the new scale became the norm and, thus, part of the Powell

117

identity. It is an interesting example of how members of an organization can adapt to new conditions without harming the collective identity. But we can also see how painful and demanding that process can be and that the first reaction is usually a strong and emotionally loaded rejection.

In the SAS case described in Chapter 5 we saw a very different pattern. The new management had an ambition to establish a new and different understanding of the airline business, which in turn would require a new organizational identity. Using rhetoric and substantial symbols, the new managers tried to help employees develop a new understanding of the business and a new corporate identity – being a customer-oriented travel company instead of a production-oriented airline. As one would expect, the new understanding was most quickly adopted by those who worked close to the customers, such as the cabin crew and the front-desk personnel. Those who were least inclined towards the change were the people who worked mainly with technical issues, and those who had a task that was strongly routinized and regulated, such as pilots and maintenance people. For the latter people, this identity was strongly tied to the technical operation of airline.

Academics who have tried to change their understanding of social science, such as from a positivist to a constructionist view, often display what can be tentatively described as a loose coupling between understanding of practice and identity. We have seen individuals accept and integrate new research practices into their existing repertoire despite the fact that the new practices harbour an identity different from their existing identity. When individuals are able to make sense of the new practices within their existing understanding, their identity remains intact. This process can progress, as more new practices are used and integrated into the repertoire. But after some time this will often lead to an 'identity crisis' and individuals have to admit that they understand research in a different way and, at the same time, have changed identity. It is surprising, however, how far the process can go before individuals fully admit that their identity has changed.

A good parallel at a collective level is the identity crisis that many radical socialist parties have undergone since 1990. On the one hand, they have been more or less forced by external realities to accept capitalism and market liberalism. On the other hand, they try to keep their identity as communists or radical socialists, and this creates contradictions and conflicts within the parties about who they are, what their identity is, and what they are supposed to do.

The need to overcome defences

In organization studies the concept of 'unlearning' is frequently used, often with a reference to Hedberg (1981). It is sometimes seen as a prerequisite for being able to learn something radically new. The concept of unlearning might evoke the idea that a person can erase his or her knowledge and start from the beginning with a clear sheet. But from our perspective on human understanding as an open but directed process, it makes more sense to think of learning something radically new as a reconstruction of an existing understanding of reality, where a modified understanding unfolds and gradually replaces the existing one. Results from phenomenographic studies indicate that people can keep the content of an earlier understanding as part of a new one (Marton and Booth, 1997). The earlier view is then related to and made sense of within the frame of the new understanding. A researcher who started his career as a positivist, but later on changed to a constructivist paradigm, will still keep his understanding of positivism, but now as something that is related to, and understood within, a constructionist view.

The 'competence trap' might be one explanation as to why people seem unwilling to change their existing understanding of work. It is inherent in the fact that it takes time for people, when adopting a new understanding, to reach the same level of productivity as they were used to within their previous understanding of work. Starting to work according to the new understanding may bring the individual back to a novice level, which contradicts the individual's current identity as a high performer. In line with Festinger's dissonance theory, the new understanding will be experienced as being less effective, and will face stiff resistance even though, seen from the outside, it would be fruitful and valuable for the company (Levitt and March, 1988). This phenomenon parallels the difficulties experienced when new technological solutions have to be utilized. In its earliest stage of development the light-bulb was clearly inferior to the gas lamp.

The concepts of unlearning and competence traps provide two explanations for the widely acknowledged observation of inertia in the process of changing understanding. We believe that emotional factors also have a significant role in explaining inertia. In discussions with psychotherapists we have found that they often encounter the conservational role of an individual's identity. Practices and beliefs seem to be firmly anchored in one's identity, and often incredibly strong influences are needed to change that identity, something that is also experienced as emotionally distressing.

Another mechanism that may be active when individuals defend their existing understanding (and identity) is what Weick (1995) described as extracted cues. When people try to make sense of something they do not do full justice to the information available. Instead, they select a few critical elements – the extracted cues – and build their sense making on these cues. We can assume that emotional motives, such as fear, or a need to confirm one's expectations or identity, have a strong impact on which cues will be selected.

In experimental psychology it has also been shown that human perception seems to be an active process, which filters out certain stimuli at the same time as it promotes other stimuli, all as a result of 'priming', which is information provided before the actual perception process being studied (Milliken and Tipper, 1998). The idea of priming has some resemblance to pre-understanding described in Chapter 4. So, what for one individual is a natural and given understanding of a situation, built from extracted cues and guided by a complex pre-understanding, might for another person be seen as an unreasonably distorted view which he or she is unwilling to accept.

The situational nature of understanding

A classic story depicts a father involved in serious talk with his young son about the importance of always telling the truth. In the midst of his educational efforts the telephone rings. The father shouts to his wife: 'If it's my boss calling, tell him I'm not at home tonight'. And so he goes back to the task of educating his son about the necessity of always telling the truth. The story illustrates how people can shift from one reality to another, and how these realities evoke completely different patterns of understanding. The fact that they are logically contradictory is something that the person does not always become aware of. In everyday life we experience many such cases, maybe not always with such apparent and drastic contradictions. A manager may display one understanding of a company issue in a public speech but in the next moment acts in a way that reveals quite a different understanding of the same issue. A person who cannot think of killing another human being, not even hurting one, can judge and act very differently as a soldier in combat. The situational nature of understanding has also been reported in several phenomenographic studies (Marton and Booth, 1997; Marton and Peng, 2005).

The most common case in organizations seems to be the one where managers understand something in one way when they talk about it and in a different way when they practise it. Argyris and Schön (1978) identified this phenomenon and coined the concepts *espoused theories* and *theories in use*. It can be seen as some kind of tactic, where people in communication with others try to appear as more 'politically correct' than they can afford to be in everyday practice. But, in a similar way as the father trying to educate his son, the manager is often not aware of the discrepancy between what is said and what is done, at least not when talking or acting.

The subordinates may also display the same discrepancy. When top management in an organization announces some new principles and practices that require changes in the behaviour of subordinates, a typical reaction may be that the subordinates do not find the new practices suitable. One reason for this may be that the subordinates think managers are requesting the new practices because they believe that their managers do not know enough about the local conditions. 'But we have been working on this for years. We know how it must be done.' If there is no strict managerial control of how subordinates work, they will probably go on working in line with their understanding of the work – they try to act reasonably in their perspective. If the top managers check up on the work practices, subordinates may produce what Argyris has called 'fancy footwork' – a term used among square dancers who try to do something special when the judges have their eyes on them (Argyris, 1990). According to Argyris, people in organizations disregard management initiatives that do not make sense to them, but this is not revealed. They try to avoid embarrassing their managers by disclosing that the managerial ambitions do not work. Managers will therefore receive the confirmation they are looking for and both parties are happy.

If we analyse such a case within the framework of understanding, we see that people deal with the new directives according to their understanding of them, but they also deal with the relationship with their boss according to their understanding of what is reasonable, and these two things represent situations that are understood differently, each one according to its specific conditions. If we accept the idea that understanding develops through reflection on one's own and others' actions, the situational character of understanding becomes reasonable. Learning to talk, particularly in public, about an issue is one kind of practice, and learning to deal with the issue in a real situation is another kind of practice, each one leading to a specific kind of reflection and sense making.

Many managers in their discussions have displayed a rational view, where a person who has acquired some insights and views in an educational programme, is expected to think and act according to those insights in all situations where they may be relevant. They expect consistency in people's understanding of the world. However, it seems that understanding which has grown from experience is tied to the situation in which it has been experienced. Understanding does not function as a logical principle that is applied to every situation where it logically should be applied. For example, an algebraic principle that seems relevant and reasonable as a solution to a problem in a mathematics lesson may not automatically be seen as relevant and reasonable to an identical problem in a real-life setting. We will discuss this more thoroughly in Chapter 7, in relation to the problem of learning that has emanated from traditional, school-type education and its application in work situations.

Hence, while we say that people act according to their understanding of reality, it would be more accurate to say that people act according to their understanding of the various realities they identify in the situation at hand. And these different understandings do not automatically form a logically consistent structure. One specific task in managing understanding could therefore be to make people become aware of such inconsistencies and facilitate the development of a larger, consistent 'whole', something that many managers try to achieve when they communicate the strategies of the organization.

When does a new understanding develop?

In educational settings we have encouraged managers to reflect upon occasions where they themselves have been subject to a shift in their fundamental understanding within a field that in some way or another is related to their work activities. An analysis of a number of such self-reflective stories revealed that some elements recur more frequently than others:

1   *Personal, concrete experiences* ('to see with one's own eyes, to be able to try for oneself, to discover something') have a distinctly stronger influence on us than the second-hand information we receive from books, media, conferences and seminars. The effect seems to be particularly strong if a person has already been confronted with the new thoughts, and in that way comes prepared. The person has read the books, and has heard about the ideas and the people behind them.

2   *Emotionally loaded experiences* have a stronger impact than purely intellectual and informative experiences. These can be happy or painful experiences. They can result from interaction with other people who create positive feelings, or emerge out of respect for a known authority. Many people refer to contexts such as: 'when I heard X talk about this, on his last visit to this country ...'. It goes without saying that the experience of listening in person to an authority who has something important to say has a stronger impact on me than if I just read his or her books, or listened to others present the same ideas. But even here it is important to be mentally prepared beforehand.

3   *Engaging in a dialogue* with other people has a stronger impact than one-way communication, such as listening to a presentation or reading a book. In dialogues people often experience social pressures to reveal their beliefs, thoughts and ideas. Such revelations are exposed to questioning from others, and the individual has to defend him- or herself against the arguments in a way that can be immediately examined and judged by the other interlocutors. In this way, it becomes more difficult to defend one's existing ideas and invalidate new thoughts and arguments.

4   A *colourful, symbolic representation* of new thoughts can contribute to their success. A clever catchword or phrase, a metaphor, a story, or a simple model have all one thing in common: they catch the meaning of a particular thought or idea and, at the same time, have a linguistic and symbolic power of attraction.

It is striking that action and experiences play a dominant role in such stories. Traditional instruments for influencing understanding that are centred on the provision of information are seldom mentioned. Although seminars are sometimes mentioned, invariably we find that these are presentations given by well-known authorities. Here, however, it is not a question of providing new information. It is more a matter of reinforcing and confirming views that are already present as a result of earlier readings and discussions. What becomes particularly visible in the stories is the importance of experiential learning. More than just traditional information is required if one seeks to change people's understandings. Personal and emotionally loaded experiences and effective dialogues seem to be crucial factors in changing understanding.

Concluding remarks

We noted that the task of influencing people's understanding is a demanding challenge. There are no direct methods by which someone can 'switch' the understanding of someone else. Changing understanding cannot be commanded or prescribed. Managers are left with indirect methods, which can be used to encourage and stimulate employees to reflect upon impressions and experiences.

Managing understanding becomes still more challenging because of various defences. It is likely that many managerial efforts fail because the power of defences has been underestimated and people are resistant to certain management initiatives. Often managers have ascribed employees' reluctance in participating in the activities prescribed to an unwillingness among them to change. Unwillingness presumes, however, that employees can identify what is being presented by the manager, examine whether or not they like it and, based on that, decide whether they should comply with it or not.

Our argument has been that it is typically not a matter of unwillingness. The employees simply do not identify with what is presented in the same way as the manager. They identify and interpret it in line with their existing understanding, and nobody can blame them for doing that. They will make sense of what is presented in a way that does not threaten their identities. This is something unforced and reasonable and should not be seen as unwillingness or opposition. Managers must realize that their task is not only to *present* new ideas or measures to be taken. Their task is also to make others *understand* the ideas and measures in a way that will support the managerial intentions. This is a difficult task but it is not a mission impossible. Maybe is it considered difficult because managers themselves do not understand this task in an adequate way and therefore choose ineffective methods for managing understanding?

SEVEN Methods and principles for managing understanding

In the previous chapter we outlined the major characteristics of understanding and the main issues involved in its transformation. The purpose of this chapter is to identify and discuss possible methods for managing understanding. We begin by identifying and describing a range of methods currently used for influencing people's action in order to achieve a desirable work performance, and evaluate their potential for managing understanding. An important conclusion from the evaluation is that while a number of methods have the potential for managing understanding, most of them are designed in a way that at best encourages a refinement but not a change in understanding. Based on our description of what constitutes understanding in Chapters 3–6, we outline a set of guiding principles for redesigning current methods so they can be utilized to actively promote changes in people's understanding of work.

Possible methods for managing understanding

In the following section we identify and describe a range of methods currently used for influencing people's action, and evaluate their potential for managing understanding. We have organized them into two main categories and four sub-categories:

Language-driven methods

- Language-based managerial methods
- Language-based educational methods

Action-driven methods

- Experience-based educational methods
- Practice-based methods

The major difference between the two main categories is that the language-driven methods primarily use language while the action-driven methods mainly use action as a means to influence understanding. The range of methods described within each sub-category is in no way exhaustive. They should rather be seen as typical representatives for the particular category in which they form a part. We discuss these methods from a management point of view, which means that the point of departure is a manager who wants to make things happen in a certain desired way. We accept here that managers' understanding of reality is reasonable from an organizational point of view, and that their intentions are likely to lead to positive effects for the organization. In real life, however, there is no guarantee that this is the case, and we will discuss this more in the last chapter.

Language-driven methods

Language-based managerial methods

Everyday communication methods

Empirical studies of managerial work (Mintzberg, 1980; Tengblad, forthcoming) show that top executives spend most of their time communicating with others. They discuss with people inside and outside the company, write emails and memos, and sometimes formulate written statements in the form of articles and formal reports. These communication tools can be seen as useful in providing organizational members with important information about their work. But managers also know that they can use everyday communication to influence the thinking and the action of their employees, and some use them very consciously for managing understanding. For example, many famous corporate leaders, such as Lee Iacocca, Andy Grove and Jack Welch, are admired for their ability to use daily communication as well as prepared formal statements to influence how people in their organizations understand the business strategy, key priorities and the importance of certain activities. For them – and many others – everyday communication has been a powerful tool in governing organizations.

Fairhurst and Sarr (1996) provided a comprehensive analysis of how managers can use everyday communication for 'framing' the minds of employees, which we interpret as exerting influence upon their understanding. As was pointed out in Chapter 1, framing can be seen as an ability to shape people's understanding in a desired way through particular conversation techniques. Fairhurst and Sarr proposed a range of such techniques, some of which are partly congruent with ingredients in classic rhetoric. For example, *contrast* can be used in communication to shape the understanding of a message by comparing it to opposite phenomena. *Stories and examples* can be used to present a more vivid representation of key points in a message, a rhetorical technique that is well known already from the parables found in the New Testament. *Metaphors* are another example of classical techniques, whereas *catch phrases* can be seen as a modern variation on that theme, developed into excellence in the field of advertising. *Spin* is a somewhat different kind of rhetorical tool that represents the emotional and empathic element in classical rhetoric. A manager can give an analysis or a discussion a positive spin to evoke positive feelings, such as pride, in listeners or readers. The discussion can also be given a negative spin to provoke disapproval or fear. By balancing positive and negative spin, the message can be given a sense of realism, and the communicator can control the message so that the presentation will end up in a positive or negative light, and thus give rise to positive or negative emotions, depending on the communicator's intentions. When it comes to what should be communicated and the timing of communicative efforts, *context sensitivity* becomes important. Managers need to identify those people and conditions that are critical for the situation at hand, and to be able to read the various signals that indicate how these people think, feel and evaluate the situational factors at hand.

However, to be able to influence other people's understanding through framing usually requires that managers have reflected in advance upon their own understanding of the phenomenon in question. Without a clear idea of what understanding should be developed, managers will not know in which direction they should frame the understanding of employees. This means that framing often becomes a delicate balancing act between being too specific or too general. On the one hand, a framed conversation should have a spontaneous character to avoid being perceived as preaching the message. On the other hand, it is not completely obvious that the framing of a message should be as clear and distinct as possible. As Fairhurst and Sarr (1996) noted, sometimes ambiguity is helpful as it leaves it open for the employees to interpret the message and add their own ingredients to it. Ambiguous goals can be helpful at the implementation of changes, since they define a direction without being too specific about how it should be done. It can also be easier to gain commitment to a general ambition than to specific actions, which may intervene in the everyday life of people.

Eisenberg (1984) used the term 'unified diversity of interpretations' to designate the eventual outcome of a manager's communication of his or her ambitions in the form of a lofty metaphor. Achieving a general commitment is an important condition for further and more specific framing efforts. Brunsson's (1985) study on decision making in organizations also lends support for being deliberately ambiguous in achieving employees' commitment to a certain understanding. He found that decision processes that follow the rational ideal, where several alternatives are presented and scrutinized in order to choose the best one, met more difficulties in the implementation phase than the 'irrational' processes with usually only one alternative and more fuzzy motives and evaluations.

Thus, by preparing oneself and planning in advance, managers can become more effective in framing the minds of others. This is the seemingly rational approach that Fairhurst and Sarr are advocating. They describe communication as primarily verbal but at the same time emphasize the complexity of communicative processes.

However, communication is not only purely verbal but is also emotional. There is a strong emotional element in communication that is intertwined with the factual part of language. The existence of an emotional dimension was noted by Aristotle. He identified *pathos* as one of his three key ingredients in good rhetoric. The emphatic element is not only expressed in words but also through the appearance and the behaviour of the communicator. Building upon psychoanalytic thinking, Hallowell (1999) discussed the role of 'the human moment', a term that covers not only what is said in a communicative situation but also how body language, behaviour and the arrangement of the setting shape the emotional atmosphere in which the verbal communication is embedded. Goleman et al. (2001) takes this idea further by claiming that the appearance and ways of acting that are displayed by a manager, and the emotional reactions that are aroused by it, are factors that to a large extent determine the success or failure of managerial communication.

In summary, there are numerous recipes for how information can be used to influence what happens in the organization, but when it comes to emotional aspects of managerial communication only general recommendations exist. It is a matter of increasing self-awareness as well as social awareness. It should be possible for managers to learn more about themselves and about how they manage relations to others in various situations. One further step might be to learn to manage social processes in a way that will create an emotional atmosphere that will support and catalyse the effect of the verbal content in managerial communication.

Managerial texts: visions, policies and other formal statements
Managers are not only using verbal communication but also a range of written texts in their attempt to influence other people's behaviour. There is a huge quantity of managerial texts in organizations that are supposed to direct

people's action. For example, managerial texts such as written corporate philosophies, strategic plans, value declarations and policy statements have been used long since in order to govern the thinking and the actions of employees.

One of the most popular managerial texts for influencing people's understanding is vision. It has received a symbolic role in the alleged paradigm shift in management described in Chapters 1 and 2. Vision as a managerial tool has also been extensively studied in management research (for an overview, see Nutt and Backoff, 1997). It is therefore worthwhile to have a closer look at what vision is and how it can be used for influencing understanding.

A vision can be seen as an attempt to create a conceptualization of the future ambitions of a corporation. According to Collins and Porras (1994), good visions contain two main elements: core ideology and envisioned future. The core ideology displays values that have been inherent in the corporate actions for a long period and signify the corporate identity. The envisioned future is shaped by 'big hairy and audacious goals'. It should evoke a visualization of a desired future that is substantially different from the present and a bold image that truly represents a challenge and stimulates an ambition to realize it.

Collins (1999) used the concept of 'catalytic mechanism' to designate vision as a managerial tool that is distinguished from traditional managerial devices for control in the sense that it is not primarily designed to regulate the achievement of specific and distant goals. It is a message to everybody, not just people in specific positions. It should evoke energy and provide a clear direction and a desired future state without specifying how to get there. It is supposed to have an ongoing influence that sometimes may produce thinking and action that is unpredictable but yet very useful. Senge (1990) used the term 'creative tension' to highlight the gap between the actual situation and a future situation that people can imagine from a vision statement. It is this gap, not too big and not too trivial, that gives rise to energy among organization members. In their extensive review of how vision can be used to influence people's behaviour in organizations, Nutt and Backoff found that visions with most impact embrace four specific characteristics:

> Possibility, desirability, actionability, and articulation emerged as the key properties of vision, and thus the key design criteria for its creation. Possibility offers a future-pull, providing a spark that animates and inspires. Desirability addresses value questions, altering the organization to shared principles that are required to energize people and prompt them to take action. Actionability addresses doability: People must be mobilized and see how they can act to support radical change. Articulation calls for superior imagery in a vision to create an attraction. (1997: 325)

The discussion so far has been primarily concerned with how a vision statement should be formulated in order to have an impact. It is still seen as an instrument of rhetoric. But what are the processes through which a vision will have an impact upon a person's behaviour? The process where written texts, such as visions, policies and instructions, are transformed into action has been the subject of a study in a police department by Ekman (2001). He noted that managerial texts became subject to approval or disapproval among the police officers through a process of 'small talk' (Gustafsson, 1994). Small talk has an everyday trivial character but it contains elements where people evaluate and comment on the norms and views being expressed in the managerial texts. These evaluations and comments contribute to the development of a shared understanding of the text, what relevance it has and what it means for their daily work practices. It is a kind of fragmented explicit reflections that contribute to the development of a shared understanding among the police officers about what a managerial text means in practice.

Ekman noted that there is often a huge discrepancy between managerial texts such as a policy statement that is supposed to govern people's actions in a particular way and how people actually understand and act upon the policy statement in question. For instance, one central policy statement that was supposed to direct the work of police officers was formulated as follows: 'Police officers are to plan their work schedule in modules, on the basis of the types of crime upon which the operating plans themselves are based' (2001: 233). According to Ekman, the message that the management tried to convey was that the police officers should plan their work around 'the crime they have to fight'. Ekman observed, however, that through small talk many police officers interpreted this policy as a possibility to plan their work 'so that it corresponds with the times when they want to work' (2001: 233). Through ongoing small talk this interpretation became shared and sanctioned by the police officers as the way to plan and conduct their work.

Methods that stimulate imaginative thinking

When managers send messages, either as part of everyday communication or in the form of carefully written statements, they 'deliver' a way of seeing things and wish their subordinates to embrace that view as their own way of understanding things. But there are other verbal methods that require a more active involvement by the 'receivers'. Such communicative methods are often used for stimulating creative thinking among employees.

If we accept the argument that understanding cannot be delivered but is created by individuals themselves, it seems reasonable for managers to use communication as a tool for inspiring employees to intensify their own creative thinking. This is the key message presented by Morgan in his book *Imaginization* (Morgan, 1993). The title is itself an invention of a new word, which Morgan uses in order to capture a specific challenge he can foresee.

As a society, we have become preoccupied with the ideas of finding ways of fixing and controlling the world around us. 'Getting organized' has meant finding the structure or solution for a situation that's going to last. ... The challenge now is to *imaginize*: to infuse the process of organizing with a spirit of imagination that takes us beyond bureaucratic boxes. We need to find creative ways of organizing and managing that allow us to 'go with the flow', using new images and ideas as a means of creating shared understandings. (1993: xxviii–xxix)

A central assumption behind the imaginization idea is that people under-stand things *as something*, which leads Morgan to emphasize the metaphor as a key management tool. By applying different metaphors to a specific situa-tion managers and others will be able to interpret that situation not in one but in multiple ways. Such manifold interpretations will enable managers and staff to reflect on their existing understanding as well as being able to develop alternative ways of understanding work.

A central element in imaginization seems to be the need to make visible a way of seeing how work can be organized, which is different from the exist-ing view. The verbal rhetoric is here combined with and maybe based upon the use of images with strong symbolic loadings. When people discover an alternative view, there is a suitable condition for providing more information that can explain and elaborate on this alternative view in comparison to the established one.

I like to talk about the process as one involving 'mirrors' and 'windows'. If one can look in the mirror and see oneself in a new way, the mirror can become a 'window', because it allows one to see the rest of the world with a fresh perspective. Or, in terms of the imagery introduced earlier, it opens new 'horizons', creating opportunities for new actions. (Morgan, 1993: 288)

However, Morgan also stresses that people must have a certain readiness for discovery and reflection. The metaphors must 'ring true' or 'hit a chord' and thus have some resonance in people's experiences and thoughts. Otherwise they become just amusing illustrations but nothing more. What is also impor-tant to notice is that Morgan claims that imaginization also contains a dimen-sion of empowerment. When people move from just following instructions to discover new and different understandings of work and how it can be orga-nized, they are likely to become empowered and start to act from their own judgements and reflections.

Another interesting method for creating imaginative thinking is various forms of visualization technologies primarily used in the area of innovation. According to Dodgson et al. (2005), visualization technologies combine a range of technologies, such as high-speed networks, image generating software and advanced curved screen projection systems. They enable professionals like engineers and architects to visualize complex data sets in advanced graphical images at a very early stage in the innovation process. In particular, visualization technologies enable people to create, design, prototype, test and successfully transform new ideas into products and services considerably faster than previously.

For example, when designing a new building, visualization technologies enable the architect to bring together a range of complex data, information, perspectives and particular preferences from various stakeholders into advanced 3D simulation models of the new building very early on in the process (Anumba et al., 2000). Such graphical images of the new building make it possible for the architect to create a shared understanding among the people involved in the project, such as architects, structural engineers, builders, contractors and client, about how it will look when finished and what particular specifications and requirement are involved in building it. A shared understanding of the new building at an early stage also makes it possible to eliminate a range of misunderstandings before the actual construction work begins.

Dialogue

Dialogue has a long tradition as a communicative method in contexts where reflection and inquiry are important elements. Classical philosophers were the first to use dialogue as a way of presenting their arguments concerning controversial issues. Dialogue has also a long history in the academic world as a method for evaluating research contributions. A particular feature of dialogue is its capacity to enable people to become aware of their own understanding of an issue by being exposed to other people's understandings of the same issue. In such situations the individual has to evaluate his or her own understanding in the collective light and defend its appropriateness or modify it, and sometimes even discard it. Becoming aware of one's own understanding through a dialogue can be similar to the process in which we become aware of our own national and ethnic culture by being confronted with people from other cultures. It is also a process that sometimes can involve psychological risk taking and moments of serious frustration.

As indicated above, if carried out properly, a dialogue can contribute to an enhanced awareness of people's present understandings, with the potential for developing and changing them. But what does a properly carried out dialogue entail? Following Gadamer, a genuine dialogue involves the process of *question and answer*, with the priority of the question over the answer. We develop our understanding through posing questions: 'Recognizing that an object is different, and not as we first thought, obviously presupposes a question whether it was this or that' (1994/1960: 362). For example, the realization that our work may differ from what we thought is based upon such a question. This realization can give rise to additional questions that encourage us to further our understanding of the work.

Moreover, a genuine question is *open* in the sense that it opens up the subject matter, such as our work, to further inquiry. The answer to an open question cannot be known completely in advance. However, although genuine questions are open, they are always posed within a particular understanding. More specifically, the questions we ask are based on a certain understanding that simultaneously opens up and confines the understanding we can develop through the questions posed. This means that the questions posed and answers given can be important sources for disclosing and making explicit the specific understanding of work within which they are formed.

What is the distinct role of question-and-answer in a genuine dialogue process? First, participants in a dialogue need to be directed towards the subject matter in order to further their understanding of it. Through its ongoing dialectic, the question-and-answer process guides the participants towards the subject matter throughout the dialogue. A second feature is that participants are following the dialogue. Again, the structure of question and answer is essential. For example, the questions that others put to us and the responses they give to our questions allow us to continually check whether we are following each other in the dialogue. A third feature is that each participant in the dialogue is oriented towards the strengths rather than the weaknesses of the others' understanding of the subject matter. This is because the purpose of the dialogue is not to win an argument but to reach a deeper understanding. For example, if someone puts forward a point of view, the other participants should explore whether it deepens their understanding of the subject matter. A closely related feature is that the focus is on participants' contributions and not on possible intentions behind what they say, although awareness of these intentions might sometimes improve the dialogue. In order to maintain such a focus each participant must be respected as an equal partner throughout the dialogue.

Finally, a successful dialogue is characterized by achievement of a shared understanding of the subject matter, which may differ from each participant's original understanding. This shared understanding is a joint effort that cannot be ascribed to a single participant. Achieving a shared understanding of the subject matter does not necessarily mean a consensus among participants. It can also mean that they agree to disagree with each other. In order to be able to reach such an agreement, each participant has to understand the others' viewpoints.

Bohm (1996) and Bohm and Edwards (1991) identified three conditions that must be met for a dialogue to possess the capacity of facilitating changes in understanding. First, its participants must *suspend their assumptions*, and hold them up before the others, thereby allowing access to scrutiny and questioning. The second prerequisite is a *willingness to see each other as colleagues*. This is necessary for creating a positive climate where people dare to be open, make themselves vulnerable without feeling the risk of being cheated or emotionally degraded. A third condition is the presence of a *facilitator* who can monitor the process and intervene when the dialogue is degenerating into a general discussion or a debate. The role of the facilitator is not to control the content of the dialogue but to maintain the necessary qualities of openness and a collegial atmosphere.

Hargrove (1998) and Isaacs (1999) identified a sequence of stages for how a group of people typically establishes a dialogue. In the first phase the participants present their viewpoints and ideas while the others listen politely. When the participants start to provide arguments to support their own claims, and supply evaluative and critical comments about other participants' viewpoints, the dialogue may run into a crisis. The participants become frustrated when they realize that not only do they have different ideas about the issues being discussed, but also that others understand things in quite different ways due to different premises and underlying assumptions. Here, the dialogue can transform into a debate, where the participants start to argue in order to show that they are right and the others are wrong, something that rarely leads to changes in understanding. But it can also transform into a more genuine dialogue described above.

Establishing a genuine dialogue is a considerable challenge for managers because in a dialogue there is no room for formal authority and power. As soon as a manager raises his voice and shows that people should adhere to his views because he is the boss, there is no dialogue any longer. Then it has transformed into an information meeting. In order for a dialogue to have a high probability of reaching the phases of reflection and constructive inquiry, managers have to choose an equal position and accept to listen more than to tell. They have to accept being influenced and maybe even be prepared to change their own understanding in order to get the opportunity to exert influence upon others.

Language-based educational methods

Educational methods are simply those being used in a setting that we identify as 'education'. It is still a question of mainly verbal communication in the oral or written form, dialogues and verbal exercises. It might also be that a manager faces some subordinates in a seminar and acts as a teacher. The difference from what in the previous section has been called managerial communication is nothing more than the labelling of the setting. However, in many cases it would seem appropriate to identify educational activities as a distinct category of methods for influencing people's behaviour.

A majority of all planned and organized competence development activities that take place in organizations belong to the category of 'language-based educational methods'. In an overview De Cieri and Kramar (2005) identified internal and external classroom teaching, workshops, seminars and computer-assisted training as the most commonly used educational methods within organizations. They all represent what we call here language-based educational methods.

A fundamental assumption underlying most of these methods is that a development of understanding is a result of a deliberate and systematic *transfer* of explicit knowledge from one source (teacher, writings, database, internet, etc.) to the learner. The transfer can be highly structured, such as a lecture, or it can be a recommended activity that is performed independently by an individual or a group, such as reading a book or checking a website on the internet. A second underlying assumption is that the knowledge acquired through such educational methods can be stored in the individual who later on can 'pull it out' and apply it to a problem or task at hand.

Hence, developing understanding is in many educational language-based methods synonymous to *increasing one's explicit knowledge*. Knowledge is assumed to exist independently of the individual in explicit forms such as theories, principles, models, explanations, and lines of reasoning, which can be transmitted to people through written or oral communication. However, what most of these methods fail to realize is the insight highlighted in Chapter 3, namely that understanding of work precedes knowledge of work. It is our understanding of work that defines what knowledge we develop and how we will use that knowledge in accomplishing our work. The failure to realize that understanding precedes knowledge means that the efforts of most educational language-based methods are likely to result in a reinforcement of existing understanding rather than in a change of understanding and thus competence renewal. Below we will try to exemplify why this is the case.

The educational research carried out by Marton and Säljö (1976) convincingly demonstrated the inherent weaknesses of the rationalistic transfer-model for influencing people's understanding of something. Their research showed that even if people internalize abstract models from different fields and are able to explicate them when asked to do so, this does not necessarily mean that they can also exploit these models when confronted with problems in their everyday life.

Watson (1996) reached a similar conclusion in his study of MBA students. He refers to a case where MBA students were asked to answer the question 'What do we know about motivation?'. He noted that students knew about concepts, models and names of researchers. Further analysis revealed that the students were able to mention and to some extent describe the principles underlying some theories of motivation but without any connections to their own experiences or practices at work.

A comparable observation is that most adults in the western world have learned how to solve mathematical equations of the first degree in school and, if faced with the challenge, a majority of them would probably even today succeed in solving some such problems. But surprisingly few of them (disregarding those who consider mathematics calculations to be a natural part of their daily work activities) have used such equations to solve problems in their daily lives. What is interesting to note is that many people claim they have used this knowledge on one occasion especially, namely when they have helped their children to solve maths equations as part of their schoolwork.

Argyris and Schön (1978) used the concepts of *espoused theories* and *theories in use* to capture a similar distinction. They noted that learning often results in explicit knowledge, which individuals possess and can explicate in certain situations, but that in different settings they choose to take advantage of totally different conceptions of reality, and therefore also different methods and analyses.

The four examples above suggest that theoretical knowledge is a resource that we can possess, but whether we exploit it or not depends on our understanding of the task and the context we face. Let us further explore the possible relationship between traditional educational language-based methods and the reinforcement of existing understanding by returning to the engine optimizers in Chapter 3. Assume that a development within their field makes it imperative to gain a new type of knowledge of engines. Employing an educational language-based method would mean that competence development should begin with an expert on the topic identifying the new knowledge and elaborating on its importance. Thereafter, the new knowledge has to be carefully formulated, structured and packaged. The next step would be for someone to develop an educational activity aimed at transferring the knowledge as efficiently as possible from the expert to the optimizers.

The result of such a developmental activity is that the optimizers would hopefully acquire the new knowledge and even try to apply it in their daily work. However, it is likely that they will adopt the new knowledge within their existing understanding of engine optimization. This means that the optimizers will continue to optimize engines based on the same principles as previously. For example, the optimizers with understanding 1 will continue to carefully optimize separate engine qualities according to certain standards, while the optimizers with understanding 2 will continue to optimize interacting engine qualities in the right order.

Increasing our explicit knowledge without questioning our underlying understanding could be considered as a more shallow way of learning. The concepts of *surface-level* and *deep-level learning,* which were established by Marton and Säljö (1976), both fit into what we refer to as refining one's understanding. The concepts have been developed in relation to scholastic settings and are concerned with how we internalize the contents of a text or other educational material. Surface-level learning can be seen as a result of an educational situation where people learn how to reproduce knowledge that is explicitly formulated in a text or other material. However, people who display a surface-level learning do not connect what is stated in the text to their own experiences. This means that the content of the text has a life of its own. It is therefore highly doubtful whether the knowledge that is the result of surface-level learning will be applied in a concrete situation.

It is more likely that deep-level learning will lead to the application of the acquired knowledge in practice. Deep-level learning means that the individual works with information and other educational material in a way that makes it possible for him or her to integrate it with previous experiences and knowledge. It leads to an understanding, but at the same time there are no guarantees that the individual will change understanding. It can still result in a refinement of existing understanding.

The same is true when it comes to the use of information technologies for developing understanding. When people make observations and search for information out of their own free will, it is natural that the search strategies and interpretations are based on their existing understanding. This means that modern information technology such as the internet can be a very powerful instrument for increasing the diffusion of information to employees, but it does not automatically lead to a change in their understanding of work.

Refining our established understanding should be seen as something valuable in most cases. To become better at performing the tasks at hand is of importance to the individual as well as the company. It is therefore no reason to portray refinement of existing understanding and, thus, competence reinforcement in a negative way. Why we have had a critical undertone in what we have described depends on the fact that people who organize training and development often do not know what kind of learning outcome they want to achieve. In those instances where the objectives are clear, they are often unrealistic with respect to the educational methods they have chosen to employ. For example, their goals are often to increase people's factual knowledge within a certain field and, at the same time, to 'change their perspective' on certain phenomena. However, given the methods commonly used, the actual outcome will probably be that the participants increase their factual knowledge within their existing understanding of work. And when

137

applying the new knowledge, the participants will receive confirmation that their behaviour is relevant and up to date and, thus, will reinforce their existing understanding without being aware of it.

As we already noted in Chapter 4, learning at work normally means that people develop their competence within their existing understanding of work. They try to interpret their observations in a way that corresponds with their existing understanding of work. Take the example in the beginning of Chapter 4, where an engine optimizer tried to explain why a colleague is perceived as being particularly competent in his line of work. Without difficulty the optimizer was able to observe that his colleague is very competent, but when he had to explain why, he grounded his reasoning in his own understanding of what it means to be a competent optimizer. People are bound in a similar way by their understanding of their work when they are faced with tasks within planned competence development activities. They then strive towards becoming better at activities, which can find a place in their own understanding of what it means to be skilful and capable at work. It follows from this that many planned training and development activities based on traditional education methods are more likely to contribute to a refinement rather than a change of understanding.

Verbal communication: a vehicle for transforming understanding?

In the mainstream management literature communication is truly recognized as a central activity for managers, particularly for those in the highest position in the organizational hierarchy. It seems to suggest that managers who need to communicate the strategic direction of the company to subordinates, its priorities and the behaviour necessary for reaching a desired outcome, should use verbal communication methods. For example, the use of managerial texts such as vision and policy statements are based on the assumption that managers and a few others work out and formulate the visions and policies and then try to transfer them to the rest of the employees. In such communicative efforts the focus is on the content of the message, in the same way as language-based educational methods focus on transferring explicit knowledge about work-related issues.

However, in Chapters 2–6 we argued that people act within their understanding of work, and all kinds of information, whether it is communicated on paper or from the mouth of a manager, will be interpreted in a way which is confined and guided by that understanding. This means that most managerial communication efforts will result in more factual knowledge about some matters and will show how the managers see things. Very few will evoke a questioning of existing understanding and, therefore, not contribute to a change in employees' understanding in any significant way.

Some of the writers referred to above recommended communicative methods that trigger a more intensive verbal and intellectual activity. In these methods, employees are no longer seen as merely passive receivers of ready-made views in the form of messages with excellent rhetorical qualities. Instead, they become an active part in an interactive process where the communication runs in two directions, and where the content communicated becomes a raw material for active verbal and intellectual elaboration. The 'imaginization' method has such qualities, provided that the target group has an active role in the process, and dialogues are by definition interactive. There are reasons to believe that these methods have a considerably higher probability of stimulating a questioning of understanding and contribute to a transformation of established understanding among the target group.

However, when communication is used to trigger people's own intellectual processes and creative thinking, the outcome cannot be fully controlled by management, which might cause anxiety among managers. On the other hand, there are numerous examples of cases where people who set the objectives and choose the methods themselves reach outcomes that the management would not have dreamed of. We will come back to this issue later in the chapter.

Action-driven methods

Experience-based educational methods

Planned and organized educational efforts aiming at developing understanding can come in many various forms. We categorized some of them as 'language-based', and the main criterion for identifying this category was a concentration upon the transfer of explicit knowledge and an adherence to the principle: theory first, followed by application. There are, however, planned and organized educational activities that are based upon other pedagogical premises and practices. In the following section we will discuss some educational methods that are *experience-based*. These methods take their point of departure in people's *actions*, which stimulates *reflection*, group-wise or individually, which is supposed to lead to some sort of insight that can remain intuitive or be made explicit as a 'formulated conclusion'.

Action Learning: learning while doing
The concept 'Action Learning' (AL) was coined by Reginald Revans, who, like many others, reacted against the inability of many traditional, educational

language-based methods to influence people's work performance in a desired way. He designed a method to be used in training programmes that is basically problem-based and takes advantage of group processes as a stimulus for reflection and constructive thinking (Revans, 1978, 1980). More recently, a range of different educational methods have been classified as AL (Marsick and O'Neil, 1999; Weinstein, 1995). While the philosophical roots of AL methods varies, they all emphasize the basic principle of 'action first' in the cycle of learning.

In a typical AL programme learning unfolds in a small group that becomes involved with a problem in an unfamiliar environment. It has to be a 'live case', tied to an identified problem in an organization and discussed in real time. The group interacts directly with the people who 'own' the problem, which means that the group functions almost like a team of consultants in relation to a client. A coach supports the group. The role of the coach can vary from merely giving procedural advice in the problem-solving process to managing the social process in the group to help the group members create a trustful and creative atmosphere.

As was pointed out above, the general assumption underlying AL is that learning starts with some kind of action. Revans identifies three different processes of learning (Alpha, Beta, Gamma), and one of them, the Gamma process, means that individuals always enter an AL programme with particular pre-understandings, which produce certain expectations about what will happen as a result of the actions taken towards the problem. If the outcomes do not fit the expectations, the group members are forced to reflect on the misfit and come to some kind of 'conclusion', which is a vital indication of learning (Revans, 1980).

According to Revans, a key condition for an effective AL programme is the degree of involvement the participants can obtain in relation to the problem or project in the host organization. Sometimes they make it become their own problem. They will then be real actors in a real-life setting and experience the same intellectual and emotional involvement in the problem solving as they would in their own daily work. Such an involvement intensifies to the reflections and gives a natural relevance to the group processes. However, it may also happen that the 'owner' of the problem keeps a distance from the small group. In those cases it is likely that the group will experience its problem-solving efforts in the same way as it would with cases and projects in more traditional educational settings.

Problem-based learning

Within university teaching problem-based learning (PBL) has been subject to a growing interest (for an overview, see Savin-Baden and Wilkie, 2004). It can be seen as a version of AL applied to the university context. One reason for the growing interest in PBL is that university teaching in areas such as management cannot practice AL in its typical form for the simple reason that students are preparing themselves for a practical work that will come later on. Similar to Action Learning, PBL is based on the principle that effective learning presupposes that individuals are involved in the problems to be solved, and that they actively search for knowledge instead of getting it served on a silver plate. It moves away from the transfer of knowledge towards an active search for new knowledge combined with independent reflection.

The students work in small groups and take on problems of an intellectual nature within a topical area that is defined by the faculty. The group has also a coach who is supposed to help the group members to manage their action and learning processes. The group members' tasks include choosing and deciding upon a problem, organizing the collective effort to search for information and producing a report. Individual actions are mixed with group meetings, where the members reflect upon the findings they have made, mainly in the literature, and try to collectively formulate an analysis of the problem.

The lecturing is carried out on predetermined educational goals, but the students have a great degree of freedom in determining how these goals will be achieved. The students are encouraged to discover controversial aspects of reality and, based on these, formulate and structure relevant problems. When they have reached consensus on a structure, the group members search for knowledge via the literature or personal contacts, and for ideas and theories that can clarify the given problem.

Donald Schön (1983, 1987) has also advocated a kind of PBL. He pointed out the need for students to experience problems that resemble situations that established professionals encounter in their daily work. In order to provide students with such a learning experience, Schön (1987) argued that we should look more closely at educational institutions that place a strong emphasis on coaching and on learning-by-doing, such as art, music and dance schools. He also introduced the idea of reflective practicum, whereby the students learn by working with concrete tasks under the watchful eye of a coach. For Schön, coaching means being able to differentiate between the varying ways in which students perceive a problem in order to assist them in perceiving the problem in a more effective way.

Laboratory training

Laboratory training is another well-established experienced-based method with the aim of making people learn more about themselves as people, and particularly about their social behaviour. The unique character of laboratory training is that the actions and the experiences that are being discussed and reflected upon are produced 'here and now' as part of the educational process and are thus shared by all the members in a training group.

Schein and Bennis (1965) describe the goals of typical laboratory training as:

1   Self-insight
2   Understanding of the conditions which inhibit or facilitate group functioning
3   Understanding the interpersonal operations in groups
4   Skills for diagnosing individual, group and organizational behaviour.

They trace the roots of laboratory training back to the ideas of Kurt Lewin. He tried to create a state of 'unfreezing' in groups by arranging educational situations that were unfamiliar to the participants, and contrasting them with the participants' taken-for-granted behaviours. Lewin is also behind the idea to improve people's social behaviour by stimulating social action, followed by feedback, that makes the participants aware of their social behaviour and how it can be improved.

The early applications of laboratory training, which started in 1946 and known as T-group training or sensitivity training, have gradually been replaced by a more varying palette of educational practices that employ the principles of action here and now, with a focus on social behaviour and systematic feedback. It can take the form of group problem-solving exercises or social games, where participants have to cooperate, handle conflicts or other challenges that evolve from the social interaction. The emphasis can be on individual behaviour in a social context, but the training activities can also focus on the group processes as such.

In later years the principles of laboratory training have been extended to activities that have a more concrete nature and where the ambition is to create collective tasks that are more structured and involve more than just social processes. It is assumed that learning will improve when the context of the experiences is perceived as more concrete and realistic. A popular example of this is 'Outdoor Adventure Experiential Learning' (Ewert, 1989), where the training groups are assigned complex tasks that involve technical problem-solving and physical work combined with organizational problems (division of work and cooperation) and all the relational problems that arise during the performance of the work. Here also the prime ambition is to learn about social issues such as cooperation and leadership, and the group members are supposed to be able to generalize the learning outcome and apply it to social situations in the organizations where they are working. To obtain this goal the adventure exercises must be repeated, and the experiences of each exercise should be subject to discussion and analysis, where the actual experiences are treated as metaphoric representations of 'real' organizational problems. If this is not done, then there is a risk that the learning achieved will be restricted to the hands-on knowledge of how to perform the particular exercise in question (Meyer, 2003; Torbert, 1991).

Self-confidence training

Self-confidence training can be seen as an interesting version of the experience-based methods. Possessing certain knowledge and mastering special skills does not automatically mean that a person is able to apply them in a real-life work situation. To be able to do that a certain degree of self-confidence is required, which makes us brave enough to employ our knowledge and skills to the fullest in accomplishing our work. Musicians, for example, are extraordinarily conscious of the fact that just because they can perform a piece of music at home without making any mistakes, does not mean they can also do it in front of an audience. The latter demands an experience-based confidence in action.

Within the world of sports one has for many years been aware of the complex relationship between potential capacity and actual performance under stress. People from the world of sports, such as Willi Railo (1986), have developed practical educational methods to build up self-esteem in practice by focusing on emotionally anchored visualizations of practice. Garfield and Bennet (1985) formulated similar developmental methods and extended the target group to individuals in management positions. Senge (1990) highlights analogous thoughts in his discussion of the concept of 'personal mastery'. He suggests that many people have the capacity to develop their own competence considerably more than they actually do. This is partially controlled by the circumstances in the organization, the degree of stimulus, but also by the individual's vision of his or her own self. Hence, a change in behaviour may not emanate from improved skills or new explicit knowledge, but rather from a changed understanding of our own capacity to use our skills and knowledge at work. People can enhance their self-confidence by doing what they are expected to do in stressful real-life situations. Having achieved results, they can observe and therefore confirm for themselves that 'they can do it'. But to reach that state, self-confidence training often uses exercises in which individuals or teams are encouraged to imagine the desired work performance, a kind of 'virtual imaginization', which seemingly can also trigger sense making about their own capacity to accomplish a particular task in a desired way.

Practice-based methods

The discussion above on how people learn from experience is of course not only valid in an organized educational setting. The same processes occur when individuals experience things in their daily work and reflect on them, individually or with others. More recently, organizational research has concentrated more and more on the learning that emerges from everyday work activities, without being deliberately designed to produce competence development. From that research we can identify some significant processes and mechanisms which contribute to an emergent learning at work. We have chosen to use the term 'practice-based methods' to cover those arrangements in organizations that nurture and enable development of understanding in different ways without being deliberately designed to do so. Below we will identify a range of these methods which are part of organizational life.

Narration as a vehicle for sharing and exploiting experience

As was reported in Chapter 5, Orr (1996) conducted an ethnographic study of service technicians at Xerox, who mostly worked alone in different client organizations. They had been traditionally educated through training programmes at Xerox, and they had technical manuals to facilitate a systematic search for causes of the problems they encountered in the client organizations. However, Orr found that more important than the 'canonical knowledge' represented in the technical manuals, were the narratives used by service technicians to develop their understanding of work. The stories they produced and were sharing expressed what they were facing in particular problem situations, how the customer had explained what had happened, and what was problematic. A story also contained possible causal chains explaining how the problem had technically arisen, what actions had been taken, and how the problem had been eliminated.

In Chapter 5 we referred to a significant event where one service technician had been asked to take care of a machine fault he had never seen before. After running through his own 'repository' of stories that could solve the problem he called for help from a qualified specialist at their unit, but the specialist was also unable to find out what had caused the problem. Orr noted that the technician and the specialist started to tell each other stories of earlier experiences of similar machine errors and finally, having found some incongruence in their stories, they were able to formulate a possible explanation to the machine fault and how to solve it.

Orr's findings confirm the implicit key message in the first part of this chapter, namely that there is a fundamental difference in the character and function between, on the one hand, the logically systematized explicit knowledge that is the raw material of traditional education and managerial communication and, on the other hand, the kind of knowledge that is developed by experiential learning and is inherent in the stories that might be seen as an important 'knowledge repository' in the service department of Xerox. Orr's study also demonstrates the limitations of the 'canonical knowledge' (handbooks and manuals) and shows us how emergent social processes constitute an important source for effective action.

Communities of practice

The service technicians at Xerox are a group of people who perform the same kind of tasks, work individually in different client organizations but also have opportunities to meet and engage in social interaction. As a group they constitute what has been called a community of practice. It consists of practitioners who identify themselves as belonging to a particular practice and conducting a similar kind of work. Researchers have primarily been interested in how such communities are able to maintain their established practices and how new members learn the game through emergent social learning processes. One central observation is that the emergent learning taking place in such communities involves not only the learning of methods and techniques of the work. Members also develop a shared understanding of their work and a social identity intertwined with the more technical learning.

Vygotsky (1978) described how the 'knowledge' in a community is continuously externalized in action, and sometimes verbally. Inexperienced members internalize what they see and what they hear and gradually grow into mature practitioners. Lave and Wenger (1991) coined the concept of 'legitimate peripheral participation' to designate the emergent procedures where new and inexperienced members are allowed to watch the work and to marginally participate in discussions on what is being done and why it is being done in this way. This process does not contribute to short-term productivity but is seen as a natural part of the social life in the community.

The process of legitimate peripheral participation may have its roots in the medieval handicraft guilds and their way of organizing learning as a relationship between a master and his or her apprentices. Today's craft education is usually a combination of traditional theoretical education and apprenticeships. There is, however, an increasing realization that planned and organized learning activities only form a small part of competence development. Watson (2001) studied how managers acquire their competence at work and found that planned and organized management training only played a minor part in becoming a manager. The emergent learning in their daily work played a significantly more important role in them becoming competent managers. He also noted the importance of the social learning that takes place at home during childhood and later on in the daily interaction at work, long before a person takes up a management position (Watson, 2001; Watson and Harris, 1999).

Looking at how new members of a community come to understand their particular practice, we can see that they acquire and internalize their knowledge, existing in the community, through processes that have not been formally organized and designed. On the other hand, the experienced members of the community may be engaged in efforts to improve and develop the established knowledge by experimenting or by learning from other communities. Part of professionals' jobs in professional communities such as medical specialties is to constantly develop their practices in their daily work. But a professional community can also use conferences, where members present research results and try to establish shared interpretations of what it means for their practice. These activities are more organized, but they are organized within the confines of the community.

Given the growing research on social learning at work and the importance of emergent learning processes in all kinds of profession, it is reasonable to suggest that managers and educators should extend their horizons and also regard competence development as emergent processes. This is exactly what has happened in the area of applied management, with its growing interest in 'learning organizations' and 'knowledge management'. But it can also be an idea for leaders to foster competence development by arranging opportunities for their employees to make discoveries on their own, which may provoke reflection and inquiry.

Arranging opportunities for discovery

Bill Bratton has become well known for the radical turnaround that he was able to produce at the New York Police Department in the middle of the 1990s and for similar radical changes at other police departments. One important ingredient in his change strategy has been not to propose ready-made solutions to problems and try to make people accept them. Instead, he confronts his managers with everyday operational problems, which evoke reflective thinking and a re-evaluation of the realities at hand.

When Bratton took charge of the New York Police Department he soon learnt that citizens using the New York subway were concerned about their safety. He also noted that his senior managers never really used the New York subway because of their free access to cars provided by the city. Bratton decided that all senior managers for a particular period of time had to use the subway for all their transportation needs, during daytime as well as at night. It was an eye-opening experience for many of the managers to be confronted with the reality that was the everyday experience of many New Yorkers. As a result of that experience he achieved a collaborative spirit and a new sense of priority in the search for ways of increasing the safety on the New York subway.

Bratton also arranged confrontational meetings between police officers and citizens in a particular district within New York. The police officers proudly presented their efforts and practices and emphasized that they had managed to keep down the number of murders and other severe crimes and that the number of criminals brought to trial had increased every year. However, it turned out that most citizens had never been in contact with severe crimes. Instead, they were more worried about the high frequency of minor crimes and the irritating experiences of anti-social behaviour. Police officers and citizens obviously understood the lawlessness in different ways, something that became surprisingly evident to the police officers involved (Kim and Mauborgne, 2003).

Using techniques that create a confrontation between groups of people has been widely discussed in the Organization Development literature. What is unique in Bratton's approach is the extension of the 'confrontation meeting' to also cover confrontations between employees and phenomena in their larger work environment. It means that managers arrange opportunities for subordinates to discover something they would not have thought about otherwise. It might be that people identify something as a problem or realize that certain practices do not work or provide the expected results.

In the 1980s Volvo Car Corporation discovered quality problems that were seen as a potential threat to the market image of Volvo as a high-quality car. In order to deal with the problem managers of the production unit bought two Oldsmobile cars and parked them side by side outside the factory entrance. Above the two cars was a board saying 'in the USA you get these two Oldsmobile for the price of one Volvo. What quality would you expect in a car twice as expensive?'

Providing opportunities for discovery may deliver the first part of a process leading to a change of understanding. The next step for management is to engage key people in dialogues and discussions, where they can help each other to reflect upon shared experiences. The manager in question will have to present problems, priorities and plans for actual measures and future development. This kind of 'peer review' takes place against a background of shared experiences and discoveries.

The underlying strategy in this method is that managers use their position of power to force people to experience things that would not take place otherwise. Hopefully the experiences will evoke reflection that can be facilitated by more organized activities. Kim and Mauborgne (2003) pointed out that this process does not necessarily include all employees. They talk about 'Tipping Point Leadership', where a manager tries to make a critical mass of people change their mind and adhere to some new solution. If a critical mass of people change understanding, the adoption of the new way of thinking and acting will spread like an epidemic. If a manager can take care of the energy unleashed here, it is possible to achieve impressive results.

Structural methods

Structural arrangement such as organizational design, work roles, lines of authority and accountability are central ingredients in influencing people's behaviour and learning at work. Every structural arrangement sends signals to the employees about what is important and what is expected from them. Sometimes the relationship between structural arrangements and learning are clearly visible and openly intentional. In other cases the relationship is more indirect and implicit. We have labelled those structural arrangements for facilitating learning in organizations as structural methods. One such method is project groups.

Managers have long since used *project groups* to improve problem solving and the implementation of solutions to organizational problems. The project group is a temporary, small unit outside the established hierarchical structure. It usually has a project leader who acts as a formal link to hierarchical decision makers. The members of the project group are chosen according to two basic criteria, namely for being competent in some important area and/or being representative of critical interests in the organization. Here we discuss projects as being minor exceptions to the normal hierarchical structure, even if organizational research more recently has been interested in cases where the project form has been the general basic principle for organizing activities (Orlikowski, 2002; Sydow et al., 2004).

While there can be an intense sharing of views and interpretations inside the project group, a very common complaint at higher managerial levels is that the learning outcome tends to stay within the particular project group. Many attempts have been made to make members of project groups share their experiences with people in the whole organization, but such efforts have usually failed. This is not surprising if we take into account the theories of social and experiential learning discussed earlier. The group members act together, and as soon as they come across something they do not have a shared experience of, they must reflect upon why they choose to do what they do. This often means that they develop some new practices or ideas and at the same time develop an understanding that gives meaning to the actions they eventually take. This learning may have an impact on their future behaviour in roles outside the project group. However, it has been shown that it is very difficult for project group members to externalize new learning in an explicit form, which is usually what is expected by higher management, and maybe the surrounding organization is not particularly interested anyway.

The above observation is very much in line with the experience of using expatriates to spread new ideas and knowledge from one country to another. Wong (2005) studied expatriates from a Japanese corporation who spent some time at subsidiaries in Hong Kong. She found that it was very difficult for the

Japanese expatriates to transfer their ideas to employees in Hong Kong due to 'collective myopia' – a condition where people in the organization have a well-established understanding of their situation and their activities. It is a situation where socialization is continuously reconfirming what is normal and no questioning of the institutional context takes place. She found that the expatriates felt uneasy in the new social context. They did not want to be seen as deviants and consequently did not push their own ideas and understanding of the situation at hand.

The role of project groups as vehicles for learning has been strongly emphasized by Nonaka (1994) in his model of knowledge creation. Teams of people work on problems that top management has assigned to them in a fairly open fashion. The team members combine their different experiences and bring explicit information from various parts of the organization, thereby creating a 'requisite variety', that is, a pool of different ideas and views which are necessary for knowledge creation, according to Nonaka. A key point in Nonaka's thinking is that the dedicated efforts of the team will make the members externalize the knowledge they bring with them, and make it available as elements in the team's discussions. If knowledge sharing on a larger scale is desired, the team members must formulate their ideas in an explicit form so that it can be used in training programmes. Alternatively, the members may participate themselves in training activities to share their thoughts and experiences with others.

Another structural method commonly used for influencing people's work performance is the *learning organization*. Örtenblad (2002) analysed an array of articles using the term 'learning organization' and was able to organize them into four main categories with the following keywords: organizational learning, learning at work, learning climate, and learning structure. The kind of learning organization we have in mind here mainly falls into categories three and four. Here, learning organization is seen as consisting of specifically designed structures, systems and control mechanisms that stimulate learning and a leadership style and a social climate that strengthen the structural arrangements for learning. Some of the most well-known writings on learning organizations, such as Garratt (1990), Pedler et al. (1991), and Senge (1990), belong to this category.

In management practice there has been a gradual shift in focus from learning organization to *knowledge management* as a means for increasing company competitiveness (for an overview see Davenport and Prusak, 1998). Here the emphasis is on *systems* rather than structure and climate. The overall aim has been to make accessible the 'knowledge' that exists among people in the organization. The focus on electronic information systems as the main instrument of achieving this means that knowledge is invariably

149

reduced to verbal statements or figures that can be shared easily. As a result, knowledge management can be used as a vehicle for refinement, but will seldom contribute to change of understanding.

Quality improvement systems represent another potential method for influencing understanding. We can exclude the bureaucratic regulation of routines inherent, for example, in certification systems such as ISO 9000, whose role is largely to guarantee to external customers or public authorities that work activities follow certain desired specifications. What we have in mind here are systems that aim for continuous improvements in quality and operational effectiveness, for example systems such as TQM and Six Sigma. The emphasis in such systems has been on their internal dynamics, where a change in one part of the system can have chain-effects, and sometimes produce amazing results.

One important principle that is used in many quality systems is 'doing things right from the beginning'. The implementation of that principle has been shown to produce remarkable productivity gains. It has, however, been hard to implement initially because of the problem of convincing people that it is actually possible to do things right the first time. The management at the Volvo Corporation factory in Sweden adopted a dramatic plan to convince people that it was in fact possible to do the right things from the beginning. They built a wall between the assembly line and the area previously used for assembly adjustments. Their stony message was that there was no opportunity for post-assembly adjustments; they *had to* make everything right the first time. This is a good example of how symbolic actions can facilitate a change in understanding.

The *balanced scorecard*, developed by Kaplan and Norton (1996), is another structural method for influencing people's behaviour. However, our own experience of using the balanced scorecard (BSC) in hospitals has not been encouraging. The accounting specialists and consultants in the hospitals made a considerable effort to show people that the BSC was intended to be an instrument for planning and follow-up of local developments in line with overall strategies. Employees in various local units were supposed to use the BSC to operationalize the general strategic ambitions, develop their own success factors and find ways of measuring them. The system would then provide them with a regular follow-up of their intentions and plans, and show how well they were doing in improving their activities. However, interviews among local staff revealed that the BSC was primarily used as a way to collect data at all organizational levels and then compile them into a report submitted to management. The BSC was thus understood primarily as another traditional accounting system. Only a few understood it as a development tool they could use for their own purposes. But this does not mean that it is impossible to make people interpret the BSC as a tool for local improvements. The instrument can be used as a development instrument. However, as long as it is used within a traditional understanding of accounting, the instrument does not do justice to its full potential.

Other structural methods for managing understanding are *reward systems*. Since understanding in itself is not easily measurable, the rewards must be tied to actions that are aligned with the desired understanding. The challenge is to encourage an understanding of overall strategy and local work that is favourable for the company. If managers succeed in this, they may be able to create a 'motivational force' that will drive people to do the right thing from a management point of view.

However, with the use of reward systems there is a risk that people act in a desired way, not because they have changed their understanding of what is favourable for the company, but because by getting the highest possible scores on the measurement they increase their likelihood of reward. The company then gets desired actions, but those actions will disappear as soon as the rewards are abolished. It is also important to note that incentives, which are not directly conditioned by specific actions, can themselves be subject to different interpretations, which sometime can lead to negative results. Classical research like that of Herzberg et al.'s (1959) demonstrated that general incentives were introduced by managers for recognizing good performance, but after being institutionalized employees came to see them as part of the general benefits of working at the corporation. This meant that they had no longer any positive effect on behaviour and only negative effects when the incentives were removed.

Culture

Contributing to the development of an organization's culture can be seen as another form of practice-based method. In Chapter 5 we discussed the parallels between culture and collective competence. A culture develops as a result of evolving practices and ongoing sense making of those practices. Shared experiences, an exchange of thoughts and ideas, and reflection give rise to patterns of shared actions and perceptions of what is wrong, what is right and what leads to success and what does not.

The shaping of culture through the evolution of practices and the sense making that follows normally proceed slowly and gradually. But there are times when the processes for some reason or other unfold at a greater speed. When people look back at these occasions they are going to perceive them as radical cultural change. A fascinating example is the dramatic changes that took place in the Soviet Union during the 1980s – an immense, spontaneous cultural change that was neither planned nor controlled by any particular actors. An example that highlights such a cultural change within industry is the change in companies from seeing environmental standards as restrictions for doing business to regarding them as an opportunity for doing business. Such changes have taken place in a multitude of companies.

Returning to more typical cultural changes, it could be claimed that if dialogue is an important method for bringing about shifts in individual understanding, the parallel to dialogue at a collective level is the more complex pattern of social interaction that takes place at many levels in a social system and through many communicative media. It is also evident that symbolic actions and the establishment of new regular practices play a role in the development of cultures. When, for example, Götaverken Arendal, a Swedish shipyard company specializing in tankers, was heavily hit by the oil crisis in the 1970s, it started to reorient its business towards residential platforms for the offshore industry. They hired project leaders (a chief production manager for one platform) who had previously worked in the construction sector. One of the project leaders set up his office in a mobile barrack on top of one of the platforms. This was something he was used to from the construction business, where no other offices were available. In this case, however, there was an elegant office block for the project leaders just a stone-throw away. For many employees, this event was of great symbolic value. It symbolized how Götaverken Arendal had taken the step from being a dock yard where tankers had been built to becoming an offshore company. It had now left the pretentious ship owners' world behind and entered the harsh reality of day-to-day economics and business.

Turning to something totally different, we can see how specific events can change the understanding of the work for a whole profession. Tennis trainers and coaches in Sweden and Germany had for many years been working to develop good players. But with the sudden and extraordinary successes of Björn Borg and Boris Becker, they apparently developed another way of thinking and undertook new activities in their work. They were not simply working with tennis players, but rather many trainers began to see themselves as training and developing aspiring world champions. Parents also changed their attitude and actively began encouraging their children to learn to play tennis. Suddenly tennis became a sport where the kids had the potential to become world champions, and this certainly led to a rush of potentially talented children to the tennis courts.

The above examples clearly show that by simply being a role model it is possible for a single person to effectively influence processes, through which meaning and a spontaneous development of practice are created. This does not necessarily mean that a leader can decide to become a role model, and then calculate on the fact that implicit learning will unfold in a certain way. People easily see through these ambitions and interpret them as non-authentic and a kind of unacceptable manipulation. Instead of providing the stimulus of spontaneous processes, it can lead to a conscious distancing from managerial initiatives.

Another possible way of developing culture is by consciously placing key individuals, who stand for an alternative understanding of the business activities, in influential positions. This can be reinforced by introducing new symbols that support the alternative understanding. However, as mentioned previously, this method is unpredictable. Implicit learning processes are inherently difficult to control in a conscious, purposive manner.

Learning from action: refinement or change of understanding?

Compared with the more traditional language-based methods, the action-driven methods seem to have a higher probability of producing an outcome where existing understanding has been changed. The typical problem of theory versus application is solved by taking one's own work practice as the point of departure. Working with real-life situations also leads to an emotional involvement which makes it more difficult to enter the role of a participant observer and to keep one's own values and worldviews apart from what is going on. Starting with action and its more or less problematic outcomes can also create a state of ambiguity that makes it more natural to be curious and to search for possible explanations and alternative action paths.

However, whether action-driven methods will lead to a refinement of or a change in people's understanding is dependent on factors beyond the actual methods. For example, if all the members in a small group share an established understanding, it is likely that they will search in the same direction and interpret information and observations in a similar fashion, unless they encounter outcomes which they cannot make sense of within their existing understanding. But there is also a risk that the group members will help each other to discard disturbing experiences and confirm that the established understanding is still valid.

If we also take into account what we know about social learning and emergent learning processes in organizations, those who have an interest in managing understanding should try to influence those processes. Based on the presentation of the practice-based methods, such as project groups, learning organizations and knowledge management, one might draw the conclusion that this is exactly what management practitioners are trying to do. On the other hand, one cannot help returning to the picture drawn in Chapter 1, namely that managers clearly see the problem, they have the methods to solve the problem but they try to apply the methods within a basically rationalistic frame of reference. As a consequence, they often fail to achieve the expected results.

Guiding principles for managing understanding

The analysis above suggests that the most distinguishing feature of the methods reviewed is the one between language- and action-driven methods. The analysis also suggests that some of the methods are more suitable for managing understanding than others. It is primarily those methods that encourage and trigger an active reflection, such as dialogue and experienced-based methods, that are most likely to facilitate a change in understanding, although the most commonly used methods for managing understanding, such as managerial communication methods and traditional educational methods, seem, at best, to merely facilitate a reinforcement of existing understanding.

A major reason why most of the methods only seem to reinforce people's existing understanding of work is that they have been developed and used within a rationalistic management perspective. This means that they are designed to actively promote the *transfer* of a particular *message*, such as the company's vision, values, policies, knowledge and skills, to a group of people to produce a desired work performance. By receiving and memorizing the particular message in question they are supposed to start to see their work in a different way and, thus change their work performance in line with managers' intentions. This feature is particularly salient when it comes to the language-driven methods such as everyday communication methods and educational language-based methods. It is the top managers, together with some key staff, who formulate visions and policy statements, which they then try to get across to the rest of the employees through various communicative means. The same is true for the educational language-based methods. It is the managers and staff experts who formulate the knowledge and skills that should be transferred to a group of people through various educational activities, such as class room teaching, seminars and book reading.

While the focus on transferring a specific content is particularly notable within most language-driven methods, it is also prominent within several action-driven methods. The focus on transferring a specific content is highly problematic because it overlooks people's understanding of work and, thus, severely hampers managers' ability to manage understanding in a desirable way. Does this then mean that we have to abandon most of the above methods? No, but it means that if we want to use them for managing understanding, they need to be *redesigned and conducted in a way that actively promote changes in people's understanding of work*. People create and develop their own understanding – it is not something that can be delivered ready-made. In other words, we need to ask how managerial communication methods, educational language-based methods, experience-based methods, and practice-based methods can be redesigned and used to provide the surprises and insights that will trigger reflections and actively promote a desirable development of people's understanding of work. Based on the discussion of the main features of understanding summarized in Chapter 6, it is possible to formulate a set of guiding principles for redesigning the above methods to enable managers to manage understanding more effectively.

First of all, when deciding which practical methods should be used for managing understanding managers need to *clarify what development of understanding they want to encourage*: a refinement of existing understanding or a change of existing understanding. Such a clarification is vital because it raises managers' awareness of which methods are most likely to lead to a desirable outcome and how the methods should be used in order to achieve the desired outcome. For example, if the goal is to encourage an existing understanding of work, managers should choose those methods that can best facilitate a reinforcement of existing understanding of work. If the intention is to rein force people's understanding of their own and the company's task, with the goal to strengthen the company's existing competence, it may be enough to use more language-driven methods, such as vision statements or policy statements, together with some traditional educational language-based methods. However, if an organization is to embark on a major corporate transformation such as that undertaken by SAS, when they transformed from an airline to a travel company (see Chapter 5), managers should choose methods that have the best chance of changing understanding. Here, they should make use of methods that are designed to produce surprises and trigger an active questioning of the existing understanding of the company's tasks. The methods used in such a transformation can range from visions to specific experience-based and practice-based methods, for example Action Learning and structural methods, in which action and reflection have a prominent role.

A second important principle when managing understanding is to *systematically identify people's understanding of work*. Knowledge about the ways in which people understand their own and the company's work informs managers about the methods they should use to manage understanding to achieve the desirable outcome. Identifying people's understanding of work is also important for modifying and revising the methods used for managing understanding. The methods that can be used for identifying understanding range from more systematic methods like the one presented in Chapter 3, which was used to identify competence in engine optimization, to more informal ways such as through everyday conversations with people.

When internal marketing was discussed in the 1980s it was mostly associated with internal information campaigns, where knowledge of marketing communication could be used to diffuse messages to staff. Perhaps it is almost as relevant to talk about *'internal market analyses'*, where management is trying to map people's thinking and reasoning in order to identify how they understand their work. The optimization example showed that even if people are not aware of their understanding of work, and therefore cannot articulate it easily, it is possible to identify their understanding through more systematic investigation. But here again the rationalistic trap is waiting. It is highly likely that managers will design questionnaires and other measurement tools that reflect their own understanding of which aspects are interesting to study and which variables are important. Then we are measuring from the management's perspective and not that of the employees.

The third fundamental guiding principle when redesigning methods to actively promote changes in people's understanding of work is to take *the employees' understanding as the point of departure*. This is because to be able to influence people's understanding it needs to be reinforced or challenged in some way or another. All the methods used in managing understanding need therefore to be specifically designed to actively promote development of employees' understanding of their work. For example, in major corporate transformations such as that at SAS, it is common to formulate the new direction in a vision statement. However, when using vision statements as a method for managing understanding, managers should not predefine it and then try to transfer it to the rest of the organization through various communicative tools. Instead, managers should start with employees' current understanding of work by inviting them to participate in the formulation of the vision. This would be a more dialogue-based way of producing and implementing visions. Several discussions between managers and other employees would be necessary for producing and implementing the vision. Such an active engagement by staff and interaction between staff and management is likely to encourage an active reflection on existing understanding at the same time as it will encourage a reflection on what an alternative understanding of work may involve. Moreover, being actively involved in the formulation and implementation of the vision is likely not only to lead to a desired understanding of work among most employees, but also to a stronger employee commitment to the new direction.

The same is true when it comes to educational language-based methods such as classroom teaching and seminars, which are used for managing understanding. For example, if managers in the department of engine optimization at the Volvo Car Corporation in Sweden want to enable the optimizers, whose understanding of work is optimizing interacting qualities of the engine, to achieve understanding from the customers' perspective, the basis for the development activities used in the classroom teaching should be the optimizers' present understanding. If they do not get the opportunity to reflect on and question their current understanding of engine optimization, it is unlikely that they will achieve the desired, more comprehensive understanding of engine optimization. If, instead, the desired understanding of work is the point of departure, the only development that is likely to take place is a transformation of attributes (knowledge skills) of the desired understanding into their present understanding of engine optimization. They would then continue to accomplish optimization in much the same way as they had done previously.

A fourth guiding principle when redesigning methods to actively promote changes in people's understanding of work is *to organize particular encounters between employees and their work as developmental triggers*, with the aim of stimulating a reflection and questioning of people's present understanding of work. When the desired outcome is to change understanding of work and if people are expected to question their own existing understanding, they must first *become aware of that understanding.* While several methods can be used for arranging developmental triggers, action-oriented methods are particularly suitable because of their strong focus on action as the primary source. Effective methods are those that mirror the thinking and action of people, so that they can become aware of their own understanding. Laboratory training, with its processes of action and feedback, typically have that capacity. Video-recording action that is afterwards shown to the actors has long since been used in the training of salespeople. Wickelgren (2005) used it in a product development team as a 'delayed mirror' to make team members become aware of the underlying patterns in their behaviour. A work problem can be used to challenge people to reflect on their current understanding of work, and many of the methods discussed earlier contain instruments and procedures that can be used to make existing understanding visible and identifiable. It is important to notice that designing methods to actively challenge people's existing understanding requires an awareness among the designers of people's existing understanding of work. The better the awareness the more likely it is that managers will be able to arrange challenging work problems that will generate the desirable change in understanding of work.

Let us use the optimizers as an example again, and assume that the aim is to enable the optimizers who understand their work as optimizing interacting qualities to acquire the understanding of optimizing from the customers'

157

perspective. One way managers can facilitate such a transformation of understanding is to introduce specific optimization problems that will stimulate the optimizers who understand their work as interacting qualities to reflect on their present understanding of work. Such challenges should lead to questions such as: why is it not possible to optimize the encountered optimization situation satisfactorily? What is inappropriate in our current way of accomplishing it?

These encounters must also be arranged in such a way that when the optimizers begin to realize the limitations and problems of their present understanding, the desired understanding of engine optimization – optimizing from the customers' perspective – is introduced as a possible alternative. However, a shift from one understanding of work to another is unlikely to take place through a single challenge or encounter between an optimizer and an arranged optimization situation. Even if the optimizers change their understanding of the arranged optimization situation and begin to understand it according to the desired understanding, it is likely they will revert to their former understanding when they encounter a new optimization situation. Therefore, the transformation of understanding is more likely to succeed if it represents a chain of changes in understanding different optimization situations rather than as a single, major change.

Concluding remark

If managers have the ambition – which is frequently claimed – to obtain competitive advantage through competence renewal, the key problem is to manage the transformation of employees' present understanding of their own and their company's task. But since most managers, educators and other specialists seem to be locked into a rationalistic management perspective, they tend to use the methods available in a way that, at best, leads to the reinforcement of their existing understanding of work. If managers want to transform understanding of work, they must choose methods that emphasize reflection and that question the existing understanding of the work. What is even more fundamental, is to redesign the methods discussed above in a way that actively promotes changes in people's understanding of work. However, being able to manage understanding effectively is not just a question of redesigning available methods. It is also about redefining leadership and management practice in fundamental ways. That challenge will be further discussed in the next chapter.

EIGHT Management: a question of managing understanding

In the two introductory chapters we discussed a far-reaching paradigm shift that has taken place within management during the two last decades. The underlying message was that managers in general should abandon the principle of managing by providing detailed instructions that restrict people's freedom of action. Instead, they should lead by making people internalize visions and ideas, and by stimulating employees to make more use of their inherent capabilities. It is about increasing people's freedom of action in order to liberate their capacity. A key driver behind the paradigm shift is a growing conviction among practitioners and researchers that organizations have become considerably more dependent on being able to manage people's understanding of work. Managers must learn how to influence people's understanding in a way that produces desirable work performance and strengthens the company's competitive advantage.

Despite the alleged paradigm shift, we still encounter several management problems that are typically associated with a management-by-rules philosophy. A core argument in this book as to why several problems from the rule-based management philosophy remain has been that managers have tried to implement the new management philosophy within a rationalistic perspective on management. By continuing to act within a rationalistic perspective, both management practitioners and researchers have to a large extent treated understanding as a 'black box'. Given the rudimentary knowledge about what defines understanding and how it forms the basis for human action, a considerable confusion exists about how people's understanding can be influenced in a way that will lead to a desirable work performance. Because of managers' insufficient knowledge about understanding and how it can be managed effectively, the paradigm shift has mainly taken place at the rhetorical but not at a practical level.

Our intention has been to use an interpretative perspective as a key to get into the black box of understanding and systematically explore its main characteristics. By adopting an interpretative approach, we tried in Chapters 2–6 to identify and illustrate what defines understanding and how it forms the basis for people's work performance and the competence they develop and use in accomplishing their work. In Chapter 7 we reviewed a range of methods currently used for directing people's action and evaluated their potential for managing understanding. Based on that evaluation, together with our description of what constitutes understanding, we proposed a set of guidelines for redesigning current methods in a way that will enable managers to manage understanding more effectively. However, as we concluded in Chapter 7, being able to manage understanding effectively is not only a question of redesigning available methods, but also of reforming leadership and management practice in crucial ways. In this chapter we try to integrate what has been stated earlier in order to carve out a more comprehensive description of what implications managing understanding have for leadership and management practice. We begin by discussing the implications for management practice. Thereafter, we discuss more specifically what implications managing understanding has for leadership. Finally, we discuss the potential obstacles and consequences for managing understanding in organizations.

Shift in focus and new priorities in management practice

If we fully accept the idea that people's behaviour is guided and confined by their understanding of work, management practice faces a number of important implications. The predominant element in these implications is a shift from focusing on the *design and content* of managerial structures, systems, processes, and methods, to paying prime attention to how these structures, systems, processes and methods, *are understood* by people in the organization. Structures and systems do not have an effect *per se*. They only become effective when they have an impact on people's actions. Since people act within their understanding of the reality at hand, effectiveness is strongly tied to how people understand structures and systems and, consequently, to how managers are able to manage understanding. In order to illustrate what implications managing understanding has for management practice, we will look at a few classical management areas below.

Strategic management

In the world of management, the concept of strategy has been discussed over many decades. In those discussions it has first and foremost been regarded as an expression of a collective intention concerning a desired future state and the line of action to reach that state. As was shown in Chapter 2, the shifting focus on what is central in strategy making illustrates fairly well the paradigm shift in management. When Ansoff published his book on corporate strategy in 1965 he clearly stated in the preface that 'This book is concerned with business strategy formulation' (1965: vii). At that time strategic thinking was an analytical process in which various analytical tools were used to produce a strategy formulation that had the character of an action plan for the future. A decade later, Ansoff (1979) had, in his book on *Strategic Management*, drifted away from strategy formulation and was instead emphasizing the problem of materializing the formulated strategy in practice. The focus on realization became even stronger when the implementation of business strategy also turned into a problem of change and 'managing resistance' (Ansoff, 1984).

With the introduction of the 'resource-based view' on strategic research (Wernerfelt, 1984), the point of departure for strategy making moved towards the capabilities of the organization. As capabilities grow from within the organization over time, and thus become something that is difficult to copy by competitors, they can be seen as a set of core competencies aimed at building competitive advantage (Hamel and Prahalad, 1994). However, in a world that is heavily influenced by the use of the internet, explicit knowledge is more and more becoming a resource available to anyone. Rather, what is a truly unique feature of an organization is its pattern of shared understanding, which enables the organization to accomplish its task in a competitive way. For example, the shared understanding that formed the collective competence among the flutemakers at Powells described in Chapter 5 is unique and cannot easily be imitated by another company. As we saw earlier, this kind of collective competence may consist of conceptualized ideas, views and narratives, but it can also be embodied in routines and established practices. To 'unlearn the past', which Hamel and Prahalad (1994) regard as a key activity in strategy development, can be interpreted as a change in a collective's understanding of its organization's task and business environment.

To understand how strategies emerge, we can return to Richard Normann's ideas, which were presented in Chapter 2 (Normann, 1975, 1977). According to his findings, a company's business strategy is not a product of a rational analysis of the economic and political conditions facing the company. It is rather an image or representation of the dominant views and ideas held by the leading actors in the company. If we translate Normann's findings to the conceptual world of this book, we might say that strategies are constructed in a more or less transparent dialogue between the most powerful actors in organizations. In this dialogue the participants are inquiring into their understanding of the business activities and the business conditions. This inquiry may lead to a renewal of their understanding, probably intertwined with attempts to reformulate the business strategy.

However, such an inquiry can take place within a dialogue that involves many more participants. For example, in 2003 IBM carried out something that resembles a dialogue involving all its employees (interview with Samuel J. Palmisano in Hemp and Steward 2004). This giant dialogue was preceded by a survey among 300 senior executives in which they evaluated to what extent four concepts should be associated with the core values of IBM. These concepts were also discussed in focus groups comprising a sample of 1,000 employees. The results from the survey and the focus groups were used to produce a new set of proposed core values for IBM:

1 Commitment to the customer.
2 Excellence through innovation.
3 Integrity that earns trust.

By participating in what was called the 'Value jam' on the company's intranet, all of IBM's employees were encouraged to comment on those core values for a period of three days. About 50,000 employees took the opportunity to express their thoughts and feelings concerning the values above. Some were critical and questioning, whereas others were more positive and tried to elaborate the meaning of the values – whether they were in line with the historical roots of IBM and whether they were in accordance with the perceived reality. The large number of comments was analysed using a specific computerized content analysis. Based on the results of the employees' comments, the top management developed a revised version of IBM's core values that better mirrored the ideas and expectations of employees:

1 Dedication to every client's success.
2 Innovation that matters – for the company and for the world.
3 Trust and personal responsibility in all relationships.

When we as outsiders read these formulations, we might think that there is not much difference, only a slightly different wording. But for those people who took an active part in the discussion of what IBM's core values are the changed wording is probably essential. The top management at IBM realized that it is not possible to *prescribe* how people should understand the essential value base of the corporation. They had to take into account the employees' existing views of what IBM stands for in their efforts to formulate new core values and develop strategic guidelines for IBM. Given the intellectual and emotional preparation that went into the 'Value jam' exercise, it is reasonable to assume that corporate strategies that are formulated on the basis of these core values will more easily become internalized by employees at various levels.

Henry Mintzberg (1989) described strategy making as a combination of (a) rational planning activities in which strategy is formulated and is supposed to provide distinct guidelines for future action, and (b) emergent processes in which people in the organization take actions, try to make sense of them and, through that, gradually reproduce or redevelop a strategy. The latter suggests that strategies can emerge without a prior designed formulation. People's action may converge into a pattern that is legitimized by the top managers as an expression of a corporate strategy. According to Mintzberg:

> These strategies all reflect, in whole or in part, what we like to call a grassroots approach to strategic management. Strategies grow like weeds in a garden. They take root in all kinds of places, wherever people have the capacity to learn (because they are in touch with the situation) and the resources to support that capacity. These strategies become organizational when they become collective, that is, when they proliferate to influence the behaviour of the organization at large.
>
> Of course this view is overstated. But it is no less extreme than the conventional view of strategic management, which may be labelled the hothouse approach. Neither is right. Reality falls behind the two. Some of the most effective strategies we uncovered in our research combined deliberation and control with flexibility and organizational learning. (1989: 34)

When top managers formulate a strategy through a planned and organized design effort, that formulation will not materialize into a real strategy unless a number of people act in accordance with it and make sense of their actions in line with the strategy. In other words, a formulated strategy will not materialize unless people in the organization develop an understanding of the business and its conditions that makes their own contribution to the strategy natural and meaningful. Managers must avoid the trap of considering strategic management as merely strategy formulation. Instead, the main challenge is to find ways of stimulating people to create an understanding that makes it meaningful to act in line with the strategy. As Mintzberg (1989) noted, developing understanding is a learning process, and our discussion of the learning that is likely to facilitate a renewal of understanding should be as relevant here as in other managerial contexts.

Organization design

Can formal design of organizations be – at least partly – determined by efforts to manage understanding? We usually discuss organization design in the context of a division of work (managerial and financial control, for example) and the need for coordination. Every kind of organization design, however, creates borders and definitions of who is inside and outside certain units. Specialization and creation of profit centres or business units helps to reduce variety and complexity in the field of activities. The other side of the coin is a social cohesiveness that can grow into isolated views and a reduced sympathy for ideas from outside the borders of the unit.

In the previous chapter we highlighted the role of dialogue as a key element in the renewal of understanding. In order for new impressions and new information to trigger an inquiry into the appropriateness of existing understanding, the social process of sharing and comparing impressions and elaborating on them in dialogues seem to be important conditional factors for managing understanding. If managers have the ambition to design organizations that have a built-in capacity to encourage reflection and a questioning of established patterns of understanding, they need to create arenas for the exchange of ideas and to confront different views. It would be better still if these confrontations emerged in a climate of mutual trust and respect.

Modern organizations are often structured to balance the need for stability and control against the capacity to cope with uncertainty and non-routine events. The use of matrix approaches and projects are common ingredients that complement the basic traditional line organization. Networks and the partial management of formally external units represent other ways of coping with complexity. The ambition here seems to be to establish channels for contact and information flow. Conflicting ideas and ambitions are taken care of by procedures for negotiation or by moving the problems to the line organization.

An example of an organizational structure that is supposed to foster dialogue and reflection is the team structure. In an action research study conducted at a large hospital, one of the authors observed that a significant obstacle for being able to develop more effective operational routines was a lack of dialogue between different professions (doctors, nurses, managers) in the hospital. No small talk was taking place at coffee-breaks or lunches in which personal views or sense making of events could be made visible and comparable. Nor were there any organized arenas where the professional groups could confront their ideas and have an open and creative discussion about operational problems. In order to facilitate a dialogue between the professional groups different forms of teams were established. Local teams were created to focus on problems at specific workplaces and process teams were formed to focus on medical processes that cut across various workplaces, clinics and supporting service units. The teams were cross-functional and represented all the professions involved. While the teams were part of the permanent organizational structure, their members come together only at regular short meetings, where problems and potential improvements were discussed. Many team members expressed their satisfaction with the team structure. They had now received an arena for dialogue that hitherto had been missing. There is no guarantee that the mere existence of a formal team structure will lead to fruitful dialogues. It is, however, a strongly facilitating condition for it.

From our point of view the design of organizational structure should take into account the need for dialogue arenas in which understanding can be made evident and questioned. The more organizations become dependent on their capacity to innovate and change, the more emphasis should be placed on creating such arenas. Structures do not guarantee the occurrence of dialogue and learning, but they provide a necessary platform for it.

Change management

It should be very evident from the discussion in Chapter 7 that managing understanding has strong implications for change management. Most of the methods for managing understanding reviewed in that chapter have an obvious application in situations where managers try to change structures or processes.

In the section on strategic management we noted how the focus has gradually moved from the design and formulation of strategies to the task of materializing the strategic intentions in practice. The latter task is to a large extent about managing understanding. The same shift in focus can be seen in change efforts in general. Organization change has, since the Tayloristic era, been discussed within the context of formal and technical changes initiated at the highest point of the corporate hierarchy. Top management used staff specialists or consultants to analyse the situation and propose appropriate formal or structural changes. It was possible to implement some of these changes regardless of whether the employees concerned liked them or not. But with an increased complexity and dependence on employees' active involvement in implementing organizational changes, the need to 'overcome resistance to change' became a key issue in change management. It was usually channelled into the task of gaining the employees' acceptance for the planned changes.

When the ambition of change management moved from redesigning structures and systems to altering employees' everyday behaviour, the need for managing understanding became more evident. In the 1980s service, customer orientation and quality improvement became essential elements in many change efforts. Here the task of gaining acceptance was usually not the problem. Who would protest against better service or quality? The managerial challenge became instead to activate changes in everyday behaviour that would give rise to improvements in service, quality or customer orientation. Employees said okay, but established behavioural patterns did not change. These changes could not be implemented in the traditional sense. Only the employees involved are able to materialize the change by starting to act in a different way. This implies that they must *change their understanding of work and alter the established daily routines and behaviour patterns*. This means that the task of managing understanding receives a key role in change management.

We can see a shift in focus, from designing and implementing the content of a planned change to arranging processes in which people are encouraged to become aware of established behavioural patterns, reconsider them and reflect upon alternative ways of understanding the tasks and taking appropriate action. Organizational change becomes a learning process, and here the methods of managing change, discussed in Chapter 7, have their relevance. On the other hand, we also discussed structural changes as a way to create platforms that could aid inquiry and search for new ways of thinking and acting. It is not a question of formal and structural changes being replaced by social learning processes. It is a question of combining the two and realizing that some formal and structural changes will remain blueprints on paper until they are materialized through learning processes that will lead to a renewal of understanding.

Motivating people at work

How can people be motivated to perform better? As in other management areas, the dominant view on how to motivate people has been based upon rationalistic assumptions. Drawing on psychological theories of human needs, researchers have for a long time tried to explain how employees evaluate and respond to various rewards that are attached to a particular work performance. In the practice of using rewards, there has been a discussion on the feasibility of using extrinsic rewards such as a rise in salary, fringe benefits and promotion for motivating people. Even in 1959, Herzberg et al. highlighted that work itself provides intrinsic rewards, which also can satisfy the psychological needs of people. Opportunities that are part of work, such as being able to solve problems, to successfully cope with challenges, and to act upon your own discretion, are rewarding and produce psychological satisfaction. It evokes commitment to the tasks and energizes people. The motivators are inherent in the tasks, work roles and job design, and social relations at work become essential instruments for motivating employees to perform better.

Another set of motivation theories has formed around the perceived relationship between the individual effort and the outcome of it. For example, equity theory was launched by Adams (1963), who proposed that the degree of effort that individuals put into a particular work activity is dependent on their perception of its fairness in relation to the outcome of the effort. Bandura (1997) took these ideas further in his discussion on self-efficacy. According to him, the amount of effort people put into a task is influenced by their perceived capacity to be able to accomplish the task successfully. Ideally, from a motivational point of view, the task should be seen as a challenge but still within the reach of what a person can expect to cope with, using a fair degree of effort.

The equity theory shows motivation is a result of social learning. How one perceives the job in relation to one's own capacity, how others perform it, or what rewards the accomplishment of it may bring are learned in a social context. We have discussed how specific cultures, such as those at IKEA and SAS, create shared understandings about specific work activities and how they should be performed. It is not too daring to assume that the same kind of learning processes that produced a shared understanding among the employees in IKEA and in SAS can also create a shared understanding of what an appropriate level of effort at work is supposed to be.

In their overview of research on motivation, Steers et al. noted that since 1990 the interest in publishing research on motivation has declined. How is it that no one has come up with any truly new theoretical approaches since the 1960s and 1970s? 'Why, then, has there been so little intellectual activity focusing on this important topic? Perhaps we have yet to develop the breakthrough ideas that can push us to the next level of understanding' (Steers et al., 2004: 383). Researchers who build upon more recent social theory with a European touch can consider this to be a healthy reaction. 'From the perspective of a view of the self as represented by contemporary social theory, it must be concluded that the whole question of motivation to work is a non-issue' (Jackson and Carter, 2000: 159).

Drawing upon our discussion of understanding, we think it would be useful to conceive of motivation as a cultural phenomenon. People who have been socialized into a particular organizational unit or a professional community often share an understanding of what is a normal workload and reasonable effort. What is generally called motivation to work could therefore be seen as a behavioural expression of a collective understanding. This does not mean that reward systems no longer play a role. But it does suggest that reward systems for the most part create minor variations around a level that has been established through socialization. The challenge of influencing people's motivation at work then becomes the same as the challenge of changing the culture in an organization.

Recruitment practices

During the last two decades there has been a reorientation of the recruitment practices within many larger companies. The traditional recruitment procedure was to analyse the competence that was required by the vacant position, advertise the position, and then carry out a selection of the applicants. When organizations became more dynamic and work roles more varied, it became increasingly difficult to identify positions with distinct and given competence requirements. Companies started to change their recruitment procedures. Instead of trying to identify exactly what competence a particular job required, companies began to recruit people with attractive general qualifications, a potential for development and a personality that fitted well in the existing culture of the organization. Trainee programmes were seen as a typical exponent of this strategy. However, even today most recruitment probably still takes its point of departure from highly specified job descriptions.

By using the engine optimization example, we have shown that competence at work can be described as people's understanding of their work. In advertisements we find formulations such as 'requiring a customer-oriented view' or 'having a global perspective'. Here the advertisers clearly state that they are searching for somebody who understands the work in a particular way. A problem, however, is that the techniques typically being used in professional selection procedures are primarily designed to analyse attributes and personal traits possessed by the applications, and not how they understand their work. This means that we do not have the same kind of systematic instruments for revealing how applicants understand phenomena related to their work. The kind of understanding that is of crucial importance for a particular job is therefore not identified at all in most recruitment efforts. For the moment, managers are more or less restricted to structured interviews for identifying how candidates understand their work.

Competence development

Our perspective on managing understanding has considerable implications for competence development practices. One key statement is that a person's competence at work should be seen as how the person *understands* the task and its context. Understanding work gives meaning to theoretical knowledge and work experience, and determines what theoretical and practical knowledge is relevant in accomplishing the work in question. It also means that understanding work forms the basis for the kind of theoretical and practical knowledge a person considers as meaningful and relevant at work.

The discussion in Chapter 7 showed that the traditional educational approaches that are used for professional training in organizations typically aim to transfer a predefined package of knowledge to employees with the hope that they will memorize it and then apply the knowledge when they encounter a situation where it is appropriate. From our perspective, the primary challenge is not to transfer packages of knowledge but, rather, to arrange opportunities for inquiry into one's established understanding of the work and to provide information as a 'raw material' in that process. Action-driven methods such as those discussed in Chapter 7 should be used as soon as it is reasonable to do so in order to intensify the questioning of established views and the search for and experimentation with alternative ideas and actions.

From earlier discussions we can also conclude that it is important for the providers of organized competence development activities to take their point of departure from the existing understanding of the target group. The activities should help the participants to become aware of their own actual understanding, which usually requires that they can compare their understanding to alternative views. Not until existing understandings have become apparent to the individuals, does it make sense to present alternative ways of understanding the work and its context. We also argued that in most cases change of understanding, and thus competence renewal, is not a one-shot discovery. Changing understanding typically includes a follow-up procedure where recurring 'educational' sessions are interspersed with periods of work, so that the intellectual questioning and discussion of understanding can be related to efforts to act according to a new understanding. This also means that competence development is mainly a process, taking place in everyday work. People understand what they are doing, and gradually make sense of conditions and actions in a different fashion. It also means that competence development should not be separated too much from the work that is being reconsidered. A person is active at work and observes his or her own actions within an understanding of that work. This understanding in turn gives meaning to the actions and confirms that the actions are reasonable. Hence, if competence concerns a *relationship* between a person and his or her work, it follows that planned efforts to develop competence should deal with that relationship. They cannot be decoupled from that relationship.

Learning is an individual process in so far that every person creates his or her own understanding of reality. But as we have noted earlier, it is rather difficult for individuals to identify and question their own understanding. It is often taken for granted and not reflected upon. Not until we are confronted with alternative patterns of understanding are we inclined to investigate our own views and maybe reconsider them. This will usually require some kind of social interaction. Consequently, learning is to a large extent a social activity.

A critical look at planned competence activities in companies leads to a couple of conclusions in addition to the ones concerning learning strategies. One is that companies today are too ambitious, and often pursue competence development in too many areas and with too many target groups. Invariably the results are less successful because resources are scattered too widely. Competence development efforts create more value to the company if they are concentrated in fewer areas and use more action-driven methods, which have a higher probability of yielding the desired outcomes. Obtaining a change in the understanding of work among specialists within the field of competence development would have a leveraging effect in this context. The methods that we have highlighted in the previous chapter have been available for a long time. But the understanding of competence development that we can find among many (but definitely not all) people in the human resource management area (and among managers in general), leads to the conclusion that they are not being used. In their understanding of competence development, other kinds of method have been seen as meaningful and appropriate. It is our hope that managers and specialists with an innovative spirit will experiment with new approaches and thereby enrich the existing body of knowledge in this area. We know that there are people who have already done it, but much remains to be done.

The paradigm shift reshapes the point of leadership

In the previous chapters we provided an extensive description of how people in organizations develop competence and choose methods of action that are based on their specific understanding of the task and its context. That that understanding forms the basis for action and competence is not only true for the employees, but also for the leaders themselves. In other words, managers' understanding of leadership forms the basis for their competence in leadership. What we argue here is that managing understanding requires *a renewal of managers' understanding of leadership itself, and thus of their competence in leadership.* Such a renewal involves more than a stronger focus on communication when leading. It means a rethinking of the relationship between the leader and the led, and a deeper inquiry into the role of leadership and the practice of leading.

Leadership becomes consultative in character

In the bureaucratic and Tayloristic tradition the leader was viewed as an architect and a builder. An effective business needs to be planned and systematically designed down to the smallest detail. Since people's work performance was thought to be governed by rules, instructions, formal work design and a system of sanctions, many managers believed they had control over the course of events. It was a question of working out good and carefully prepared blueprints for the company and its systems, structures and formalized procedures and then implementing them. The leader's key role was therefore in consultation with experts and staff specialists, to design systems and structures and then deal with the disturbances that unfortunately always occur.

According to the new paradigm, instead of exerting detailed control over employees' behaviour, systems and routines should act as a broad framework for them. Within this framework there are degrees of freedom that employees are supposed to make use of in order to maximize customer satisfaction and at the same time improve quality and monitor the costs. It is a question of taking care of people's inherent driving forces, their commitment and sense of responsibility. The core leadership task is to guide and stimulate people to develop and maintain a particular understanding of their work and its context that will lead to a desirable work performance. In that way leadership becomes, by necessity, more *consultative* in character.

Chris Argyris's (1970) classic description of the consultant role can be used to concretize what consultative leadership may involve in practice. He identifies three main functions:

1   The consultant should *make valid information become apparent* – and here valid means relevance for the problems at hand. One way the consultant can achieve this is to conduct his own observations and investigations and inform the client organization about the results. But it can also be achieved by arranging various social interactions, such as meetings, confrontations and role play activities, that encourage and sometimes entice employees into gathering and providing the relevant information themselves. It may mean that employees discover new things or dare to discuss matters that were previously taboo or matters they have refused to acknowledge as existing in the past.

2   The second task is to *create commitment* in the sense of making employees take up a standpoint and develop a conviction that can form the basis for powerful action. The consultant should not be content with having informed the people in question. The consultant also needs to provoke them to clarify their views and make explicit how they feel about what is being discussed. In our vocabulary, we would express it as stimulating people to reflect upon the information and make up their mind concerning how it relates to their existing understanding of the reality in question.

3   When it comes to take up a standpoint, Argyris emphasizes that organization members must have a *free choice*. Nobody in a consultative position can force them to take up a particular standpoint. Every attempt in that direction will lead to a make-believe game in which employees no longer behave openly and honestly but, rather, present themselves as

171

representing ideas that are not truly their own. This lack of honesty is a prime source of ineffectiveness in organizations because a considerably amount of energy is consumed in playing unproductive make-believe games (Argyris, 1990).

In a typical managerial situation the subordinates do not have a free choice of action. A manager has the authority to take decisions that force the subordinates to act in a specific way. But the manager pays a price because people are then likely to understand their actions as 'this is something we must do in this way'. Acting upon such premises does not produce commitment among the actors and does not create a feeling of responsibility for the job they perform. In an organizational environment, where managers become more and more dependent on rapid actions at lower levels and local ingenuity and improvisation to meet customer needs, there is a strong need for commitment and responsibility on the employees' part. For organizations in such an environment it is therefore very dangerous if their people learn to do exactly what has been prescribed to them and don't need to care for the consequences of their actions. Consequently, although managers can use imperative directives, this method should be restricted to situations in which no other option is available.

In Chapters 4–6 we based our discussion on the view that the learning that produces a renewal of understanding is an individual and creative process, which mostly takes place in a social context. Information and impressions function as stimuli and the raw material in this process, where people form their understanding of reality. Taking this insight as our point of departure, we note that traditional prescriptive management thinking has emphasized the task of *creating a reality for people*, whereas the new paradigm describes the leader's role as to *guide people to create their own reality*. Instead of discovering the truth and handing it over to the employees through various means of communication, a consultative leadership role becomes a question of guiding, explaining, supporting and stimulating the processes of reshaping employees' understanding of their task and its context.

It is possible to recognize the step from a prescriptive to a more consultative role not just in management but also in many other areas in society. It represents a key element in a major value shift that is taking place in society, and it can be seen as forming a core principle in the paradigm shift that has taken place in the field of management. Let us look at a few examples.

The role of supervisor or middle manager has in one sense gained more significance in organizations since managers are more frequently assigned responsibility for a particular section, team, unit or department. Being in charge of a unit means managers are responsible for its daily operations, monitoring the quality of its products or services, improving and developing its work procedures, and handling relationships with other parts of the total work process in the organization. In the new management paradigm, this responsibility is supposed, to a considerable degree, to be carried forward to subordinates. For this to be realized, the supervisors or middle managers cannot take all the responsibility on themselves. Instead, they have to delegate work activities, give the initiative to group discussions, establish follow-up routines and reward systems that stimulate the employees to take responsibility themselves, and then rely upon their capacity to cope with and resolve their problems. This means that the management job becomes more consultative – it becomes a matter of *encouraging, guiding and supporting* other people in their handling of the tasks that were previously considered to be those of the managers and specialists. What counts is not whether managers can accomplish these tasks themselves, but rather how they can make other people carry out those tasks in a desirable and effective way. This is a change of principle and has considerable importance for leadership practice.

The new conditions also apply to general managers with complete responsibility for a business area, such as a CEO of a corporation, or the head of a local sales company or any other profit centre unit. Even if the general managers carry out specific leadership tasks themselves, such as certain business negotiations or the recruitment of key staff members, a considerable part of their work consists of letting subordinate managers take responsibility in carrying out their designated leadership tasks. Here also we witness a development towards the establishment of management teams in which the general manager, together with the subordinate managers, discuss the development and strategic direction of the business. Here, the top manager is not only a decision maker, but to an increasing degree also a 'seminar leader' who arranges and leads continuing discussions on what the business is about, where it is heading, and how it can be developed and improved. The difficult task in this context is not that of declaring in a powerful way how things should be. The challenge lies instead in making subordinate managers and their employees understand why they are supposed to do things in a particular way – to grasp the full meaning of it and incorporate that into their work performance. The powerful and bold decision maker has become an advocate of ideas within a social framework of long-term trusting relationships and mutual learning. Introducing and advocating ideas requires a *consultative role*: managers may still be ambitious in reaching certain goals, but at the same time they realize that they do not necessarily know everything themselves. The only way is to *act with mutual respect within the framework of a trustful dialogue.*

The transition from a prescriptive to a more consultative leadership role has clear parallels in the world of education. In Chapter 7 we discussed the traditional language-based educational methods in which the teacher is the knowing expert who transfers knowledge to less knowledgeable pupils. Within modern didactic theory, the view of the learner as a passive receiver of pre-packed knowledge is to a large extent abandoned. Instead, it is generally acknowledged that learning is an active process in which people create their own understanding of reality, which can result in a reinforcement, modification or renewal of their former understanding. If people create their understanding of work through an individual learning process, the teacher's role becomes very much one of creating opportunities for making discoveries and helping students to interpret events and experiences with the aim of actively developing their understanding. The teacher's role has therefore taken on a consultative character. Instead of designing an elegant package of knowledge and then carrying out the transfer, teaching has become a matter of stimulating and supporting an ongoing learning process in the individual.

Within the world of medicine we can observe an emerging critique against the traditional physician's role, in which the doctor is an elevated expert who investigates symptoms and then decides about the remedy. In that role, the patient is nothing more than an object of treatment. The traditional critique reveals a lack of empathy, in the sense that doctors are unable and unwilling to enter into the patient's life situation. But the critique also highlights a need for a more trusting dialogue, where both parties respect each other's knowledge, where the treatment is seen as more of an agreement in which the patient is clear about the meaning and the motives behind a proposed treatment. Moreover, patients are now more knowledgeable about their own bodies and illnesses, and as a result demonstrate increased independence and take responsibility for themselves. Consequently, the role of the doctor is becoming more consultative.

In labour market policy and its implementation in employment offices and work rehabilitation centres we can see a similar pattern. Many unemployed people find it unsatisfactory to be regarded as objects that are moved around from one training course to another. Instead, they want an interested and empathic agent, who is able to understand their situation and help them to find constructive solutions that will get them back into the workforce. Here representatives of the agencies are required to take a consultative role. They need to enter into a trustful dialogue with the job seekers and support them in their own process of finding a way into the workforce again. This might in some cases include efforts to change the job seekers' understanding of themselves, their abilities, and of specific jobs and labour market conditions.

The conclusion of the discussion so far is that since the 1980s we have seen a growing interest in a consultative approach. This interest is not confined to the relations between managers and subordinates in companies. It can also be traced in many areas, where traditional experts, often in combination with a formal authorization, have been able to prescribe the conditions for other people. A higher level of knowledge and self-confidence among citizens, together with a stronger appreciation of individual freedom and independence, have also contributed to the creation of new conditions for the roles of leaders and experts. *This means that we do not see the emergence of consultative leadership as a particular fashion or management fad, but rather as an expression of a deeper value shift in our society.*

Consultative leadership will necessarily mean managing understanding

As long as leaders considered their task was to create a reality for people, the judgement of their competence was based on their ability to design and build structures, systems and routines that made employees function according to their intentions. This idea was built on the belief that structures and systems were the proper instruments for influencing human behaviour in organizations. As was stated in Chapter 2, within the new management paradigm this basic presumption is now changing in a profound way. *Human behaviour is not controlled by structures, systems and prescriptions as such. Instead, it is how people understand those structures, systems and prescriptions that determine their behaviour.*

The modified presumption becomes more relevant as people in organizations are given greater freedom to make their own judgements and act upon their own discretion. We have observed that the ideas of consultative leadership and the management of understanding have received the fastest and most enthusiastic support among people in professional organizations and the so-called knowledge-intensive firms, that is schools, universities, hospitals, IT companies, consultant companies, accountancy firms and law firms. The employees in these organizations are highly educated and through their personal expertise they have developed greater self-confidence, status and pride. For them, the role of management is primarily to provide general conditions and guidelines. They do not see management interference as a necessary component of their daily routine.

Building structures and systems will always be an important task for managers. But the design and construction of them only form a small first step in the process of management. The task that remains is to influence how employees' understand those structures and systems: What is the point of having them? Why are they so important? How are they supposed to be used? It is, after all, the people in the organization who are supposed to use them in order to achieve efficiency and effectiveness in their work performance.

175

Employees must therefore integrate the systems and structures into their own ways of understanding how the company can become more competitive, how work activities can be made more efficient and how the quality of work can be improved. To lead then means to care for the development of people's understanding of their work and its context.

As we have noted many times before, managing understanding is not only a simple information problem. Developing people's understanding in a desirable way requires more than just elegant information. Since people create their own understanding, leaders cannot merely prescribe how people should understand their reality. They will be forced to choose a consultative role in the same way as a teacher in an educational setting. They can arrange opportunities for others to receive information and reflect on it, they can show possible ways of interpreting impressions, but every individual will develop his or her own understanding based on their existing understanding of reality.

In the new management paradigm, *managing understanding therefore becomes a key function in leadership*. Based on what we showed in Chapters 3–6, namely that people's understanding of work forms the basis for the competence they develop and use in accomplishing their work, many would perhaps regard the core task of the new leadership as developing competence. Seeing understanding as the basis for individual and collective competence also implies that the traditional conception of competence development must be widened. Competence development should not be confined to specific HRM activities, detached in time and space from the ordinary work. Instead, developing employees' competence becomes an integrated part of the leadership function. When leaders influence employees' understanding of work they also contribute to the competence development in the organization. To put it the other way round, the development and maintenance of the core competencies that are a prerequisite for the competitive advantage of the firm will depend on the capacity of its leaders to influence employees' understanding of their work.

Those who want to become successful leaders must therefore develop their competence in managing understanding. Drawing on the discussion in the previous chapters, we can identify a number of key activities that a leader must master in order to be skilful in managing understanding:

- *Identify and describe* how people understand important phenomena at work and use it as a point of departure for enabling them to become aware of their existing understanding. In this way managers can help them to develop and transform their understanding.
- Provide opportunities for people in the organization to be *confronted and acquainted with* new ways of thinking, new approaches and methods to cope with problems related to their work. One important part of this is for the leaders to present their own understanding of environmental trends, challenges and strategies in a way that can have an influence on the understanding of others.

- Develop processes that enable people *to reflect* on their experiences, ideas and lines of thought and through that develop their own understanding.
- Find methods that *stimulate trust, involvement and participation* and provide the necessary conditions for people to be able to question and modify their understanding of work.
- *Redesign and use* existing methods for influencing human behaviour in a way that actively promote changes in people's understanding of work.
- *Actively experiment and try to develop new* and more effective methods for managing understanding.

In order to master these activities leaders are required to develop a new understanding of what leadership means as well as to find new methods and instruments to develop skills in using them. However, using a consultative approach may be a demanding and painful experience for many people. At the end of the day it is the managers who take full responsibility for the business results, but with the consultative approach they do not have full control of the mechanisms that contribute to the results. The consultative role offers opportunities to guide and stimulate employees to develop their understanding of work, but limits the possibility to control the *outcome* of those efforts.

Are leaders then losing their power?

Does this then mean that leadership in managing understanding loses its power and control over the work processes in organizations? To some extent, yes. But it can also be argued that managers have never had complete control of activities that lead to business results. While the methods and instruments used within rationalistic perspectives do not always produce the intended outcomes, they appear to provide a *feeling of being in control* of the business activities and their outcome. In his study of popular management ideas, Huczynski (1993) found that one key characteristic of popular management ideas was that they clearly identified the executive as the key person and the one who designs and controls processes and makes things happen. It is therefore likely that many of the popular management ideas often work as an instrument for leaders to confirm and strengthen their view of themselves as being in control of what is happening.

We have noted similar reactions among academic teachers who have participated in problem-based and experience-based educational activities. They become frustrated when they are unable to control the learning of their students, and learning is left to the discretion of the students. But to what extent do teachers really control the learning process by specifying a list of required readings and providing a set of carefully designed exercises that should lead to expected outcomes? They *do control the educational efforts*, but does it mean that they also control the learning process of the students? By using traditional managerial instruments, leaders tend to think they are controlling the processes, but in truth they are only controlling the instruments that are supposed to have an impact on people's behaviour. The last link in the chain is still hidden in the fog. In managing understanding it becomes much more visible that leaders are not in control of the outcome. This insight can sometimes cause uncertainty and stress. On the other hand, in many areas, such as in the world of finance, people learn to accept uncertainty and can cope with an outcome that is impossible to control. It therefore seems reasonable to assume that managers should be able to learn to live with a higher level of conscious uncertainty. In other words, in a leadership based on managing understanding, managers acquire a greater degree of realism of what they can influence and what they cannot when it comes to people's work performance in organizations.

In truth, leaders do not lose their control and power. They usually have a positional power as formal managers, which mean that they have the authority to make decisions that prescribe their subordinates' actions. But, as discussed earlier, this way of controlling action can have harmful side-effects. When employees cease to use their own ingenuity and judgement capacity, and start to do what they are told to do, they tend to leave the responsibility to those who formulated the prescriptions. The positional power has no value, however, when it comes to making people question and renew their understanding. You cannot order people to think differently. But having the formal management position provides opportunities to set the agenda and take initiatives. As was described in Chapter 7, managers can use their formal power to create arenas for discussion and encourage people to participate in certain activities that can provoke reflection and a questioning of one's own understanding. A manager who initiates dialogue can to some extent also set the agenda, formulate the problem, and be well prepared to defend his or her position with good arguments. This offers many advantages. However, if the manager tries to 'decide' what is right or appropriate and thereby does not follow the social rules of a genuine dialogue, then he or she immediately destroys the necessary climate of openness and respect, which is fundamental for developing and transforming understanding effectively.

A need for showing strong conviction

Leaders can be assumed to have reached their positions at least partly because they display the attributes that are regarded as central for good leadership. Charisma is an interesting concept in this context. House (1977) identified the characteristics that he considered were shared by those classified as charismatic leaders. These included a strong belief in one's own basic viewpoints, self-confidence, dominance and an ambition to exert influence upon others. Later, he also argued that charisma was a strong common denominator in descriptions of visionary, transformational and inspiration leadership theories (House and Howell, 1992). Bass (1998) made the same point concerning transformational leadership.

Renewal of understanding seems to be an important ingredient in transformational leadership efforts, even if that particular concept is not used in the descriptions. In our perspective, it seems reasonable to accept that leaders who try to influence others to develop new ways of understanding should themselves demonstrate a strong conviction. This cannot be achieved only by 'using the right words'. Organizational members will detect from subtle elements in the communication if the statements represent the leader's authentic view, or if he or she is just preaching a message received from above. This is in line with the ideas of 'authentic leadership' presented by Luthans and Avolio (2003). Authentic leaders display congruence between their espoused ideas and values and their actions. Our discussion in Chapter 7 about how to achieve effectiveness in managing understanding also highlighted the importance of combining language-driven and action-driven methods in order to show and confirm the validity of what is said or written.

Renewal of leaders' own understanding

The discussion above has been pursued from a manager's point of view. We have argued that according to the new management paradigm leaders will have to take on the challenge of making people renew their understanding. In such a discussion it seems taken for granted that the leader has the 'right' understanding of the phenomenon in question. Of course, it is easy to find examples of companies that have run into trouble just because key managers understood the business, the competitive situation, the technological development etc., in a way that led to actions that were harmful to the company's performance. This leads to a dilemma. On the one hand, leaders should have a strong conviction and deeply internalized views in order to be effective in inspiring others to change their understanding. On the other hand, leaders must have an open and inquiring approach to 'how it really is', and they must be ready to question their own understanding as a result of reflections that grow from interactions with employees. This situation is similar to the one of researchers who are expected to work hard on developing theories but at the same time keep a critical distance and be ready to question the theory. There is no simple solution to this dilemma.

In the same way as managers, in line with our discussion in Chapter 7, should provide opportunities for employees to participate in activities that have some probability of evoking critical reflections and questioning of established understanding, managers themselves should also take the opportunity to participate in such activities. Senge et al. (2005) discussed this need for 'seeing one's seeing'. The basic strategy for the individual manager is to become aware of one's own basic pattern of pre-understanding. This is very difficult to accomplish for an isolated individual. They therefore advocate the use of highly authentic dialogues, in which the participants cooperate in 'suspending their views' so that they become visible and vulnerable to questioning. The most typical learning that most leaders are involved in, identified by Senge et al., is similar to that which we have described as refinement of present understanding. 'It's quite possible to simply gather information that confirms our pre-existing assumptions – indeed it's common. We "download our mental models" ... and see what we're prepared to see' (2005: 88). What is needed to break away from our existing understanding is a 'retreat' to a situation which stimulates reflection and releases the process of 'presencing'. This is when one's actions receive a new meaning. Senge et al. refer to dramatic experiences in which the established understanding breaks down, opening up the way for new and radical reflections, which can grow into new ways of seeing reality. When we experience a shift in our understanding of some basic issues, a process of 'realizing' starts to work, where one will assign new meanings to problems and activities. They become something different from what they were before.

Our own experience of leadership development is that executives usually expect new methods and techniques that fit into their existing understanding of business and their role as managers. We have seen the frustration expressed when they are confronted with ideas that are said by many to be important but which cannot be integrated within their existing understanding of management. But we have also experienced the satisfaction that people sometimes show when they have experienced a breakdown of their established understanding and begun the process that Senge et al. called 'realizing', when they see that they must choose a new road and try quite different solutions. They are physically in the same world, but they see a completely different world with which they have to cope. Hopefully, the practice of leadership development will provide more opportunities for critical investigation of leaders' own understanding and help leaders to 'see their seeing'.

Avoiding the rationalistic trap

Throughout this book we have emphasized the need for management to acknowledge the importance of managing understanding in organizations.

The most likely reaction among a majority of managers will probably be something along these lines: 'Oh yes, of course! We know this already'. As became evident in Chapter 1, there is no doubt that managers have identified people's viewpoints and competence as being important, and cultural factors are often referred to in the explanation of why things happen the way they do. In a similar way managers also emphasize the use of communication methods such as rhetoric and visions as vital elements in a leader's work. Consequently, it is likely to be easy for managers to accept the concept of understanding as designating something of importance in the sphere of management.

But we also say that managing understanding involves more than just identifying understanding as a new object for management efforts. It represents a *different understanding of management itself*. In Chapter 2 we discussed the difference between a *rationalistic* and an *interpretative* perspective on management. It was claimed that they represented two basic ways of understanding what it means to manage organized activities.

One of us wrote a doctoral dissertation in the 1970s on strategies for organizational change (Targama, 1978). Based upon empirical evidence from 34 change projects in industrial companies, four kinds of strategy were empirically identified, and a central question was: How do companies choose strategy for change? In the analysis, a theoretical contingency model for choice was developed and presented in the form of a decision tree. It was said to represent a decision procedure depicting how one could go about it, if one had an ambition to make a rational choice based upon the knowledge available. But it was openly stated that it was just a theoretical model that was *not* confirmed by the empirical observations. Instead, the analysis clearly showed that choice of strategy was a kind of established practice – 'This kind of change is made in this way' – without reflecting upon available alternatives or other elements of rational analysis. The thesis was published and sold in quite large numbers of copies to practitioners. From discussions and seminars it became clear that what practitioners picked up from the dissertation was the rational decision tree. It was what they considered to be the result of the research! This is one small example of what we here call the 'rationalistic trap'. Managers pick up new information, but it is interpreted within their existing understanding of management. It contributes to refinement of their existing understanding but not to a transformation of it.

There are therefore good reasons to believe that most managers will fall into the trap of regarding understanding as one object among others that can be managed with traditional management efforts. Competence is seen as a set of knowledge and skills that leaders try to develop through traditional educational efforts. Customer orientation or quality thinking is 'implemented' by the use of project approaches that have been modelled on traditional organizational changes concerning structures, systems and training programmes. Visions and strategies are communicated through information campaigns, where the executives tell the employees how 'things' should be and how one should think. No one is protesting or resisting the ideas and therefore everything seems to be fine.

Many researchers have described the rationalistic perspective as an ideological foundation of management. One of the more ambitious attempts is Shenhav's (1999) study of the engineering foundations of management thinking. In order to trace the roots of management, he analysed American periodicals on industrial matters from the late nineteenth century to recent time. He found that articles on management increased dramatically from 1880. The writing had at that time a clear engineering approach to management, and it also applied concepts and models from the world of mechanical engineering, not from the field of economics. Gradually, a whole body of knowledge was developed, based upon these concepts and models (systems, planning, standardization, control, and labour). Its roots in mechanical engineering also provided a connection with science as well as moved management from the capitalists to the engineers. Among the ideological elements of management he finds an emphasis on order and systematization as opposed to chaos and uncertainty. The human element is seen as an uncertain and disturbing factor in a rationally designed and controlled working system.

Huczynski (1993) emphasizes a few other characteristics (among others) of American management thinking in his study of management ideas:

1 The focus on the leader as the key actor, the decision maker and the one controlling what is happening.
2 Emphasis on individuals rather than collectives and that the behaviour of individuals can be predicted from attributes that are measurable in a similar way as performance can be categorized and measured.
3 The focus on functionalism. Leaders do not act on the basis of their own will and power – they are only mediators of the necessity (emanating from competition, etc.). Conflicts are suppressed.

The American management thinking with its engineering-oriented language and models of thought, its obsession with control, its functional, unitary perspective and its individualistic view did gradually conquer the world of business. Today, it is a canonized body of knowledge and practice, taken for granted by almost all managers and the surrounding society. It is a body of knowledge and an ideology that has been internalized and embodied in the people in organizations. It has shaped the understanding of leadership and organizing, and many other phenomena, among managers as well as others.

Consequently, it is no surprise that leaders try to manage understanding by the use of traditional rationalistic methods such as providing explicit knowledge and running information campaigns and, thus, fall into the rationalistic trap. Since the world of management is so strongly dominated by the rationalistic ideology, it is extremely easy to fall into the trap. All surrounding structures and systems, administrative and financial routines, HRM practices and reward systems have been created within the understanding of management as a rationalistic and engineered form of behaviour. It is therefore very tempting to lead in accordance to the rationalistic perspective, and to be seen as 'doing the right things'.

However, as was pointed out in Chapter 1, if one falls into the rationalistic trap there is a high risk that the management efforts will lead to a failure. The trap is also very deceitful, since it typically does not lead to any dramatic and visible failures. Employees do not protest against the quality campaigns, and people do not complain when it doesn't lead to the changes in behaviour that management was hoping for. This outcome is bearable and does not arouse investigations that blame the managers for having spent a lot of resources on something that did not produce any results. More often, perhaps, the employees are blamed for being unwilling or not committed. Managers can usually show that the projects *have been carried out according to plan*. Information has been given, seminars have been held, middle managers have received slide packs to inform their subordinates, etc. Top managers seem also more interested in promoting the implementation of new ideas than making a thorough follow-up of what is already history.

The 'undetected failure' can, in the long run, lead to a situation in which employees start to see the organization as consisting of two separate worlds, namely a rhetorical world and a real world. In *the world of rhetoric*, fashionable concepts and models, new theories, and visions and missions rule. In that world new ideas and changes are continuously discussed. In *the real world of everyday work*, however, productivity measures, competitive pressure and return on investment are the dominating position. In this world it is not enough to use fancy concepts and bold statements; one has to act fast and with force. It is a matter of having routines that work and people who know the ropes. We are in great danger and waste resources unnecessarily if our efforts to change and renew stop at the rhetorical level and do not become integrated in people's understanding of their reality.

To avoid a split between rhetoric and reality it is important that efforts to influence understanding do not only become part of the world of rhetoric. It is necessary for managers to find methods that make people question their understanding and develop new ways of understanding their work in line with what was described in Chapter 7. And maybe this will require, in the first place, that managers question their own understanding of management.

To conclude, our main thesis is that in the new management paradigm it is not enough to attend to and positively consider phenomena such as competence, cultural patterns, customer orientation, visions and values, which all in some sense are related to a particular understanding of the work. Leaders will have to:

- make clear what understanding means,
- investigate and find out how people develop and change understanding,
- find workable ways of influencing the learning processes by which people develop and change their understanding.

It is not until then that leaders will be capable of managing understanding in an effective way, and that managing understanding will become a forceful ingredient in the efforts to develop the competitive strength of the company.

Leaders have to climb down from the pedestal

Within the rationalistic management tradition leaders have been seen as the active ones who are presumed to influence a group of passive followers. In this perspective, the leader stands above the ones being led. This 'from above' view of leadership has been strongly reinforced by the tendency to personalize organizations in the media. A CEO of a company is often treated in the media as more or less synonymous to the company itself. Using various techniques, the potent leader is supposed to guide the employees in performing their work in such a way that their performance will deliver the results expected by the company owners and shareholders. When managing understanding becomes a key issue, the role of the leader changes and becomes more indirect and interactive. One important aspect is that the leader and the led should not be considered as two separate entities, but rather as actors within an interactive totality. The leaders, as well as the people being led, are parts of the social process in which their understanding develops. Through the formal position, the leader has an advantage in the process, but he or she is still only part of the shared creation of meaning.

In contemporary organizations, the quest for greater effectiveness has not decreased but rather increased. Managing understanding should therefore not be confused with the idea that managers should drop their tough requirement for results and hope that everything will work out well anyway. The fact that top managers, in order to meet the demand of greater speed and flexibility in today's business environment, have tried to organize and design jobs that give more freedom to employees to plan and choose what they regard as the best actions for carrying out their work, rather than expecting employees to blindly follow detailed prescriptions about how to carry out their work, can probably be seen as an effort to increase effectiveness. While it is true that giving employees greater discretion requires that leaders refrain from controlling all details, it does not mean that leaders should stop monitoring productivity and quality. It just means that productivity and quality requirements must be given a different *meaning*. Leaders must create conditions for a more genuine participation, such as engaging employees in strategic discussions concerning how the company should cope with competition and in the formulation of productivity requirements. The instruments and routines for follow-up and control must be understood as shared tools for monitoring the achievements of the company.

To have efficient operations and at the same time develop and renew the business will lead to conflicting demands on the social processes in the organization. The need for a mutual commitment and shared understanding is particularly salient when it comes to the truly long-term issues, such as understanding the corporate vision and the core values, on the one hand, and to the very short-term issues, such as the daily operational work, on the other hand. But when it is a matter of developing and renewing an existing vision, it might be fruitful to have people with different ways of understanding the reality in question. This will bring a broader spectrum of ideas and judgements. For a leader, it means tolerating a certain degree of pluralism in understanding, and accepting that extra efforts are needed in dialogues and collective problem-solving.

We have earlier emphasized that managing understanding means that leaders need to take on a more consultative role. It requires some humility and a more genuine interest in the thoughts and views of other people. At the same time the leader must realize his or her limited capacity to influence the understanding of others. However, it is important to emphasize that the leader is also supposed to be active and energetic in getting things done. This is because while managing understanding, as we have described it here, may lead to a more human leadership, it will not do so at the expense of effectiveness and competitive strength. Instead, the insights about what understanding is, how it unfolds and how it can be developed and transformed will enable leaders to take care of and use human ingenuity to cope with the challenges of the business world.

Climbing down from the pedestal also involves a shift from an outside to an inside perspective on managing understanding. As pointed out before, within the rationalistic perspective the manager is seen as a scientist and someone who regards managing organizations and its related problems as scientific problems in a natural scientific sense. A fundamental dimension in the natural scientific management orientation is *an outside perspective* on what is being managed. In an outside perspective all business problems, such as strategy, learning and competitors, are treated as external objects that can be described objectively and then manipulated and controlled from above.

For example, when formulating a company's strategy, managers and staff specialists and consultants try to analyse the company's environment as objectively as possible. Based on that analysis, they go on to inform the employees about the company's strategic directions by first formulating the desired direction in an elegant vision statement and then transmitting it to the employees through fancy booklets, videos and dramatic speeches. In other words, in an outside perspective understanding is treated as an external object to be managed. In this case as a neat information package that can be easily transmitted with sophisticated communication devices.

But as we discussed throughout this book, understanding is not particularly effective to manage from the outside. It is better managed from *the inside*, that is, managers need to be part of the understanding they are trying to develop among the employees. If they try to manage understanding from the outside, they really don't know what is going on inside people's understanding of work. Managing understanding from an outside perspective may mean that managers, as Shotter expressed it, 'become disempowered by [their] own analysis' (1993: 149). Therefore, to be able to influence employees' understanding to a greater degree managers need to get 'inside' the employees' understanding of their work. They have to be part of the employees' understanding in order to facilitate the development and transformation of their understanding of work into a shared understanding that will generate a desired work performance.

Managers have by tradition been appointed on the basis of a superior factual knowledge, a capacity to structure problems and formulate solutions and for being active and energetic. In shifting management towards managing understanding, the key qualifications of leaders will include skills in dealing with the social processes in which understanding is created. In truth, analytical and social capacities have always been intertwined in managerial practice. But if managers are to guide social processes and at the same time respect the understanding of others, they will face greater challenges in coping with both technical and emotional elements. It seems likely therefore that managers, to a larger extent than previously, have to train and develop their capacity to understand and deal with group dynamics.

When leaders and other employees participate in the social processes in which understanding is challenged, questioned and sometimes transformed, it means that leadership, at least at the ideological level, will be practised by many in a group. The idea that leadership can be practised by many is similar to the notion of *shared leadership* developed recently by researchers such as Pearce and Conger (2003). Instead of regarding leadership in terms of a specific set of attributes and behaviours of the leader, they argue that leadership should be seen as an *'activity* that is shared or distributed among members of a group or organization. For example, depending on the demands of the moment, individuals can rise to the occasion to exhibit leadership and then step back at other times to allow others to lead' (2003: xi, italics in original). Leadership for managing understanding should therefore not only be defined by a particular position in a hierarchical line of authority. It is also to large extent determined by individuals' particular competence and their capacity to influence peers' understanding of work and how to accomplish it.

The idea of shared leadership can be interpreted as an erosion of the leadership role but it can also be seen as a 'natural' development in a democratic society, where human equality is acknowledged in parallel to accepting the legitimacy of the leadership position. Being able to take care of more ideas and reflective thoughts can also be seen as a valuable asset from an effectiveness point of view. In a management based on managing understanding, leadership may be somewhat less dramatic and lose some of its prestige. The leadership role will certainly not become easier but may become more interesting and challenging.

However, climbing down from the pedestal is easier said than done. Previously we pointed out that it may be extremely difficult for leaders to avoid the rationalistic trap. Climbing down from the pedestal is likely to be equally difficult and perhaps even more difficult than avoiding the rationalistic trap. This is so because climbing down from the pedestal means that managers not only have to change their understanding of management – what it is about and how to practise it – but they also have to change their *self-understanding and identity*, that is, who they are. As was pointed out in Chapter 5, while we always live and embody an understanding of reality, we are not born with such an understanding but are socialized into it. Through socialization we develop an understanding of the world in which we live and act, which we hold in common with our fellow human beings. This internalized, common understanding of our world becomes the basic framework for making sense of our actions and who we are.

Most managers (at least in the western world) have been socialized into some form of market economy. Their internalized understanding of the market economy provides them with both management as a phenomenon and as a context to which management belongs. This means that their pre-understanding of the market economy largely defines their understanding of management and therefore how they 'do' leadership and how they see themselves as leaders.

As has been indicated in various places in this book and elsewhere, the prevalent understanding of successful leadership in most market economies can be characterized in the form of *a male individual who is a tough fighter and rational expert*, legitimated by hierarchical authority (Bendix, 1956; Fletcher and Käufer, 2003; Kalifatides, 2002; Sandberg, 2001a). Since a failure to display the above characteristics may be seen as a sign of weak leadership, most managers may not be prepared to change their leadership style. But even more important, a failure to display the above characteristics may not only be regarded as a sign of weak leadership, but may also be experienced by many male leaders as a failure to be a 'real man'. Changing their self-understanding of what a 'real man' is provides a formidable challenge to most male leaders. While it can be argued that women are less burdened by such an understanding of leadership, and are therefore in a better position to embrace the new leadership role related to managing understanding, it is well known that the prevalent understanding of what characterizes good leadership severely impedes, and sometimes even denies, women the opportunity to advance into leadership positions (Cockburn, 1991; Collinson and Hearn, 1996; Kanter, 1977). It should also be noted that it is not only difficult for leaders themselves to embrace the new leadership role described here. It may be equally difficult for 'non-leaders'. Many people used to traditional, authoritarian leadership styles may have difficulty in accepting and regarding a more dialogue-based leadership style as real and valuable. The new leadership style will also have a profound impact on the 'followers'. Now they become part of leadership itself. It is therefore highly likely that many employees, at least initially, will be reluctant to embrace the new leadership role required for managing understanding.

Some problematic power issues in managing understanding

As has been described, when managing understanding, the locus of control changes from hierarchical to more horizontal relations. Staff members and their managers are involved in an ongoing dialogue about what the company's task involves, what it means and how it should be accomplished. To produce a concerted social action, staff members need to a considerable degree to comply with the negotiated shared understanding. If there is too much disagreement, not much will be achieved.

We have argued that when managing understanding managers need to maintain a healthy tension between control and resistance and between different points of view. At the same time as the people involved in creating and maintaining a shared understanding need to comply to that understanding in order to get something done, they must also be able to resist and express viewpoints that deviate from the managers' and the majority's understanding of work. Sennett (1998) argued in a similar vein. With reference to Coser's (1976) study *The Function of Social Conflict*, Sennett argued that conflict and disagreement may create stronger bonds between people than a complete agreement about what the work is about, how it should be done, etc. There are, however, several problematic power issues involved when changing the locus of control. Below we point out what we regard as three central power issues that may arise in managing understanding.

Tightening of the 'iron cage'

One such issue is the 'iron cage' problem. In his study of an organizational change from bureaucracy to self-managed teams, Barker found that workers in self-managed teams created a concertive control of themselves through a negotiated consensus about what their work involved and rules about how it should be carried out on a daily basis. According to Barker, such a concertive structure 'resulted in a control more powerful, less apparent, and more difficult to resist than that of the former bureaucracy. The irony of the change in this postbureaucratic organization is that, instead of loosening, the iron-cage of rule-based rational control, as Max Weber called it, actually became tighter' (1993: 408). This is because 'concertive workers must invest part of themselves in the team: they must identify strongly with their team values and goals, its norms and values. If they want to resist their team's control, they must be willing to risk their human dignity, being made to feel unworthy as a "teammate". Entrapment in the iron cage is the cost of concertive control' (1993: 436).

There is also a risk that managing understanding will not only encourage the development of concertive control but also invite and bolster the emergence of what Courpasson (2000) called 'soft bureaucracies'. Courpasson's study of French organizations indicated that organizations tend to incorporate the use of soft management techniques, such as value, culture and visions, which we have suggested can be used for managing understanding, within existing bureaucratic framework. This means that they create a double form of domination and control: a concertive control centrally managed through bureaucratic authority.

Power without authority

Another, highly related power issue in managing understanding is that it can lead to what Sennett (1998) called 'power without authority'. In managing understanding there is an encouragement that the responsibility for doing the job properly to a large extent moves away from the manager to staff members. This is particularly true when it comes to self-managed teams. In self-managed teams and in organizations that have embraced a shared leadership, many managers try to facilitate and coach the staff members to carry out the work properly, and by doing so 'avoid being held responsible for his or her action; its all on the player's shoulder' (1998: 114). According to Sennett, a particular problem that arises in power without authority is that it allows leaders to dominate 'employees by denying legitimacy to employees' needs and desires' (1998: 115).

The risk of manipulation

A third problematic issue is that many of the methods suggested for managing understanding can easily be used to manipulate other people against their will or even without their awareness of it. As we all know, tools and methods can be used for many different purposes. A knife can be a very helpful and valuable tool for improving daily life, but it can also be used to kill people. The evaluation of a method or an approach on a scale from good to bad cannot be directly derived from its inherent characteristics. In Chapter 7, dialogue was highlighted as a positive method for managing understanding. The dialogue as a method truly has many positive attributes. Provided that the participants have an open mind and a willingness to scrutinize each other's claims, there is an opportunity for learning to take place that will enrich all parties' understanding of the world around them. But in order for that to happen, *all parties* must have that openness.

A dialogue is a kind of language game, where all participants are active in making claims but also active in listening. This is, however, also the case in the typical salesperson–customer relationship, where the salesperson is playing the dialogue game, informing, arguing and listening. But every action step is here taken from a tactical perspective. The salesperson has been trained in advance to find effective arguments against every possible comment or opinion. What seems on the surface to be an honest dialogue is, at a deeper level, a planned, manipulative language game.

So, we come back to the crucial role of authenticity, as a prerequisite for leaders and for others practising the principles of managing understanding. To exert influence upon others' understanding of the world is legitimate in the management of organizations as well as in political activities. But somewhere the practice of managing understanding can go beyond what is seen as legitimate and become an unethical, manipulative practice. Identifying the borderline in this context will be one of the challenges for the management in the future.

In sum, throughout this book we have mainly discussed how understanding can be managed with the aim of improving work performance in one way or another. However, as the problematic issues above indicate, managing understanding is not only about finding out effective methods of actively promoting the development of specific understandings of work. It also needs to include an ethical awareness and a mindfulness of the political power games involved in managing understanding. It is therefore important that leaders develop an awareness of these and other problematic issues so they at least can lessen their impact when confronted by them in managing understanding.

Conclusion

In this book we have argued for the need to pay more attention to the significant role understanding plays in organizations. We have tried to show in which ways the concept of understanding can help us to see many traditional management problems in a new light.

The interest of what we call understanding has existed for a long time. Even in the 1970s the management literature pointed to the insight that people's understanding of reality is of great importance for what happens in organizations. However, due to strong rationalistic management thinking, understanding remained something of a 'black box' for a long time. It was easy to notice that it was important for human actions, but it was hard to advance it much further. The increased emphasis on competence and knowledge during the last two decades has evolved in a similar fashion. Everyone acknowledges that it is important, but at the same time they are rather unclear what it stands for.

Our ambition has been to identify and describe the contents of the black box. We have tried to show what understanding is, its relation to human action and competence, and its implications for management practice. A discussion on how understanding unfolds, develops and changes formed the platform for an analysis of the methods that can be used to encourage people to change their understanding of something so that they can improve performance at work. We have argued that the concept of understanding should be highly valuable and useful for management thinking, particularly when we take into account the paradigm shift within management that was our point of departure at the very beginning of the book.

Our principal thesis has been that if we fully accept that understanding forms the basis for people's work performance and the competence they develop and use in accomplishing their work, managing understanding becomes the main task for management. In other words, management becomes a question of managing understanding with the aim of *influencing employees' understanding of the their own work and that of the company in such a way that a shared understanding is achieved, which in turn will guide the development of specific learning processes and competence, which together constitute the ability of the organization to achieve competitive advantage.* Hence, the chief task in all areas of management, such as strategy, organization design, change management, HRM and innovation, becomes managing understanding in one way or another. This means that management as a whole needs to be redesigned for the task of managing understanding.

Redesigning management for managing understanding cannot be achieved through a specific new method, containing eight action steps. It is more a question of reconsidering existing methods and practices within management. In Chapter 7 we evaluated a range of methods that are suitable for managing understanding. Based on that assessment, and in conjunction with what constitutes understanding, we outlined a set of guiding principles for redesigning current methods in a way that will assist managers in managing understanding more effectively. It is likely that those principles can also function as guidelines for redesigning management as a whole, in a similar way as they do for redesigning current methods, to actively promote a desirable development of people's understanding of work.

The greatest challenge when redesigning management is to avoid falling into the ever present rationalistic trap. If we fall into the trap we are back at square one again. But those managers who are able to avoid the trap and are bold enough to experiment and try to develop a leadership for managing understanding are likely to become more successful leaders in business and in society at large.

References

Adams, J.S. (1963) 'Towards an understanding of inequity', *Journal of Abnormal and Social Psychology*, 67: 422–36.

Alvesson, M. (1993a) 'Organizations as rhetoric: knowledge-intensive firms and the struggle with ambiguity', *Journal of Management Studies*, 30: 997–1016.

Alvesson, M. (1993b) *Cultural Perspectives on Organization*. Cambridge: Cambridge University Press.

Alvesson, M. (1995) *Management of Knowledge-Intensive Companies*. Berlin: Walter de Grutyer.

Alvesson, M. (2002) *Understanding Organizational Culture*. London: Sage.

Alvesson, M. (2004) *Knowledge Work and Knowledge-Intensive Firms*. Oxford: Oxford University Press.

Alvesson, M. and Berg, P.O. (1992) *Corporate Culture and Organizational Symbolism*. Berlin: Walter de Gruyter.

Alvesson, M. and Björkman, I. (1992) *Organisationsidentitet och organisationsbyggande. En studie av ett indus-triföretag (Organizational Identity and Organizational Construction: A Study of an Industrial Company)*. Lund: Studentlitteratur.

Alvesson, M. and Deetz, S. (2000) *Doing Critical Management Research*. London: Sage.

Alvesson, M. and Kärreman, D. (2000) 'Varieties of discourse: on the study of organizations through discourse analysis', *Human Relations*, 9: 1125–49.

Alvesson, M. and Sköldberg, K. (1999) *Toward Reflexive Methodology*. London: Sage.

Alvesson, M. and Thomson, P. (2005) 'Post-bureaucracy?', in S. Akroyd, R. Batt, P. Thomson and P.S. Tolbert (eds), *The Oxford Handbook of Work and Organization (pp. 485–507)*. Oxford: Oxford University Press.

Alvesson, M. and Willmott, H. (1996) *Making Sense of Management: A Critical Introduction*. London: Sage.

Andrews, K. (1971) *The Concept of Corporate Strategy*. Homewood, IL: Dow Jones–Irwin.

Ansoff, H.I. (1965) *Corporate Strategy*. New York: McGraw-Hill.

Ansoff, H.I. (1979) *Strategic Management*. New York: John Wiley.

Ansoff, H.I. (1984) *Implanting Strategic Management*. Englewood Cliffs, NJ: Prentice-Hall.

Anumba, C.J., Bouchlaghem, N.M., Whyte, J. and Duke, A. (2000) 'Perspectives on an integrated construction project model', *International Journal of Cooperative Information Systems*, 9: 283–313.

Aoki, M. (1988) *Information, Incentives and Bargaining in the Japanese Economy*. Cambridge: Cambridge University Press.

Argyris, C. (1970) *Intervention Theory and Method: A Behavioral View*. Reading, MA: Addison-Wesley.

Argyris, C. (1990) *Overcoming Organizational Defenses: Facilitating Organizational Learning*. Needham, MA: Allyn & Bacon.

Argyris, C. and Schön, D.A. (1978) *Organizational Learning: A Theory of Action Perspective*. Reading, MA: Addison-Wesley.

Armstrong, M. (1991) *A Handbook of Personnel Management Practice*. London: Kogan Page.

Ashkanasy, N., Hartal, C.E.J. and Daus, C.S. (2002) 'Diversity and emotion: the new frontiers in organizational behaviour research', *Journal of Management*, 28: 307–38.

Atkinson, P. (1988) 'Ethnomethodology: a critical review', *Annual Review of Sociology*, 44: 441–65.

Atkinson, P., Coffey, A. and Delamont, S. (2003) *Key Themes in Qualitative Research: Continuities and Change*. Walnut Creek, CA: AltaMira Press.

Bäcklund, A.-K. (1994) *Just-in-time: Hur industriella rationaliseringsprocesser formar arbetsdelning och kompetens* (*Just-in-time: How Industrial Rationalisation Processes Influence Work Division and Competence*). Lund: Lund University Press.

Balota, D. and Marsh, E.J. (2004) *Cognitive Psychology*. New York: Psychology Press.

Bandura, A. (1997) *Self-efficacy: The Exercise of Control*. New York: Freeman.

Barker, J. (1993) 'Tightening the iron cage: concertive control in self-managing teams', *Administrative Science Quarterly*, 38: 408–37.

Barley, S.R. (1996) 'Technicians in the workplace: ethnographic evidence for bringing work into organization studies', *Administrative Science Quarterly*, 41: 404–41.

Bass, B.M. (1998) *Transformational Leadership: Industrial, Military, and Educational Impact*. Mahwah, NJ: Erlbaum Associates.

Baumard, P. (1999) *Tacit Knowledge in Organizations*. London: Sage.

Beckérus, Å., Edström, A., Edlund, C., Ekvall, G., Forslin, J. and Rendahl, J.-E. (1988) *Doktrinskiftet: Nya ideal i svenskt ledarskap* (*The Doctrinal Shift: New Ideal in Swedish Leadership*). Stockholm: Svenska Dagbladets Förlags AB.

Bendix, R. (1956) *Work and Authority in Industry*. Los Angeles: UC Press.

Bengtsson, J. (1989) 'Fenomenologi: vardagsforskning, existensfilosofi, hermeneutik' ('Phenomenology: everyday research, existential philosophy, hermeneutics'), in P. Månson (ed.), *Moderna samhällsteorier: Traditioner riktningar teoretiker* (pp. 67–108). Stockholm: Prisma.

Bengtsson, J. (1993) 'Theory and practice: two fundandamental categories in the philosophy of education', *Educational Review*, 45: 205–11.

Bengtsson, J. (1995) 'What is reflection? On reflection in teacher profession and teacher education', *Teachers and Teaching*, 1: 23–32.

Benner, P.E. (1984) *From Novice to Expert: Excellence and Power in Clinical Nursing Practice*. San Francisco: Addison-Wesley.

Berg, P.-O. (1986) 'Symbolic management of human resources', *Human Resource Management*, 25: 557–79.

Berger, P.L. and Luckmann, T. (1981/1966) *The Social Construction of Reality*. Harmondsworth: Penguin.

Bernstein, R.J. (2002) 'The constellation of hermeneutics, critical theory and deconstruction', in R.J. Dostal (ed.), *The Cambridge Companion to Gadamer*. New York: Cambridge University Press.

Blumer, H. (1969) *Symbolic Interactionism*. Englewood Cliffs, NJ: Prentice-Hall.

Bohm, D. (1996) *On Dialogue*. London: Routledge.

Bohm, D. and Edwards, M. (1991) *Changing Consciousness: Exploring the Hidden Source of the Social, Political and Environmental Crisis Facing the World*. San Francisco: Harper.

Bourdieu, P. (1977) *Outline of a Theory of Practice*. Cambridge: Cambridge University Press.

Bourdieu, P. (1990) *The Logic of Practice*. Cambridge: Polity Press.

Boyatzis, R.E. (1982) *The Competent Manager*. New York: John Wiley.

Brown, J.S. and Duguid, P. (1991) 'Organizational learning and communities of practice: toward a unified view of working, learning and innovation', *Organizational Science*, 1: 40–57.

Brunsson, N. (1985) *The Irrational Organization*. Chichester: John Wiley.

Burrell, G. and Morgan, G. (1979) *Sociological Paradigms and Organisational Analysis*. Aldershot: Gower.

Calás, M. and Smircich, L. (1996) 'From the woman's' point of view: feminist approaches in organization studies', in S. Clegg, C. Hardy and W. Nord (eds), *Handbook of Organization Studies* (pp. 218–58). London: Sage.

Castells, M. (1996) *The Rise of the Network Society*. Oxford: Blackwell.

Chandler, A.D. (1962) *Strategy and Structure: Chapters in the History of the Industrial Enterprise*. Cambridge, MA: MIT Press.

Clark, T. and Clegg, S. (2000) *Changing Paradigms: The Transformation of Management Knowledge for the 21st Century*. London: HarperCollins Business.

Cockburn, C. (1991) *In the Way of Women*. London: Macmillan.

Collins, J.C. (1999) 'Turning goals into results: the power of catalytic mechanisms', *Harvard Business Review*, July–August.

Collins, J.C. and Porras, J.I. (1994) *Built to Last: Successful Habits of Visionary Companies*. New York: Harper Business.

Collinson, D. and Hearn, J. (1996) *Men as Managers, Managers as Men*. London: Sage.

Cook, S.N. and Brown, J.S. (1999) 'Bridging epistemologies: the generative dance between organizational knowledge and organizational knowing', *Organization Science*, 10: 382–90.

Cook, S.N. and Yanow, D. (1993) 'Culture and organisational learning', *Journal of Management Inquiry*, 2: 373–90.

Cooper, C. (ed.) (2002) *Fundamentals of Organizational Behaviour*. London: Sage.

Coser, L. (1976) *The Functions of Social Conflicts*. New York: Free Press.

Courpasson, D. (2000) 'Managerial strategies of domination: power in soft bureaucracies', *Organization Studies*, 21: 141–61.

Cyert, R.M. and March, J.G. (1963) *A Behavioral Theory of the Firm*. Englewood Cliffs, NJ: Prentice-Hall.

Dall'Alba, G. (1987) 'The Relation between Cognitive Learning Strategies and Learning Outcomes in Secondary Science'. Unpublished PhD thesis, Monash University, Melbourne.

Dall'Alba, G. (2002) 'Understanding medical practice: different outcomes of a pre-medical program', *Advances in Health Sciences Education*, 7: 163–77.

Dall'Alba, G. and Sandberg, J. (1996) 'Educating for competence in professional practice', *Instructional Science*, 24: 411–37.

Dall'Alba G. and Sandberg, J. (in press) 'Unveiling professional competence: a critique of stage models', *Review of Educational Research*.

Davenport, T.H. and Prusak, L. (1998) *Working Knowledge: How Organizations Manage What They Know*. Boston, MA: Harvard Business School Press.

Deal, T.E. and Kennedy, A. (1982) *Corporate Cultures: The Rites and Rituals of Corporate Life*. San Francisco: Addison-Wesley.

De Cieri, H. and Kramar, R. (2005) *Human Resource Management in Australia*, 2nd edn. North Ryde: McGraw-Hill Australia.

Deetz, S.A. (1992) *Democracy in the Age of Corporate Colonization: Developments in Communication and the Politics of Everyday Life*. New York: State University of New York Press.

Denzin, N.K. (1997) *Interpretive Ethnography*. Thousand Oaks, CA: Sage.

Denzin, N.K. and Lincoln, Y.S. (eds) (1994) *Handbook of Qualitative Research*. Thousand Oaks, CA: Sage.

Denzin, N.K. and Lincoln, Y.S. (eds) (2000) *Handbook of Qualitative Research*. Thousand Oaks, CA: Sage.

Derrida, J. (1981/1972) *Positions* (translated by Alan Bass). London: The Athlone Press.

DiMaggio, P.J. and Powell, W.W. (1983) 'The iron cage revisited: institutional isomorphism and collective rationality in organizational fields', *American Sociological Review*, 48: 147–60.

Dodgson, M., Gann, D. and Salter, A. (2005) *Think, Play, Do: Technology, Innovation, and Organization*. Oxford: Oxford University Press.

Dreyfus, H.L. and Dreyfus, S.E. (1986) *Mind over Machine: The Power of Human Intuition and Expertise in the Era of the Computer*. New York: Free Press.

Edström, A., Norbäck L.-E. and Rendahl, J.E. (1989) *Förnyelsens ledarskap (Renewing Leadership)*. Stockholm: Norstedts.

Eisenberg, E. (1984) 'Ambiguity as a strategy in organizational communication', *Communication Monographs*, 51: 227–42.

Ekman, G. (2001) 'Constructing leadership in small talk', in S.-E. Sjöstrand, J. Sandberg and M. Tyrstrup (eds), *Invisible Management: The Social Construction of Leadership* (pp. 224–239). London: Thomson.

Ekstedt, E. (1988) *Humankapital i brytningstid: Kunskapsuppbyggnad och förnyelse för företag* (*Human Capital in Transition: Knowledge Development and Renewal of Companies*). Stockholm: Allmänna förlaget.

Eliasson, G., Fölster, S., Lindberg, T., Pousette, T. and Taymaz, E. (1990) *The Knowledge-Based Information Economy*. Stockholm: Almqvist & Wiksell International.

Ellström, P.-E. (1992) *Kompetens, utbilding och lärande i arbetslivet: Problem, begrepp och teoretiska perspektiv* (*Competence, Education, and Learning in Working Life: Problems, Concepts and Theoretical Perspectives*). Stockholm: Publica.

Ely, R.J. and Thomas, D.A. (2001) 'Cultural diversity at work: the effects of diversity perspectives on work group processes and outcomes', *Administrative Science Quarterly*, 46: 227–73.

Ewert, A. (1989) *Outdoor-Adventure Pursuits: Foundations, Models and Theories*. Columbus, OH: Publishing Horizons.

Fairhurst, G.T. (2005) 'Reframing *The Art of Framing*: problems and prospects for leadership', *Leadership*, 1: 165–85.

Fairhurst, G.T. and Sarr, R.A. (1996) *The Art of Framing: Managing the Language of Leadership*. San Francisco: Jossey-Bass.

Felstead, A., Gallie, D. and Green, F. (2002) *Work Skills in Britain 1986–2001*. Nottingham: Department of Further Education and Skills.

Festinger, L. (1957) *A Theory of Cognitive Dissonance*. New York: Harper & Row.

Fielding, N.G. (1988a) 'Competence and culture in the police', *Sociology*, 22: 45–64.

Fielding, N.G. (1988b) *Joining Forces: Police Training, Socialization, and Occupational Competence*. London: Routledge.

Fletcher, J.K. (1999) *Disappearing Acts: Gender, Power and Relational Practice at Work*. Cambridge, MA: MIT Press.

Fletcher, J.K. (2002) 'The Paradox of Post Heroic Leadership: Gender, Power and the "New" Organization'. Paper presented at the Academy of Management Annual Meeting, Denver, CO.

Fletcher, J.K. and Käufer, K. (2003) 'Shared leadership: paradox and possibility', in C.L. Pearce and J.A. Conger (eds), *Shared Leadership: Reframing the Hows and Whys of Leadership* (pp. 21–47). Thousand Oaks, CA: Sage.

Flick, U. (2002) *An Introduction to Qualitative Research*. London: Sage.

Foucault, M. (1972) *The Archeology of Knowledge*. London: Routledge.

Freidson, E. (2001) *Professionalism: The Third Logic*. Oxford: Polity Press.

Frost, P.J. (ed.) (1985) *Organizational Culture*. Newbury Park, CA: Sage.

Fuller, S. (2002) *Knowledge Management Foundations*. Oxford: Butterworth-Heinemann.

Gadamer, H.-G. (1977) *Philosophical Hermeneutics* (translated by David E. Linge). Berkeley: University of California Press.

Gadamer, H.-G. (1994/1960) *Truth and Method* (translated by Sheed and Ward Ltd). New York: Continuum.

Garfield, C.A. and Bennet, H.Z. (1985) *Peak Performance: Mental Training Techniques of the World's Greatest Athletes*. Los Angeles: Jeremy P. Tarcher.

Garfinkel, H. (1967) *Studies in Ethnomethodology*. New York: Prentice-Hall.

Garfinkel, H. (ed.) (1986) *Ethnomethodological Studies of Work*. London: Routledge.

Garratt, B. (1990) *Creating a Learning Organization: A Guide to Leadership, Learning and Development*. Cambridge: Director Books.

Geertz, C. (1973) *The Interpretation of Cultures*. London: Fontana Press.

Gherardi, S. (2000) 'Practice-based theorizing on learning and knowing in organizations', *Organization*, 7: 211–23.

Giddens, A. (1984) *The Constitution of Society: Outline a Theory of Structuration*. Cambridge: Polity Press.

Giddens, A. (1993) *New Rules of Sociological Methods: A Positive Critique of Interpretive Sociologies*. Cambridge: Polity Press.

Gilpin, R. (2000) *The Challenge of Global Capitalism: The World Economy in the 21st Century*. Princeton, NJ: Princeton University Press.

Giorgi, A. (1992) 'The Theory, Practice and Evaluation of the Phenomenological Method as a Qualitative Research Procedure for the Human Sciences'. Quebec: University of Quebec at Montreal.

Goleman, D., Boyatzis, R. and McKee, A. (2001) 'Primal leadership: the hidden driver of great performance', *Harvard Business Review*, December.

Gustafsson, C. (1994) *Produktion på allvar* (*Production of Seriousness*). Stockholm: Nerenius & Santerus.

Habermas, J. (1972) *Knowledge and Human Interest*. London: Heinemann.

Hallowell, E.M. (1999) 'The human moment at work', *Harvard Business Review*, January–February.

Hamel, G. and Prahalad, C.K. (1994) *Competing for the Future*. Boston: Harvard Business School Press.

Hannertz, U., Liljeström R. and Löfgren, O. (eds) (1982) *Kultur och medvetande* (*Culture and Consciousness*). Stockholm: Akademilitteratur.

Harding, S. (1986) *The Science Question in Feminism*. London and New York: Cornell University Press.

Hargrove, R. (1998) *Mastering the Art of Creative Collaboration*. New York: McGraw-Hill.

Harley, B., Hyman, J. and Thomson, P. (2005) 'The paradoxes of participation', in B. Harley, J. Hyman, and P. Thomson (eds), *Participation and Democracy at Work* (pp. 58–54). New York: Palgrave.

Harvey, D. (1989) *The Condition of Postmodernity: An Inquiry into the Origins of Cultural Change*. Oxford: Blackwell.

Hedberg, B. (1981) 'How organizations learn and unlearn', in P.C. Nystrom and W.H. Starbuck (eds), *Handbook of Organizational Design* (pp. 3–27). New York: Oxford University Press.

Hedberg, B. and Jönsson, S.A. (1978) 'Designing semi-confusing information systems for organizations in changing environments', *Accounting, Organizations & Society*, 3: 47–64.

Hedberg, B. and Sjöstrand, S.-E. (eds) (1979) *Från företagskriser till industripolitik* (*From Corporate Crises to Industrial Politics*). Malmö: Liber.

Hedberg, B., Nystrom, P. and Starbuck, W.B. (1976) 'Camping on seesaws: prescriptions for a self-designing organization', *Administrative Science Quarterly*, 21: 41–65.

Hedberg, B., Sjöberg, S. and Targama, A. (1971) *Styrsystem och företagsdemokrati* (*Information Systems and Corporate Democracy*). Göteborg: BAS.

Heidegger, M. (1962/1927) *Being and Time*. New York: Harper & Row.

Heidegger, M. (1992) *History and the Concept of Time* (translated by Theodore Kisiel). Bloomington: Indiana Press.

Hellgren, B. and Melin, L. (1993) 'The role of strategist's way-of-thinking in strategic change processes', in I.J. Hendry, G. Johnson and J. Newton (eds), *Strategic Thinking: Leadership and the Management of Change* (pp. 47–68). Chichester: John Wiley.

Hemp, P. and Stewart, T.A. (2004) 'Leading change when business is good (an interview with Samuel J. Palmisano)', *Harvard Business Review*, December.

Heritage, J. (1984) *Garfinkel and Ethnomethodology*. Cambridge: Polity Press.

Herzberg, F., Mausner, B. and Snyderman, B. (1959) *The Motivation to Work*. New York: Wiley.

Hiefitz, R. and Laurie, D. (1999) 'Mobilizing adoptive work: beyond visionary leadership', in J. Conger, G. Spreitzer and E. Lawler (eds), *The Leader's Change Handbook* (pp. 55–86). San Franscico: Jossey-Bass.

Hirschorn, L. (1990) 'Leaders and followers in a postindustrial age: a psychodynamic view', *The Journal of Applied Behavioral Science*, 26: 527–42.

Hofer, C.W. and Schendel, D. (1978) *Strategy Formulation: Analytical Concepts*. Minnesota, MN: West.

Hosking, D.-M. and Morley, I.E. (1991) *A Social Psychology of Organizing*. New York: Harvester Wheatsheaf.

House, R.J. (1977) 'A 1976 theory of charismatic leadership', in J. Hunt and L. Larsson (eds), *Leadership: The Cutting Edge* (pp. 187–207). Carbondale, IL: Southern Illinois University Press.

House, R.J. and Howell, J.M. (1992) 'Personality and charismatic leadership', *Leadership Quarterly*, 3: 81–108.

Huczynski, A.A. (1993*) Management Gurus: What Makes Them and How to Become One.* London: Routledge.

Husserl, E. (1962/1931) *Ideas: General Introduction to Pure Phenomenology* (Translated by W.R. Boyce Gibson). London: Collier Macmillan.

Husserl, E. (1970/1900–01) *Logical Investigations* (Vol. 2) (translated by J.N. Findlay). London: Routledge & Kegan Paul.

Husserl, E. (1970/1936) *The Crisis of European Sciences and Transcendental Phenomenology* (translated by D. Carr). Evanston, IL: Northwestern University Press.

Hutchin, E. (1993) 'Learning to navigate', in S. Chaiklin and J. Love (eds), *Understanding Practice: Perspectives on Activity and Context*. London: Cambridge University Press.

Isaacs, W. (1999) *Dialogue and the Art of Thinking Together*. New York: Doubleday.

Jackson, N. and Carter, P. (2000) *Rethinking Organisational Behaviour*. Harlow: Pearson Education.

Jacobs, R. (1989) 'Evaluating Managerial Performance: The Need for More Innovative Approaches'. Paper presented at the meeting of the European Foundation for Management Development on Knowledge as a Corporate Asset: An International Perspective, Barcelona, Spain.

Janis, I.L. and King, B.T. (1954) 'The influence of role playing on opinion change', *Journal of Abnormal and Social Psychology*, 49: 211–18.

Kalifatides, M. (2002) *Modern företagsledning och omoderna företagsledare (Modern Management and Not-so-modern Managers)*. Stockholm: EFI.

Kamprad, I. (1976) *En Möbelhandlares Testamente (A Furniture Trader's Code)*. Älmhult: IKEA.

Kanter, R.M. (1977) *Men and Women of the Corporation*. New York: Basic Books.

Kanter, R.M. (1990) *When Giants Learn to Dance*. London: Urwin Hyman.

Kaplan, R.S. and Norton, D.P. (1996) *The Balanced Scorecard: Translating Strategy into Action*. Boston, MA: Harvard Business School Press.

Keller, E.F. (1985) *Reflections on Gender and Science*. New Haven, CT: Yale University Press.

Kilduff, M. (1993) 'Deconstructing organizations', *Academy of Management Review*, 18: 13–31.

Kim, W.C. and Mauborgne, R. (2003) 'Tipping point leadership', *Harvard Business Review*, April.

Knight, D. and Morgan G. (1991) 'Corporate strategy, organizations and subjectivity: a critique', *Organization Studies*, 12: 251–73.

Kögler, H.H. (1999) *Critical Hermeneutics after Gadamer and Foucault* (translated by P. Henrickson). Cambridge, MA: MIT Press.

Kotter, J.P. (1995) *The New Rules: How to Succeed in Today's Post-Corporate World*. New York: Free Press.

Kuhn, T.H. (1962) *The Structure of Scientific Revolutions*. Chicago: University of Chicago Press.

Kusterer, K.C. (1978) *Know-How on the Job: The Important Working Knowledge of 'Unskilled' Workers*. Boulder, CO: Westview Press.

Lave, J. (1993) 'The practice of learning', in S. Chaiklin and J. Lave (eds), *Understanding Practice: Perspectives on Activity and Context* (pp. 3–32). Cambridge: Cambridge University Press.

Lave, J. and Wenger, E. (1991) *Situated Learning: Legitimate Peripheral Participation*. Cambridge: Cambridge University Press.

Levitt, B. and March, J. (1988) 'Organizational learning', *Annual Review of Sociology*, 14: 319–40.

Lincoln, Y.S. and Denzin, N.K. (2003) 'The seventh moment: out of the past', in N.K. Denzin and Y.S. Lincoln (eds), *The Landscape of Qualitative Research: Theories and Issues* (pp. 611–40). Thousand Oaks, CA: Sage.

Littler, C.R. and Innes, P. (2003) 'Downsizing and deknowledging the firm', *Work, Employment and Society*, 17: 73–100.

Livingston, E. (1987) *Making Sense of Ethnomethodology*. London: Routledge & Kegan Paul.

Luthans, F. and Avolio, B. (2003) 'Authentic leadership development', in K.S. Cameron, J.E. Dutton and R.E. Quinn (eds), *Positive Organizational Scholarship: Foundations of a New Discipline* (PP. 241–258). San Francisco: Benett-Koeler.

Marsick, V.J. and O'Neil, J. (1999) 'The many faces of action learning', *Management Learning*, 30: 159–76.

Martin, J. (1994) 'The organization of exclusion: institutionalization of sex inequality, gendered faculty jobs, and gendered knowledge in organizational theory and research', *Organization*, 1: 401–31.

Martin, J. (2002) *Organizational Culture: Mapping the Terrain.* Thousand Oaks, CA: Sage.

Marton F. and Booth, S. (1997) *Learning and Awareness.* Mahwah, NJ: Erlbaum Associates.

Marton, F. and Peng, Y.W. (2005) 'The unit of description in phenomenography', *Higher Education Research & Development*, 24: 335–48.

Marton, F. and Säljö, R. (1976) 'On qualitative differences in learning: outcome and processes', *British Journal of Educational Psychology*, 46: 4–11.

Marton, F. and Svensson, L. (1979) 'Conceptions of research in student learning', *Higher Education*, 8: 471–86.

Marton, F., Dahlgren, L.O., Svensson, L. and Säljö, R. (1977) *Inlärning och omvärldsuppfattning* (*Learning and Worldview*). Stockholm: Almquist & Wiksell.

Mayo, E. (1933) *The Human Problems of an Industrial Civilization.* London: Routledge.

McClelland, D.C. (1973) 'Testing for competence rather than for "intelligence"', *American Psychologist*, 1: 1–14.

McGregor, D. (1960) *The Human Side of Enterprise.* New York: McGraw-Hill.

Mead, G.H. (1934) *Mind, Self and Society from the Standpoint of a Social Behaviorist.* Chicago: Chicago University Press.

Meindl, J.R., Ehrlich, S.B. and Dukerich, J.M. (1985) 'The romance of leadership', *Administrative Science Quarterly*, 30: 78–102.

Merleau-Ponty, M. (1962/1945) *Phenomenology of Perception* (translated by C. Smith). London: Routledge & Kegan Paul.

Meyer, J. (2003) 'Four territories of experience: a developmental action inquiry approach to outdoor-adventure experiential learning', *Academy of Management Learning and Education*, 2: 352–63.

Meyer, J. and Rowan, B. (1977) 'Institutional organizations: formal structure as myth and cermony', *American Journal of Sociology*, 83: 340–63.

Miles, R.E. and Snow, C.C. (1978) *Organizational Strategy, Structure, and Processes.* Tokyo: McGraw-Hill Kogakusha.

Milliken, B. and Tipper, S. (1998) 'Attention and inhibition', in H. Pashler (ed.), *Attention* (pp. 191–222). Hove: Psychology Press.

Mintzberg, H. (1980) *The Nature of Managerial Work.* Englewood Cliffs, NJ: Prentice-Hall.

Mintzberg, H. (1989) *Mintzberg on Management.* New York: Free Press.

Mintzberg, H. (1994) *The Rise and Fall of Strategic Planning.* New York: Free Press.

Mohanty, J.N. (1989) *Transcendental Phenomenology: An Analytic Account.* Oxford: Blackwell.

Moon, J.A. (1999) *Reflection in Learning and Professional Development.* London: Kogan Page.

Moran, D. (2000) *Introduction to Phenomenology.* London: Routledge.

Morgan, G. (1980) 'Paradigms, metaphors and puzzle-solving in organization theory', *Administrative Science Quarterly*, 25: 605–22.

Morgan, G. (1983a) *Beyond Method: Strategies for Social Research.* Beverly Hills, CA: Sage.

Morgan, G. (1983b) 'More on metaphor: why we cannot control tropes in administrative science', *Administrative Science Quarterly*, 28: 601–7.

Morgan, G. (1986) *Images of Organizations.* London: Sage.

Morgan, G. (1988) *Riding the Waves of Change: Developing Managerial Competencies for a Turbulent World.* San Francisco: Jossey-Bass.

Morgan, G. (1993) *Imaginization: The Art of Creative Management.* Newbury Park, CA: Sage.

Neef, D. (1998) *The Knowledge Economy*. Boston, MA: Butterworth-Heinemann.

Neuman, D. (1987) *The Origin of Arithmetic Skills: A Phenomenographic Approach*. Göteborg: Acta Universitatis Gothenburgensis.

Newell, A. and Simon, H. (1972) *Human Problem Solving*. Englewood Cliffs, NJ: Prentice-Hall.

Newell, S., Robertson, M., Scarbrough, H. and Swan, J. (2002) *Managing Knowledge Work*. New York: Palgrave.

Nonaka, I. (1994) 'A dynamic theory of organizational knowledge creation', *Organization Science*, 5: 14–37.

Normann, R. (1975) *Skapande Företagsledning* (*Management for Growth*). Stockholm: Aldus.

Normann, R. (1977) *Management for Growth*. Chichester: Wiley.

Novotony, H., Scott, P. and Gibbons, M. (2001) *Rethinking Science: Knowledge and the Public in an Age of Uncertainty*. London: Sage.

Nutt, P.C. and Backoff, R.W. (1997) 'Crafting Vision', *Journal of Management Inquiry*, 6: 308–28.

Ogbonna, E. (1992) 'Organization culture and human resource management: dilemmas and contradictions,' in P. Blyton and P. Turnbull (eds), *Reassessing Human Resource Management* (pp. 74–96). London: Sage.

O'Keefe, B.J. (1988) 'The logic of message design: individual differences in reasoning about communication', *Communication Monographs*, 55: 80–103.

O'Keefe, B.J. (1997) 'Variation, adaptation, and functional explanation in the study of message design', in G. Philipsen (ed.), *Developing Communication Theories* (pp. 85–118). Albany, NY: SUNY Press.

Orlikowski, W.J. (1993) 'Learning from notes: organizational issues in groupware implementation', *The Information Society Journal*, 9: 237–50.

Orlikowski, W.J. (2002) 'Knowing in practice: enacting a collective capability in distributed organizing', *Organization Science*, 13: 249–73.

Orr, J.E. (1996) *Talking about Machines: An Ethnography of a Modern Job*. Ithaca, NY: ILR Press.

Örtenblad, A. (2002) 'A typology of the idea of learning organization', *Management Learning*, 33: 213–30.

Osborne, D. and Gaebler, T. (1992) *Re-inventing Government*. Reading, MA: Addison-Wesley.

Palmer, R.E. (1969) *Hermeneutics: Interpretation Theory in Schleiermacher, Dilthey, Heidegger and Gadamer*. Evanston, IL: Northwestern University Press.

Pawlowsky, P. (2001) 'The treatment of organizational learning in management science', in M. Dierkes, A. Berthoin Antal, J. Child and I. Nonaka (eds), *Handbook of Organizational Learning and Knowledge* (pp. 61–88). Oxford: Oxford University Press.

Pearce, C.L. and Conger, J.A. (eds) (2003) *Shared Leadership: Reframing the Hows and Whys of Leadership*. Thousand Oaks, CA: Sage.

Pedler, M., Burgoyne, J. and Boydell, T. (1991) *The Learning Company: A Strategy for Sustainable Development*. London: Lemos & Crane.

Peters, T. (1978) 'Symbols, patterns and settings: an optimistic case for getting things done', *Organizational Dynamics*, 7: 3–23.

Peters, T. and Waterman, R. (1982) *In Search of Excellence: Lessons from America's Best-Run Companies*. New York: Harper & Row.

Pettigrew, A. (1985a) *The Awakening Giant*. Oxford: Basil Blackwell.

Pettigrew, A. (1985b) 'Contextual research: a natural way to link theory and practice', in I.E. Lawler III and Associates (eds), *Doing Research That is Useful for Theory and Practice* (pp. 228–48). San Francisco: Jossey-Bass.

Polanyi, M. (1958) *Personal Knowledge: Towards a Post-critical Philosophy*. London: Routledge.

Pondy, L.R. (1978) 'Leadership is a language game', in W. Morgan, and M.M. Lombardo (eds), *Leadership: Where Else Can We Go?* (pp. 87–99). Durham, NC: Duke University Press.

Porac, J.F., Thomas, H. and Baden-Fuller, C. (1989) 'Competitive groups as cognitive communities: the case of the Scottish knitwear manufacturers', *Journal of Management Studies*, 26: 397–416.

Porter, M. (1980) *Competitive Strategy: Techniques for Analyzing Industries and Competitors*. New York: Free Press.

Potter, J. and Wetherell, M. (1987) *Discourse and Social Psychology: Beyond Attitudes and Behaviour*. London: Sage.

Prasad, A. and Prasad, P. (2002) 'The coming age of interpretive organizational research', *Organizational Research Methods*, 5: 4–11.

Prasad, P. (1993) 'Symbolic processes in the implementation of technological change: a symbolic interactionist study of work computerization', *Academy of Management Journal*, 36: 1400–29.

Primoff, E.S. and Sidney, A.F. (1988) 'A history of job analysis', in S. Gael (ed.), *The Job Analysis Handbook for Business, Industry and Government* (Vol. 1, pp. 14–29). New York: John Wiley.

Railo, W. (1986) *Willing to Win*. Amsterdam: Amas Export.

Raven, J. (1984) *Competence in Modern Society*. Edinburgh: Dinwiddie Grieve. Göteborg: Acta Universitatis Gothoburgensis.

Renström, L. (1988) Conceptions of Matter: A Phenomenographic Approach. Göteborg: Acta Universitatis Gothoburgenesis.

Revans, R.W. (1978) *The A.B.C. of Action Learning*. Salford: University of Salford.

Revans, R.W. (1980) *Action Learning*. London: Blond & Briggs.

Roethlisberger, F.J. and Dickson, W.J. (1939) *Management and the Worker: An Account of a Research Program conducted by the Western Company, Hawthorne Works, Chicago*. Cambridge, MA: Harvard University Press.

Rorty, R. (1979) *Philosophy and the Mirror of Nature*. Princeton, NJ: Princeton University Press.

Ruggles, R. (1998) 'The state of the notion: knowledge management in practice', *California Management Review*, 40: 80–9.

Rumelt, R.P., Schendel, D.E. and Teece, D.J. (eds) (1994) *Fundamental Issues in Strategy*. Boston, MA: Harvard Business School Press.

Salzer, M. (1994) *Identity Across Boarders: A study in the IKEA-World*: Linköping: Linköping Studies in Management and Economics.

Sandberg, J. (1994) *Human Competence at Work: An Interpretative Approach*. Göteborg: BAS.

Sandberg, J. (2000) 'Understanding human competence at work: an interpretative approach', *The Academy of Management Journal*, 43: 7–25.

Sandberg, J. (2001a) 'Leadership rhetoric or leadership practice?', in S.-E. Sjöstrand, J. Sandberg and M. Tyrstrup (eds), *Invisible Management: The Social Construction of Leadership* (pp. 28–48). London: Thomson.

Sandberg, J. (2001b) 'The constructions of social constructionism', in S.-E. Sjöstrand, J. Sandberg and M. Tyrstrup (eds), *Invisible Management: The Social Construction of Leadership* (pp. 167–87). London: Thomson.

Sandberg, J. (2001c) 'Understanding the basis for competence development', in C. Velde (ed.), *International Perspectives on Competence in the Workplace* (pp. 167–87). Dordrecht: Kluwer Academic Press.

Sandberg, J. and Pinnington, A. (forthcoming) 'Competence in professional practice: an ontological framework'.

Sandberg, J. and Targama, A. (1998) *Ledning och forstaelse: Ett kompetenspersektive pa organisationer* (*Leadership and Understanding: A Competence Perspective on Organizations*). Lund: Studentlitteratur.

Savin-Baden, M. and Wilkie, K. (eds) (2004) *Challenging Research in Problem-based Learning*. Maidenhead: Open University Press.

Schein, E. (1985) *Organisational Culture and Leadership: A Dynamic View*. San Francisco: Jossey-Bass.

Schein, E.H. and Bennis, W.G. (1965) *Personal and Organizational Change through Group Methods*. New York: John Wiley.

Schön, D.A. (1983) *The Reflective Practitioner: How Professionals Think in Action*. New York: Basic Books.

Schön, D.A. (1987) *Educating the Reflective Practitioner: Towards a New Design for Teaching and Learning in the Professions*. San Francisco: Jossey-Bass.

Schumpeter, J.A. (1934) *The Theory of Economic Development: An Inquiry into Profits, Capital, Credit, Interest, and the Business Cycle*. Cambridge, MA. Harvard University Press.

Schutz, A. (1945) 'On multiple realities', *Philosophy and Phenomenological Research: A Quarterly Journal*, 5: 533–75.

Schutz, A. (1953) 'Common-sense and scientific interpretation of human action', *Philosophy and Phenomenological Research: A Quarterly Journal*, 14: 1–37.

Schutz, A. (1967) *The Phenomenology of the Social World*. Evanston, North Western University Press.

Schwandt, T.A. (1994) 'Constructivist, interpretivist approaches to human inquiry', in N.K. Denzin, and Y.S. Lincoln (eds), *Handbook of Qualitative Research* (pp. 118–37). Thousand Oaks, CA: Sage.

Schwandt, T.A. (2003) 'Three epistemological stances for qualitative inquiry: interpretativism, hermeneutics and social constructionism', in N.K. Denzin and Y.S. Lincoln (eds), *The Landscape of Qualitative Research: Theories and Issues* (pp. 292–331). Thousand Oaks, CA: Sage.

Scott, R.W. (1995) *Institutions and Organizations*. Thousand Oaks, CA: Sage.

Selznick, P. (1957) *Leadership in Administration*. New York: Harper & Row.

Semin, G.R. and Gergen, G.J. (1990) 'Everyday understanding in science and daily life', in G.R. Semin and G.J. Gergen (eds), *Everyday Understanding: Social and Scientific Implications* (pp. 1–18). London: Sage.

Senge, P.M. (1990) *The Fifth Discipline: The Art and Practice of Learning Organization*. New York: Doubleday.

Senge, P.M., Scharmer, C.O., Jaworski, J. and Flowers, B.S. (2005) *Presence: Exploring Profound Change in People, Organizations, and Society*. New York: Currency, Doubleday.

Sennett, R. (1998) *The Corrosion of Character: The Personal Consequences of Work in the New Capitalism*. New York: Norton.

Shenhav, Y. (1999) *Manufacturing Rationality: The Engineering Foundations of the Managerial Revolution*. New York: Oxford University Press.

Shotter, J. (1993) *Conversational Realities: Constructing Life through Language*. London: Sage.

Silverman, D. (1970) *The Theory of Organisations*. London: Heinemann.

Silverman, D. (1991) 'On Throwing Away Ladders: Re-writing the Theory of Organisations. Paper presented at the conference Toward a New Theory of Organizations, Keele University. UK.

Silverman, D. (1998) *Harvey Sacks: Social Science and Conversation Analysis*. Cambridge: Polity Press/ New York: Oxford University Press.

Simon, H. (1945) *Administrative Behavior*. New York: Macmillan.

Smircich, L. and Morgan, G. (1982) 'Leaderhip: the management of meaning', *Journal of Applied Behavioural Science*, 18: 257–73.

Smircich, L. and Stubbart, C. (1985) 'Strategic management in an enacted world', *Academy of Management Review*, 4: 724–36.

Snow, C.C. and Hrebiniak, G.L. (1980) 'Strategy, distinctive competence, and organizational performance', *Administrative Science Quarterly*, 25: 317–36.

Spencer, L.M. and Spencer, S.M. (1993) *Competence at Work: Models for Superior Performance*. New York: Wiley.

Spender, J.-C. and Grant, R.M. (1996) 'Knowledge and the firm', *Strategic Management Journal*, 17: 5–9.

Spiegelberg, H. (1976) *The Phenomenological Movement: A Historical Introduction (Vols I & II)*. The Hague: Martinus Nijhoff.

Stålsby-Lundborg, C.R., Wahlström, R. and Dall'Alba, G. (1999) 'Ways of experiencing asthma management: variations among practitioners in Sweden', *Scandinavian Journal of Primary Health Care*, 17: 226–31.

Starbuck, W. (1992) 'Learning by knowledge-intensive firms', *Journal of Management Studies*, 29: 713–40.

Steers, R.M., Mowday, R.T. and Shapiro, D.L. (2004) 'The future of work motivation theory', *Academy of Management Review*, 29: 377–87.

Susskind, R. (1996) *The Future of Law: Facing the Challenges of Information Technology*. Oxford: Clarendon Press.

Svensson, L. (1976) *Study Skill and Learning* (Göteborg studies in educational sciences, 19). Göteborg: Acta Universitatis Gothoburgensis.

Svensson, L. (1977) 'On qualitative differences in learning: III. Outcome and processes', *British Journal of Educational Psychology*, 47: 233–43.

Sydow, J., Lindkvist, L. and DeFilippi, R. (2004) 'Project-based organizations, embeddedness and repositories of knowledge', *Organization Studies*, 25: 1475–89.

Targama, A. (1978) *Former för administrativt utvecklingsarbete (Forms of Organizational Change Work)*. Gothenburg: BAS.

Taylor, F.W. (1911) *The Principles of Scientific Management*. New York: Harper.

Tengblad, S. (forthcoming) 'Is there a "new managerial work"? A Comparison with Henry Mintzberg's classic study 30 years later', *Journal of Management Studies*.

Thomson, P. and Warhurst, C. (1998) *Workplaces of the Future*. Basingstoke: Macmillan Business.

Torbert, W.R. (1991) *The Power of Balance: Transforming Self, Society and Scientific Inquiry*. Newbury Park, CA: Sage.

Tsoukas, H. (1996) 'The firm as a distributed knowledge system: a constructionistic approach', *Strategic Management Journal*, 17: 11–25.

Van Maanen, J. (1995) *Representation in Ethnography*. Thousand Oaks, CA: Sage.

Veres, J.G., Locklear, T.S. and Sims, R.R. (1990) 'Job analysis in practice: a brief review of the role of job analysis in human resources management', in G.R. Ferris, K.M. Rowland and R.M. Buckley (eds), *Human Resource Management: Perspectives and Issues* (pp. 79–103). Boston, MA: Allyn & Bacon.

von Krogh, G., Roos, J. and Slocum, K. (1994) 'An essay on corporate epistemology', *Strategic Management Journal*, 15: 53–71.

Vygotsky, L. (1978) *Mind in Society: The Psychology of Higher Mental Functions*. Cambridge, MA: Harvard University Press.

Watson, T.J. (1996) 'Motivation: that's Maslow, isn't it?', *Management Learning*, 27: 447–64.

Watson, T.J. (2001) 'The emergent manager and processes of pre-learning', *Management Learning*, 32: 221–35.

Watson, T.J. and Harris, P. (1999) *The Emergent Manager: Becoming a Manager in the Modern Work Organization*. London: Sage.

Weber, M. (1964/1947) *The Theory of Social and Economic Organisation*. New York: Free Press.

Weick, K.E. (1979) *The Social Psychology of Organizing*. Reading, MA: Addison-Wesley.

Weick, K.E. (1995) *Sensemaking in Organizations*. Thousand Oaks, CA: Sage.

Weinstein, K. (1995) *Action Learning: A Journey in Discovery and Development*. London: Harper Collins.

Wernerfelt, B. (1984) 'A resource-based view of the firm', *Strategic Management Journal*, 5: 171–80.

Wenger, E. (1998) *Communities of Practice: Learning, Meaning, and Identity*. Cambridge: Cambridge University Press.

Wenger, E. (2003) 'Community of practice and social learning systems', in D.S. Nicolini, S. Gherardi and D. Yanow (eds), *Knowing in Organizations: A Practice-based Approach* (pp. 76–99). Armonk, NY: M.E. Sharpe.

Whipp, R. (1996) 'Creative deconstruction: strategy and organization', in S. Clegg, C. Hardy and W. Nord (eds), *Handbook of Organization Studies* (pp. 218–58). London: Sage.

Wheeler, H. (2002) *The Future of the American Labor Movement*. New York: Cambridge University Press.

Wickelgren, M. (2005) *Engineering Emotion: Values as Means in Product Development*. Göteborg: BAS.

Willmott, H. (1997) 'Rethinking management and managerial work: capitalism, control and subjectivity', *Human Relations*, 50: 1327–59.

Winograd, T. and Flores, F. (1986) *Understanding Computers and Cognition: A New Foundation for Design*. Norwood, NJ: Ablex.

Wong, M.M.L. (2005) 'Organizational learning via expatriate managers: collective myopia as blocking mechanism', *Organization Studies*, 26: 325–50.

Woodruffe, C. (1990) *Assessment Centres: Identifying and Developing Competence*. London: Institute of Personnel Management.

Zald, M.N. (1996) 'More fragmentation? Unfinished business in linking the social sciences and the humanities', *Administrative Science Quarterly*, 40: 251–62.

Zemke, R., Raines, C. and Filipczak, B. (eds) (2000) *Generations at Work: Managing the Clash of Veterans, Boomers, Xers, and Nexters in your Workplace*. New York: AMACOM.

Index